T0309251

The Great Mental Models, Volume 2

The Great Mental Models

VOLUME 2

Physics, Chemistry, and Biology

RHIANNON BEAUBIEN
and Shane Parrish

PORTFOLIO · PENGUIN

Portfolio / Penguin
An imprint of Penguin Random House LLC
penguinrandomhouse.com

First published in hardcover by Latticework Publishing, Inc., Ottawa, in 2020

This updated and revised edition first published in the United States by Portfolio, 2024

Most Portfolio books are available at a discount when purchased in quantity
for sales promotions or corporate use. Special editions, which include
personalized covers, excerpts, and corporate imprints, can be created when
purchased in large quantities. For more information, please call (212) 572-2232
or email specialmarkets@penguinrandomhouse.com. Your local bookstore
can also assist with discounted bulk purchases using the Penguin Random House
corporate Business-to-Business program. For assistance in locating a participating
retailer, email B2B@penguinrandomhouse.com.

Illustrations by Marcia Mihotich, London

A portion of this work has appeared online at fs.blog.

LIBRARY OF CONGRESS CATALOGING-IN-PUBLICATION DATA
Names: Beaubien, Rhiannon, author. | Parrish, Shane, author.
Title: The great mental models. Volume 2, Physics, chemistry,
    and biology / Rhiannon Beaubien and Shane Parrish.
Other titles: Physics, chemistry, and biology
Description: [New York] : Portfolio/Penguin, [2024]
Identifiers: LCCN 2024014107 (print) | LCCN 2024014108 (ebook) |
    ISBN 9780593719985 (hardcover) | ISBN 9780593720028 (ebook)
Subjects: LCSH: Science. | Reasoning. | Cognitive maps (Psychology)
Classification: LCC Q172 .B43 2024 (print) | LCC Q172 (ebook) |
    DDC 500—dc23/eng20240723
LC record available at https://lccn.loc.gov/2024014107
LC ebook record available at https://lccn.loc.gov/2024014108

Printed in the United States of America
1st Printing

Book design by Daniel Lagin

Contents

BIOLOGY

The Great Mental Models, Volume 2

Introduction

The world is beautiful, fascinating, and full of curiosities, but it doesn't have to be completely mysterious. Humans may not know everything about the world, and indeed it often feels like we have just scratched the surface, but we have figured out some fundamentals about how everything on this planet operates. It is those fundamentals that make up *Farnam Street*'s latticework of mental models, a way of approaching new ideas and situations, problems and challenges with a toolkit of valuable knowledge.

In volume 1 of *The Great Mental Models*, we introduced nine general-thinking concepts to get you started on the journey of building a foundation of timeless knowledge. Those models had broad applicability, and we hope you were inspired and excited to apply them to achieve better results with fewer problems as you tackled both opportunities and challenges in your life.

In volume 2 of *The Great Mental Models*, we continue the journey and explore fundamental ideas from physics, chemistry, and biology. These disciplines offer an exceptional amount of insight that we can apply across all areas of our lives to improve our careers, our relationships, and ourselves.

The truths about the physical world, from the forces that allow us to manipulate energy to the behaviors that drive the actions of all organisms, are constants that can guide our choices.

In *Storm in a Teacup: The Physics of Everyday Life*, Helen Czerski tells the story of the *Fram*, a boat designed "to work with nature instead of against it."[1] In the late 1800s, there was immense curiosity about the North Pole. But the ships that were sent to try to get there would get stuck in the ice of the Arctic, freezing in place. As the ice around the ships grew, it put incredible pressure on the hulls, eventually breaking them apart. No one could get to the North Pole without encountering ice, and the total amount of ice and corresponding pressure to be dealt with was essentially an unknown. No ship had the hull strength to handle the upper limits of potential ice pressure. A Norwegian scientist named Fridtjof Nansen came up with the idea for the *Fram*, a truly unique ship. "She had a smooth curvy hull, almost no keel, and engines and rudder that could be lifted right out of the water. When the ice came, the *Fram* became a floating bowl. And if you squeeze a curved shape like a bowl or a cylinder from below, it will pop upward. If the squeeze from the ice got too much, the *Fram* would just be pushed upward to sit on it."[2] Nansen did not try to improve on the design of existing boats. Instead, he let the reality of ice expansion determine the design of his ship.

The *Fram* floated across the Arctic Ocean for the next three years, not quite making it to the pole, but collecting reams of valuable scientific data. She got closer to the pole than any ship previously and provided conclusive evidence that the Arctic was an ocean. All of this success was due to trying to answer one question: How can I work with the world, not against it? As Czerski concludes, "Instead of fighting the inexorable expansion of the ice, [the *Fram*] had used it to ride across the top of the world."[3]

Taking action that works with the world is more effective, less stressful, and ultimately more rewarding. We don't waste our time fighting to accomplish the impossible.

About the Series

The *Great Mental Models* series is designed to inspire and challenge you. We want to give you both knowledge and a framework for making it useful.

One of our goals for the series is to provide you with a set of tools built on timeless knowledge that you can use again and again in daily life.

We present dozens of mental models, spread across four volumes, that define and explore the foundational concepts from a variety of disciplines. We then take the concept out of its original discipline and show you how you can apply it in nonintuitive situations.

We encourage you to dive into new ideas not only to augment your knowledge toolbox but also to leverage what you already know by applying it in new ways, to give yourself a different perspective on the challenges you face.

In the first book, we explained that a mental model is simply a representation of how something works. We use models to retain knowledge and simplify how we understand the world. We can't re-learn everything every day, and so we construct models to help us chunk patterns and navigate our world more efficiently.

Farnam Street's mental models are reliable principles that you can see at work in the world time and again. Using them means synthesizing across disciplines and not being afraid to apply knowledge from different areas far outside the milieu they usually cover.

Not every model applies to all situations. Part of building a latticework of mental models is educating yourself regarding which situations are best addressed by which models. This takes some work and is not without error. It's important to constantly reflect on your use of models. If something didn't work, you need to try to discover why. Over time, by reflecting on your use of individual models, you will learn which models will best help you tackle which situations. Knowing why a model works will help you know when to use it again.

About This Book

This book explains and explores the core mental models from physics, chemistry, and biology. A degree in these subjects is not required, though if you happen to have one, you might see parts of your discipline in a new light. The models we have chosen from these fields are foundational, relevant far beyond their normal academic applications. We take time in each chapter to explain the science and situate the concepts in real-world examples. We want you to see each concept in action and to be inspired to find analogous uses in your own life. To achieve this goal, we discuss how using the model as a lens will help you by applying the science to stories and themes in history.

As you go through this book, you will begin to see patterns and understand that both natural systems and people organize themselves in a limited number of ways. What applies in biological growth applies in economic growth. What governs chemical reactions relates to any process of creation. Furthermore, lessons for an individual have relevance for teams and organizations. As you learn the models, identifying the forces at play in any situation will become easier. You'll see things that others don't and avoid costly mistakes.

Some of the models in this book function like metaphors, especially in the physics section. Our aim is to show you how to use these models to uncover forces at play in your life. When a problem seems too complex or the behavior of people too mysterious, these models offer insight into the why. The more you know, the easier it is to design solutions that will work.

Other models, many from biology, have a more literal application. Although useful for understanding why certain things are the way they are, these models have a more direct application to human behavior. They can be mapped to your life experiences to give you ideas for better ways to solve common problems. For example, the forces that explain inertia are used more metaphorically to understand why some erroneous beliefs continue to persist, while the concept of cooperation can be applied quite literally to identifying business opportunities.

Finally, it is important to remember that all these science models are value-neutral. They can be used to illuminate both the positive and negative aspects of any situation. It's up to you to ask yourself: What can this model show me about what not to do? Where will it help me find a better way forward?

You will know the differences in how to apply each model through the stories we have chosen to explain them. Each example offers insights on where the model can apply. You can take the elements of each story as a signpost directing you to find similar situations in your life where the lens of a particular model will be most useful.

The most important thing to remember is that these models are tools. You are meant to try them out, play with them, and learn what you can use each of them to fix. Not all tools are useful for all problems, and just like a traditional toolbox has a hammer when you need to pound a nail and a wrench for when you need to turn a bolt, you'll learn through practice which tools are useful in which situations. Starting with curiosity is the best way to do that. As you begin each chapter, be open to learning and updating your knowledge. Then, practice. Pick a new model every day, apply it to a situation you are in, and see if you can improve your understanding and decision-making. Finally, reflect. Take some time to evaluate your successes and failures. In doing so, you will begin to learn the full potential of the tool kit you are building.

Let's get started.

PHYSICS

Nothing in life is to be feared,
it is only to be understood.
Now is the time to
understand more,
so that we may fear less.

—MARIE CURIE[1]

Relativity

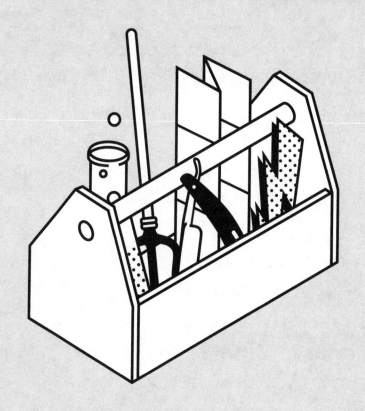

Put it into perspective.

The theory of relativity is founded on empathy. Not empathy in the ordinary emotional sense; empathy in a rigorous scientific sense. The crucial idea is to imagine how things would appear to someone who's moving in a different way than you are.

—STEVEN STROGATZ[1]

We often think someone is wrong because they see things from a different perspective than we do. Relativity helps us to understand that there is more than one way to see everything. That doesn't mean everyone's perspective is equally valid, only that we might not have the most complete view into a problem or situation.

Thought Experiments That Changed the World

The science of relativity is best explained through two famous thought experiments—one conducted by Galileo and the other by Albert Einstein. Each describes a situation that demonstrates the reality of differing perspectives.

Thought Experiments

In volume 1, we dedicated a chapter to thought experiments because they are such valuable mental models. Frequently used
as tools by scientists, thought experiments let us take on the
impossible, evaluate the potential consequences of our actions,
and reexamine history to make better decisions. They are rigorous applications of the scientific method to determine what we
can infer from what we can imagine.

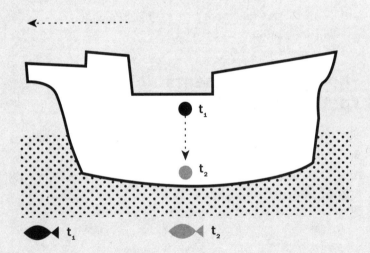

In the 1630s, Galileo discovered that any two observers moving at constant speed and direction will obtain the same results for all mechanical experiments they perform.

Galileo's original thought experiment describes a scientist on a ship moving at constant velocity. The scientist is belowdecks with no portholes to give him a frame of reference for the movement of the ship. When this scientist drops a ball from waist level, he will notice only the vertical movement caused by gravity. He will observe that the ball drops to the floor of the ship. However, there is also a horizontal movement that the scientist doesn't perceive. Both the scientist and the ball are also moving the distance covered by the ship as the ball is falling to the ground.

An outside observer, someone standing on a nearby beach or a fish in the water, can detect the complete movement of the ball because their perspective is different. By being outside the ship, they see a more complete version of reality. The scientist on the boat would have to make a conscious effort to remember that both he and the ball are moving with the ship. Before you conclude that the motion of the ship should be obvious to the scientist, consider how often you reflect on your movement through space every day. Right now, you probably feel as though you're stationary. However, if you're on Earth, you're moving around the sun at sixty-seven thousand miles per hour. Galileo developed this thought experiment partly thanks to his belief that Copernicus was right and that the Earth itself is in motion that we do not feel.

Perspective influences what we perceive as reality and how we understand the world. Galileo's thought experiment is one you can use all the time. Imagine the scientist performing experiments on the boat and ask yourself: Now what does a fish see? And how does that relate to what the scientist experiences? Imagine being either one, or a bird in the sky, and you start to get an idea of how multiple eyewitness accounts of the same robbery can be so different.

To use this yourself, imagine seeing a situation through the eyes of all the participants. Changing your perspective and looking at things through the eyes of others not only reveals blind spots but also creates empathy.

In the early 1900s, Einstein used another famous thought experiment when developing his theory of special relativity, which linked mass and energy using the formula $E = mc^2$. This formula demonstrates that energy is equivalent to mass times the speed of light squared. With this theory, Einstein stated that the speed of light is fixed within any frame of reference moving at a constant velocity, and therefore there is no fixed frame of reference from which one can measure the physical laws. This is what Galileo had argued, but his ideas were put aside in the 1700s in favor of a view that said there was an absolute frame of reference. Einstein's theory of special relativity revived Galileo's ideas.

Einstein's thought experiment to describe special relativity illustrated the concept that observers in relative motion experience time differently. This means that two events can happen simultaneously from one observer's perspective and at different times from another observer's perspective. Both are right. Here is the experiment:

Imagine you are watching a train go by. Lightning strikes each end just as the train's midpoint is passing you. The lightning strikes are each the same distance from you, so you correctly conclude that the two bolts of lightning hit the train at exactly the same time.

Later on, you catch up with your friend, who was on the train. "Crazy that two bolts of lightning struck your train at exactly the same time," you say.

"What are you talking about?" she responds. "The front of the train got hit by lightning first."

You dismiss her interpretation. After all, you witnessed the whole thing. But here is what was happening for her:

She was sitting at the midpoint of the train. If the train had been stationary, she would have observed the two lightning strikes being simultaneous like you did. However, because the train was moving, the light from the rear strike had farther to travel to reach her. She perceived the light from the strike at the front first. So, she correctly concluded that the lightning strikes were not simultaneous; the one in front happened first.

These are two valid interpretations of the same event. Both are correct. The difference arises because of the perspective of each person.

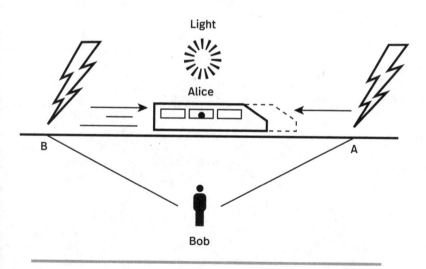

Your perspective informs your experience.

Our perspective is very much unique to us, as both Galileo and Einstein so vividly demonstrated. In the day-to-day world that we live in, this means not only that you are seeing what nobody else sees but also that you do not automatically, unconsciously see through the eyes of others. There is an objective reality, but none of us can perceive it in totality without doing a little work. Is it any wonder we make suboptimal decisions?

Perspective-Taking in Psychology

Perspective-taking in psychology refers to the ability to perceive a situation from an alternative point of view. We are not born with this ability. It develops throughout childhood. There are two broad types of perspectives that we learn: differing physical perspectives, such as that the view out your neighbor's window is different than yours; and conceptual perspectives, such as that people have different feelings or beliefs that in turn influence their perspectives. Some conditions can negatively impact the development of the ability to fully understand a different perspective. And while we are capable of appreciating the wide variety of perspectives that exist, we are often lazy about developing this ability.

The Subjectivity of Perspective

You are always going to have an imperfect perspective. You can't see everything at once. Nor will you be able to completely trust that everything you do see is viewed by others. In concrete terms, relativity highlights a subjectivity of perspective that explains partly why eyewitness testimonies have lost their credibility over the years.

When considering an eyewitness testimony during a trial, there are many aspects to consider in order to understand that person's perspective. First, there are the physical aspects: How good is that person's vision? What was the light like at the time? How long did they have to observe the person in question? But there are also a host of psychological ones: What mood was the person in? Were they rushing to get somewhere? Had they just had a fight with their spouse? Do they have an incentive to take a certain position? And what about the biases: Do they consider certain ethnicities more likely to commit crimes? How predisposed are they to being helpful with police? All of this factors into what a witness believes they saw and helps explain why two witnesses can have remarkably different accounts of the same situation, as in *Rashomon*.

Rashomon, the classic Japanese film, is an excellent exploration of the differences in the testimonies of several eyewitnesses to the same crime. A samurai is found murdered in a forest. A bandit is accused of the crime. During the subsequent trial, the bandit, the samurai—speaking through a medium—his wife, and a woodcutter who observed the whole incident each give testimony. Each story is different, partly due to the self-interest of each of the characters, and partly because each can understand the events that play out only through a single perspective—their own.

Rashomon is interesting because the end does not give the viewer "the truth." The audience does not get any closure on what happened, which is an accurate portrayal of life. They are simply left with the contradictory testimonies and the implication that each of these has become the truth for the person telling them.

In addition, our memories are not infallible. We often think of memories as being like a video recording, capturing a scene with perfect fidelity. The truth is far more complicated. Our memories are highly subjective and malleable. We often misattribute memories, such as a witness thinking something that they read in the news about a crime is something they witnessed. We are also highly suggestible, such as when a police officer asks us a leading question or uses emotive language.

Our memories of the past are also distorted by what we know now, such as when a witness learns a new piece of information and feels they knew it at the time.[2] These and other common memory distortions feed into the subjectivity of eyewitness reports. People rewrite and reshape their memories, often to fit their existing beliefs. We often feel committed to our original perception and unconsciously adjust our memories to support what we think we originally saw.

When juries hear eyewitness testimony, they must sort through the limits and influences on that person's perspective and consider how self-interest and time have distorted the person's memory. It is no small feat. One example of the challenge is chronicled here.

On the morning of July 4, 2000, twenty-year-old Chris Kinison was killed in a convenience store parking lot in Ocean Shores, Washington, USA. Minh Duc Hong was charged with the crime. Hong was visiting the area to see a fireworks show with his twin, Hung Hong. Both were Asian Americans, and Kinison was white. During the subsequent trial, a dozen eyewitnesses provided testimony. As David A. Neiwert explains in *Death on the Fourth of July*, "For every bit of testimony, it sometimes seemed, there arose a view of events that conflicted with the description provided by previous witnesses, creating a web of questions about competing self-interests, and the extent to which they colored different witnesses' testimony."[3] Many witnesses described seeing things they physically could not have, which was determined once their positioning during the violence was mapped out. Others were clearly biased by their relationship with the victim—a local—versus the accused, who was from out of town. Racial bias was a huge factor, and in his book, Neiwert makes the case for Minh Hong first being a victim of a hate crime, whose subsequent actions were really about defense.

According to witnesses, Kinison waved a Confederate battle flag at Hong and his friends and shouted racial slurs. He also made threatening gestures, indicating a desire to harm Hong, who took a knife from the convenience store, fearing for his safety. When Kinison physically assaulted Hong's brother, Hong used the knife on him. Kinison had previous accusations of racist violent threats.[4]

Many of the witnesses had been drinking, and many admitted to being scared. These distortions meant that the jury did not get a reliable, consistent account from each witness. They had to piece together what might have happened. The jury then had to evaluate the credibility of how each witness saw the crime and the laws of physics governing the physical perspectives. One life had already ended. The future of another one was completely dependent on how the jury untangled the testimony through the limits of their own perceptions.

After deliberation, the jury could not reach a verdict and the judge declared a mistrial. The jury revealed that they had deadlocked 11–1 in favor of acquittal. What's interesting, though, is the ambiguous end to the story. The jurors continued to be comfortable with the position they took, believing that Minh Hong acted reasonably in self-defense. The local sheriff's office recognized that Hong had been the victim of a hate crime and the officers committed to an education program so they could deal with similar situations better in the future. But, Neiwert further writes, "If there is any lingering sentiment in Ocean Shores, it is a quiet dismay at the outcome of Minh Hong's trial. Even though the Grays Harbor jury found otherwise, many in town, especially those who knew Chris Kinison, believe an injustice was done."[5]

The multiple and conflicting perspectives displayed in the trial of Minh Hong are a common phenomenon. We have all been in situations in which we have a totally different perspective on events than the person standing next to us. It's important to be aware of and compensate for different perspectives if you want to get the most complete picture possible of the situation you are in. What you see is never all there is.

> When people thought the earth was flat, they were wrong. When people thought the earth was spherical, they were wrong. But if you think that thinking the earth is spherical is just as wrong as thinking the earth is flat, then your view is wronger than both of them put together.
>
> —ISAAC ASIMOV[6]

Through the Eyes of Others

The limits of perspective are fundamental to how the world works. Considering multiple perspectives is the best chance we have to understand. Given that you can't go back in time to situate yourself differently, what can you do to augment your perspective? This is where thought experiments come in handy. Think back to Galileo's scenario of the scientist conducting experiments on the boat. The scientist cannot hang out in the ocean and watch the boat go past. Our scientist can, however, imagine what the view would be like from the perspective of a fish.

Thought experiments don't have to be confined to what already is or even what's possible. The scientist, when considering the perspective of the fish, can also imagine the boat as being made of glass and the water as easy to see through as air. Or he need not limit the experiment to the visual perspective of the fish. After all, we don't gain perspective only with our eyes, but through the lens of our experiences, biases, desires, and more. This can explain a lot of human behavior.

When you see someone doing something that doesn't make sense to you, ask yourself what the world would have to look like to you for those actions to make sense. While we all see our own version of events, the goal is to enlarge our perspective to be a closer representation of reality by removing some of the factors that cloud our judgment. One of the best ways to do this is by noticing and observing the details of what is going on around you.

> It is good to know something of the customs of various peoples, so as to judge our own more soundly and so as not to think that everything that is contrary to our ways is ridiculous and against reason, as those who have seen nothing have a habit of doing.
>
> —DESCARTES[7]

We bring our sensibilities into what we see. The problem is, most of us usually forget this. We are so used to being on Einstein's train that we forget it is there. But traveling to new places far outside our normal experiences can jolt us into remembering our train, seeing it in a new light, understanding better its size and shape, and reminding us that not everyone is on it.

One story that drives home the point that considering others' perspective can substantially enrich our own is that of Rifa'a Rafi' al-Tahtawi, an Egyptian who traveled to Paris in the late 1820s and recorded in detail the minutiae of what he saw in his book *An Imam in Paris*. This book tells us a lot about Parisian society in the late 1820s. We can learn loads about the social customs and idiosyncrasies of the urban French and how they reconciled scientific development with religious sensibilities.

We can also, however, draw some conclusions about the author al-Tahtawi. His book is more like a report, a gathering of facts about a foreign culture. He was an observer who was seeking to understand not only the French but how what he could see related to French culture and France's influence in the world. In doing so, he hoped to gain useful knowledge that he could bring back to Egypt to encourage development. His time in France changed his perception of his own culture, and when he returned he instituted teachings based on the things he had learned from observing the French.[8] Daniel L. Newman explains in his introduction to al-Tahtawi's book, "In the end, al-Tahtawi stayed in Paris for five years and the experiences, know-how and skills acquired during his Paris days . . . were to have a decisive and lasting impact on the cultural and scientific development of his native country." Al-Tahtawi had multiplied his perspective, and in doing so contributed to significant change in Egypt.

We frame things through our perspective. How others frame

things is not an unobstructed description of reality but rather their individual perspective. Making efforts to understand someone's view helps you understand their frame, their set of beliefs and biases that guide how they see their world, and the actions they take.

The core concepts of relative perspective and framing have a broad application. When someone gives you something—an opinion, a report, an article, a plan—consider how it is framed. Who is involved in this information, and what do you know about their vantage point? Knowing the factors that influence how a person frames issues helps you understand their perspective and how you can use it to augment your own.

Al-Tahtawi's experiences of trying to understand his own culture by juxtaposing them against those of another demonstrates the value of considering other perspectives and comparing them with your own. Namely, that you get a more complete picture of the context in which you are operating and where opportunities might be. This is why the publishing industry relies heavily on editors, and why research needs peer review to be credible. Outside views combine to make a better product.

Perspective often comes from distance or time. If you're attempting to solve a problem and you're stuck, try shifting your vantage point. Try zooming in to see more details or zooming out to see fewer details.

One reason we offer helpful advice to friends is because we are not them. They often get caught up in all the irrelevant details of a situation that we can't see. Lacking the confusion these irrelevant details add, we often see things for what they are.

Another way to change your perspective, aside from looking at the situation through the eyes of others, is to extend the timeline. What does this situation look like in the weeks, months, and years ahead? Assuming different perspectives allows you to gain a more complete understanding of what's really going on.

Conclusion

Relativity is the idea that our perceptions and judgments are not absolute, but are instead shaped by our unique vantage points and frames of reference. It's the understanding that our experiences are subjective.

We each inhabit a particular web of experiences. This context shapes how we see the world, what we notice and what we overlook, what we value and what we dismiss. Two people can look at the same event and come away with vastly different interpretations based on their unique frames of reference.

Consider two people standing in the same room: They each experience the same absolute temperature differently. One can feel hot while the other feels cold, even though the temperature is the same. Similarly, consider political debates: Our beliefs are shaped by our unique experiences and social contexts. A policy that seems like common sense to an urban progressive might feel like complete nonsense to a rural conservative, and vice versa. In this way, understanding relativity is key to fostering empathy and finding common ground.

However, relativity is not the same as relativism—the idea that all perspectives are equally valid. Recognizing the relativity of our perceptions doesn't mean we don't have to make judgments about validity. Rather, it's a call to examine our own assumptions, seek out diverse perspectives, and expand our frames of reference.

We all have blind spots—things we cannot see. Understanding that our perceptions are relative allows us to open ourselves to other ways of seeing. If you're wondering where to get started, try asking others what they see that you can't. Apply your judgment to their responses and update your beliefs accordingly.

Reciprocity

Give and take.

For every action, there is an equal and opposite reaction.

—NEWTON'S THIRD LAW

Reciprocity can be summed up like this: When you act on things, they act on you. For every action there is an equal and opposite reaction. When pushed on by others, we push back. The harder we push others, the harder they push back. While this is a simple principle, the implications are anything but simplistic.

Reciprocity demonstrates why win-win relationships are the way to go, why going positive and going first puts people on your side, why it's a good idea to use the least force possible to secure an outcome, and why a lot of companies don't permit their employees to accept gifts. This model also demonstrates why we should view giving as being as valuable as receiving. It prompts us to rewrite the Golden Rule to say, "Do unto others knowing that something will be done unto you."

So what exactly is reciprocity?

In physics, reciprocity is Newton's third law, which states that for every force exerted by object A on object B, there is an equal but opposite force exerted by object B on object A. Every force involves the interaction of two objects in which the force asserted by one is reciprocated with an equally powerful and directionally opposite force by the other object. Forces always occur in pairs of the same type, and it is not possible for one object to exert a force without experiencing a reciprocal force.

When I land on the ground after jumping, I am exerting a force on the ground. At the moment of my landing, the ground is applying a force on me that is equal but opposite in direction. The earth applies a force on me even when I am just standing. This force is gravity. But the gravitational force exerted on me by earth is reciprocated by me through the force I am exerting on the earth.

In the natural world, this third law of Newton's explains jet propulsion. The word "propulsion" comes from two Latin terms meaning "forward" and "drive"—propulsion is a force that drives an object forward.[1] Jet propulsion works by forcing a jet of fluid, such as gas produced by burning fuel, in one direction, to generate a force in the opposite direction. This is the primary process behind how jet engines, rockets, and guns work.

Jet propulsion works only if the forward push is stronger than the forces acting on the object, like air friction and its own weight. The greater the force in comparison to drag (the amount of force opposing the motion), the faster the object can move. Octopi and squid force water through their mantle and out through a siphon at a high speed that compensates for their weight and the viscosity of the water. As the animal asserts a force on the water, the water exerts a force on the animal, and this makes the octopus or squid move.

Consider the tackle in American football. The force that the defender puts on the receiver's body to bring him to the ground is equivalent to the force felt by the defenseman's body during the tackle. You can't initiate force without having a force put on you. For the tackle, this is very important. If the tackler felt nothing, there would be no incentive for him to be strategic in the application of his force on the receiver. And who would want to be a receiver if this were the case? If the person who initiates the force feels nothing—much better to be him.

Since this is not the case, the tackle should be more about using the least amount of force required to bring the receiver to the ground. It's better for the receiver, and it's also better for the player doing the tackling, because the more force you apply to others, the more damage you do to yourself.

Quid pro Quo

Sometimes, if you want to understand how pervasive a concept is, you can look at the vernacular of a society. English speakers from Commonwealth countries have many expressions that suggest the basics of reciprocity are foundational for how we expect our society to function. "Quid pro quo," Latin for "something for something," appeared in regular usage in the sixteenth century. We also have "give and take," "tit for tat," and "If you scratch my back, I'll scratch yours." The meaning behind these expressions, which implies an expectation of reciprocity, is perhaps best summed up by another Latin phrase: "do ut des," translated as, "I give, so that you may give."

What We Give

The relationship between what we do and what we get is commonly known as karma. It would be amazing if every time you did something good for the world, you received a corresponding amount of positive effect in your life. We all know that unfortunately this is not true. Sometimes positive intentions produce negative results, or bad things happen to people who do good things for other people.

Although the connection between good deeds and a good life isn't perfect, there is a documented relationship between the two. Using the model of reciprocity can help us understand why people benefit themselves when they work for what they believe is good. The life of Norman Bethune, a Canadian surgeon, is one that can teach us a lot about the nuances of reciprocity.

Bethune grew up wanting to be a surgeon, inspired by his doctor grandfather. During the First World War, he completed his studies while also providing medical support on the battlefield as a volunteer. In the 1920s he practiced medicine in the United States and Canada, eventually settling in Montreal. He initially specialized in thoracic surgery and developed a solid reputation as a surgeon. However, he had an ongoing commitment to helping people beyond what he did in his practice—a goal he pursued in a variety of ways.

During the early 1930s, while in Montreal, Bethune provided free medical services to the poor and established a free clinic, which he ran once per week. He vocally advocated for universal health protection, explaining that many medical issues were created by poverty and negligent employers. In addition, and unique for the time, he used radio broadcasts to educate the public on tuberculosis. Bethune volunteered his time, energy, and intelligence to try to bring about meaningful improvements in the lives of the most impoverished.[2]

During the 1930s, he also became a supporter of communism and joined the Communist Party, mostly on account of what he saw of the benefits of the Soviet socialized health-care system. These political beliefs took him further afield in his efforts to improve access to and outcomes in health care.

In 1936 in Spain during the Spanish Civil War, Bethune designed and developed the first-ever mobile blood transfusion unit. This vehicle could draw and store blood, was used to give transfusions, and most important, could be used on the front lines of the battlefield. It was a remarkable innovation that saved countless lives and inspired the medical approach used in World War II.

All the work that Bethune did in Spain, and later China, was nonprofit. The mobile blood unit and all his other surgical innovations and inventions did not make Bethune any money.

In 1938 Bethune went to China, again trying to help people. China was fighting a war with the Japanese, the Second Sino-Japanese War, and Bethune's belief in communism led him to deploy his efforts in support of Mao Tse-tung and the Communist Party of China. He was made commander of all Chinese medical forces and immediately set about modernizing the existing primitive health care in China.

Helping the Chinese in their fight, he again deployed his practice of bringing the surgeon to the battlefield, designing mobile operating equipment and improving the survival rate of the injured. He also extensively trained doctors and nurses and established hospitals in areas that had neither. In their article, "The Medical Life of Henry Norman Bethune," Jean Deslauriers and Denis Goulet write, "His courage, determination and will to fully employ his talents of ingenuity, aggressiveness and selfless response to social concerns when the time came is truly remarkable."[3] He accomplished so much in his eighteen months in China that when he died of septicemia after operating on a soldier, Mao delivered his eulogy, describing him as "a man who is of value to the people."[4]

Bethune's achievements continue to be regarded as heroic by the Chinese. The first hospital he founded still exists, and his story is mandatory learning for primary school students in China.

Bethune's story, however, is not solely one of accolades and recognition, heaps of positive effects achieved as a result of a life spent trying to bring about good. His death at age forty-nine was directly caused by his efforts to improve health outcomes on the battlefield when he accidentally cut his finger while operating on a wounded Chinese soldier, which resulted in a bacterial infection. The fact that he was a communist led him to be written out of Canadian history during the Cold War years, when communism was seen as a direct threat to Western democracy.

Normally one would talk about a life like Norman Bethune's in terms of sacrifice. He sacrificed personal relationships, social acceptance, and ultimately his life to take actions in accordance with his beliefs and values. But using the lens of reciprocity suggests there is another way to interpret the story.

In a paper on the health benefits of volunteering in adults, the authors explain, "Research has found that participation in voluntary services is significantly predictive of better mental and physical health, life satisfaction, self-esteem, happiness, lower depressive symptoms, psychological distress, and mortality and functional inability."[5] Multiple studies have demonstrated the positive consequences of volunteering that are conferred on the volunteer. We may volunteer for a variety of reasons, based on our interests, goals, or values, but regardless, we reap health benefits when we do so.

The studies on the positive aspects of volunteering on the volunteer bring to mind the concepts we outlined in the science of reciprocity, like how forces always occur in pairs. Although volunteering is not governed by the laws of physics, using reciprocity as a metaphor can help us understand why volunteering appeals to so many people. And consequently, why some people make the choice to help others at seemingly great cost to themselves.

The research on volunteering makes it clear that when we give, we get. We improve our physical health; we feel better about ourselves and our place in the world. We evaluate our lives as having more meaning. One way of understanding people who take the kinds of actions that Bethune did, which on their face seem to risk so much, is that they receive a benefit from the world proportional to what they put out there. It's not a benefit that can always be measured in legacy or reward. Sometimes those things come; for Bethune, although North America struggled for decades to appreciate him as the dedicated medical innovator he was on account of his political views, China continues to go all out in its appreciation of his contributions to their country.

However, perhaps the benefit is better conceptualized as the reciprocity received by the individual in terms of the satisfaction they have regarding the choices they've made.

The act of doing good for others not only helps them but also causes the doer to feel good. In terms of Bethune's story, he was not motivated by recognition but rather by a genuine desire to help people, which gave him an exceptional amount of energy and drive. It is very possible that he didn't evaluate his life as one of sacrifice, but instead derived satisfaction from his efforts.

Many, many men have been just as troubled morally and spiritually as you are right now. Happily, some of them kept records of their troubles. You'll learn from them—if you want to. Just as someday, if you have something to offer, someone will learn something from you. It's a beautiful reciprocal arrangement.

—J. D. SALINGER[6]

Tit for Tat

Tit for tat is a strategy that, according to game theory, is the most effective choice for iterated games based on cooperation or defection. Both players benefit if they cooperate, but one benefits and the other loses if only the one defects, and both lose to a lesser extent if they simultaneously defect. As abstract as such games sound, they have important implications for understanding everything from group selection in biology to cooperation in economics. Under tit for tat, a player begins by cooperating, then in subsequent iterations replicates whatever their opponent did last time. So if their initial cooperation is punished with defection, they will then reciprocate. In games that are not iterated and only consist of a single round, defection is thought to be the best strategy.

Tit for tat was codified as a game theory strategy by mathematical psychologist Anatol Rapoport, but it builds upon our instinctual notions of reciprocity. It teaches us that our best option when dealing with people we cannot trust entirely is to reciprocate their choices. Seeing as we can rarely place full trust in anyone, especially if they stand to gain by screwing us over, we lean toward tit for tat. In general, we view this as fair and just. If someone helps us, we're quite happy to assist them the next time they need help. But if they ignore our plight when we need help, we're highly unlikely to care in the inverse situation. For this reason, evolution tends to select for cooperative behavior in groups—it benefits everyone in the long run.

However, straightforward tit for tat is not as effective as the strategy known as tit for tat with forgiveness. This strategy involves occasionally cooperating in the face of defection. It is easy for two opponents to get stuck in a cycle of mutual defection, from which they cannot escape unless and until one decides to cooperate. If both are using tit for tat, a cycle of cooperation will then commence.

Life is an iterative and compounding game. In the words of businessman Peter D. Kaufman, it pays to "go positive and go first." Also, remember that people make mistakes. Assuming there is no maliciousness, it pays to forgive.

The Rise of the "Win-Win"

In the physical world, the law of reciprocity works 100 percent of the time. The harder you punch a wall, the more force pushes against your fist, the more damage is caused to both you and the wall. In the biological world, reciprocity doesn't have the same perfect record. However, it has been discovered to work much more often than not, and thus harnessing it has significant long-term benefits.

Evolutionary biologists argue that our tendency to engage in reciprocal behavior is a natural product of evolution. You are more likely to survive if you receive help from others. And you are more likely to receive that help if you have offered assistance in the past. So, the genes that encode the reciprocal instinct were more likely to be passed on. And thus, the fact that the human species has made it to now is directly dependent on our building social interactions that are reliable, useful, and trustworthy.

Humans engage in two types of reciprocity with each other: direct, which is "I help you and you help me"; and indirect, which is either a pay-it-forward concept ("I help you and then you help someone else") or about reputation building ("I help you, building a reputation as one who helps, so that someone else will help me in the future"). Both work.

Loss Aversion

Loss aversion is one of the principles that govern the value of outcomes. Daniel Kahneman explains it like this: "When directly compared or weighted against each other, losses loom larger than gains." According to Kahneman, people are willing to risk losing $100 for every $250 of potential gains. The loss aversion coefficient is 1:2.5.[7] This asymmetry between the power of positive and negative expectations or experiences has an evolutionary history. Organisms that treat threats as more urgent than opportunities have a better chance to survive and reproduce. When it comes to reciprocity, we need to understand, "We are driven more strongly to avoid losses than to achieve gains."[8] This is why putting ourselves out there, engaging people who might dismiss or reject us, is so scary. Because in the one-off situation, the pain it will cause is perceived as stronger than the positive feelings of acceptance. The trick is to start looking at outcomes in the aggregate instead of focusing on each unique situation.

While reciprocity isn't as reliable when it comes to humans as it is with physics, the concept can help you achieve better outcomes.

Sometimes we go first and go positive and get nothing back, as is the case if we smile at a stranger walking on the street. Most times they'll smile back at you, but occasionally, you're met with a scowl. It's easy to forget the times our smile elicited a smile in response and remember the times when we received nothing in return, and so we stop smiling. However, the small loss we occasionally experience because of putting ourselves out there and not having it reciprocated is more than compensated for by the gains the rest of the time. If you want to get an idea of the true value of engaging in positive reciprocal behavior, just make a list of your outcomes in any given week.

Life is easier and more enjoyable when we start and maintain win-win relationships with everyone. Helping others helps us. And as we explained, reciprocity has been part of our biological makeup for a very long time.

> Tsze-Kung asked, "Is there one word with which to act in accordance throughout a lifetime?" The Master said, "Is not reciprocity such a word? What you do not want done to yourself, do not do to others."
>
> —CONFUCIUS[9]

Let's go back to the eastern Mediterranean around 1250 BCE. The bulk of the power in the region was held by the four kings of Egypt, Hatti (a region in present-day Turkey), Assyria, and Babylon. They didn't like each other much—in fact, "they deeply distrusted each other and frequently squabbled."[10] Demonstrating military prowess was often a way that a king achieved legitimacy in the eyes of his subjects, and there were constant conflicts, from skirmishes to full-on battles, between these four areas. Fighting was the norm.

Then, one day, as Trevor Bryce chronicles in his article on the Eternal Treaty, fifteen years after a "great military showdown" between the Egyptians and the Hittites, an interesting thing happened. The two kings decided to enter into the world's first-known peace treaty.

The treaty was not about peace in the global sense, stemming from a desire to have a world without war. It was about peace in the immediate sense: two parties trying to establish a mutually beneficial relationship. The treaty, known as the Eternal Treaty, was the laying out of a directly reciprocal relationship between two civilizations.

Egypt was led by Ramesses, whose primary goal was to build "monumental construction projects, and to build his kingdom's wealth through trade and the exploitation of its mineral-rich regions."[11] He had other security issues, most notably the Libyans to the west. So his interest in the treaty was to give himself some space to accomplish the legacy that mattered to him. The reality is, if you're fighting with everyone all the time, you have to spread your resources along many fronts, and you likely don't have time to do anything else. One less border to defend was an opportunity to put his efforts elsewhere.

The Hittites had a similar problem, in the form of a growing military threat from the Assyrians. In addition, their ruler Hattusili had usurped the throne from his nephew and was badly in need of some external power to legitimize his rule. Ramesses commanded great respect in the region, and his acknowledgment of Hattusili's leadership would go a long way toward maintaining stability. In pursuing the treaty with Egypt, "his hope was that Ramesses' endorsement of his own position, and by implication that of his lineal descendants, would provide some security against future challenges."[12]

The treaty contained provisions for future military support, the kind of alliance in which an attack on one is an attack on the other. Assyria, despite having both interest and a good position, did not, in fact, invade Hatti during Hattusili's reign, so "quite possibly, the Egyptian-Hittite alliance did prove an effective deterrent against such an enterprise."[13]

Reciprocity based on self-interest is still reciprocity. Engaging in positive behavior to then be a receiver of positive behavior is about the long game. For both Ramesses and Hattusili, the benefits of trying to develop an alliance were clear. It gave them both an opportunity to exit fighting that consumed resources and allowed them to focus those resources on long-term stability and their legacies. Over time, the likelihood of reciprocal interactions increases, and thus it's a much better strategy to try to make them positive. The more people you help, the more people you will have willing to help you.

Schadenfreude

"Schadenfreude" is a German word that has the literal translation of "damage-joy" and the more nuanced definition of delight or satisfaction at another person's misfortune or suffering. As Tiffany Watt Smith writes in *Schadenfreude: The Joy of Another's Misfortune*, equivalent concepts pop up in proverbs and words from numerous countries: France, Japan, Holland, Denmark, Israel, China, Russia, and ancient Greece and Rome.

Schadenfreude is closely linked to our sense of reciprocity. We feel it most strongly when someone's misfortune seems earned, as penance for their misdeeds. No one of sound mind would feel joy at the sight of an elderly lady tripping in the street or a dog getting its paw stepped upon. But when a homophobic politician accidentally tweets a link to gay porn? That's when we feel a sense of glee and feel less need to hide it. Schadenfreude is not sadism—it's a normal feeling that ties to our evolutionary programming and sense of fairness. We even use it as a form of bonding.[14]

According to research, schadenfreude is tied to three things: aggression, rivalry, and justice.[15] First, our sense of belonging to a particular group leads us to feel aggression toward anyone outside our tribe. The misfortune of those perceived as outsiders brings us satisfaction because we perceive it as benefiting our own group, even if it might not. Second, seeing things go wrong for other individuals gives us a stronger sense of our own superiority because we look and feel better in comparison. We naturally position ourselves within hierarchies based on every possible quality and are highly sensitive to where we stand in relation to others. Any sign of their inferiority transpires to be a plus for us.[16] Status is always relative.

Finally, we experience schadenfreude when our sense of reciprocity is satisfied—when we feel someone deserves come-uppance. We may not be willing or able to enact vengeance our-selves, but we're delighted when it seems the universe has done it for us. Sometimes we are content to bide our time until this happens, as our sense of reciprocity is so strong that we expect people to get what they deserve sooner or later. Research sup-ports this, suggesting that we feel more schadenfreude when we think someone deserves misfortune.[17]

Conclusion

Reciprocity underlies everything from basic human kindness to the most complex systems of trade. At its core, reciprocity is the simple idea that we treat others as they treat us—that we give what we get. But from this simple principle grows a vast web of social interactions and expectations that shapes nearly every aspect of our lives.

A lot of people seem to expect the world to just hand them things without putting in any effort. This is a poor strategy because it doesn't align with the human behavior you can observe around you every day. Reciprocation teaches us that if you give people cynicism and curtness or nothing at all, you are likely to receive the same. But if you give people opportunity and the benefit of the doubt, you will, more often than not, be on the receiving end of the same behavior.

Become what you want to see in the world, and the world will give it back to you. If you want an amazing relationship with your partner, be an amazing partner. If you want people to be thoughtful and kind to you, be thoughtful and kind to them. If you want people to listen to you, listen to them. The best way to achieve success is to deserve success. Small changes in your actions change your entire world.

One of the biggest misperceptions about reciprocity is that people should sit around waiting for others to go first rather than unlocking the power of reciprocity in their favor by going positive and going first without expectation.

Reciprocity reminds us that our actions tend to come back on us. It's an important reminder that we are part of the world, and thus our actions do not happen in isolation but are instead part of an interconnected web of effects.

Thermodynamics

Reduce chaos and find order.

A cold sink is essential. . . . In this sense, the cooling towers of a generating station are far more important to its operation than the complex turbines or the expensive nuclear reactor that seems to drive them.

—PETER ATKINS[1]

Thermodynamics refers to a set of laws that provide the ultimate foundation for how the world really works. It helps us understand randomness and disorder in systems and explains the conversion of energy from one form to another, the direction heat will flow, and the availability of energy to do work. One of the most useful aspects of thermodynamics is that it applies to all systems everywhere in the known universe, giving it a broad applicability. All work requires energy, and all systems are headed toward equilibrium.

To explore how the model of thermodynamics might give us new insights, we need to explain the four laws that comprise the theory. Here they are:

1. The first law of thermodynamics states that energy cannot be created or destroyed; it can only be transferred or changed from one form to another, such as from light to heat. The first law is known as the law of conservation of energy, and it deals with the transfer of energy. There are two forms of energy exchange—heat and work. Heat is energy exchange through thermal interaction and work is energy exchange by any process other than heat. Whereas work can be completely con-

verted into heat, heat cannot be completely converted into work.

2. The second law of thermodynamics states that entropy (a measure of disorder simply understood as energy unable to be used to do work) of an isolated system always increases. Isolated systems are those that spontaneously progress toward the state of maximum entropy of the system, also described as thermal equilibrium—no net heat flow between objects. The entropy of the universe only increases with time. One of the impacts of this law is that we need to expend energy to create order. Without the deployment of energy, all things move away from order.

3. The third law of thermodynamics states that as temperature approaches absolute zero, the entropy of a given system approaches a constant value.

4. The fourth law of thermodynamics is known as the zeroth law. This is because it was formulated after the first three laws but is fundamental to and assumed by the others. It states that if two objects are in thermal equilibrium with a third object, then those two objects are also in thermal equilibrium with each other.

Aside from powering most of the world, the laws of thermodynamics have many metaphorical applications. We can recognize that we will be influenced by the behavior of the people around us; therefore, it's important to be wise in choosing who they are. Entropy reminds us that energy is required to maintain order. You need to anticipate things falling apart and focus on prevention.

The energy state of an economy—that is, its temperature—largely determines what its members can do and how fast they can do it. Temperature—the average kinetic energy of the moving molecules in a gas—affects every chemical process and every physical property associated with life. It influences not only the cost of doing business, but the speed at which tasks can be accomplished, and perhaps most importantly the range of adaptive options available. Temperature is, in other words, the crucial link between energy and time, the two components of power.

—GEERAT VERMEIJ[2]

Putting Up Walls

Much of thermodynamics is about equilibrium, including the fact that two systems of different temperatures, when exposed to each other, eventually become the same temperature.

If thermal equilibrium is desirable, we can expend our efforts to maximize the exposure of the two systems to each other. Conversely, to keep them from reaching a state of equilibrium, some sort of insulating barrier is required. Like the experience of using a thermos to keep coffee hot, insulators can slow down the temperature change but cannot stop it completely.

The physical world, all of it, only ever has one destination: equilibrium.

—HELEN CZERSKI[3]

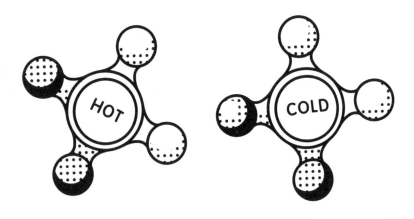

Much of thermodynamics is about equilibrium, including the fact that two systems of different temperatures, when exposed to each other, eventually become the same temperature.

What if we consider the equilibrium of two systems not between two containers of different-temperature water, but two societies with different values?

If we want to encourage equilibrium, then we can think of sharing as transfer of energy. There are three physical modes through which to transfer energy: radiation, convection, and conduction. There are clear analogies of how these modes are used socially to achieve equilibrium across boundaries. For example, radio and TV radiate ideas across borders. Teacher-student exchanges act as intellectual and social convection currents. Brands and foreign aid conduct values. Mixing cultures gives them common ground. We move toward social equilibrium when we share ideas and values that have the same foundations.

Sometimes, however, for various political or cultural reasons, we decide we don't want social or cultural equilibrium and so choose to erect an insulator in hopes of keeping the two systems from mixing. Humans have been putting up border walls for millennia. These walls often serve a physical and psychological purpose and are a line demarcating some sort of contrast. Us and them. My land, your land. Our values, your values. Our resources, your resources. The walls, however, never seem to work. From Hadrian's Wall to the Great Wall of China to the Berlin Wall, these complex, expensive structures stopped the movement of neither people nor ideas. Why? Because contrast is hard to maintain. It is hard to keep groups of people from sharing ideas, customs, or language, just as it is difficult and expensive to keep a cube of ice solid on a hot summer day. Through social structures such as trade and marriage, borders tend to be places of exchange and social evolution. Two different states, whether of matter or people, will be impacted by what they are exposed to. An ice cube will undergo a temperature change if left outside in warmer air, and similarly a group of people will undergo changes in custom based on whom they interact with outside their group.

> Division shapes politics at every level—the personal, local, national and international. Every story has two sides, and so does every wall. It's essential to be aware of what has divided us and what continues to do so, in order to understand what's going on the world today.
>
> —TIM MARSHALL[4]

The Romans, building Hadrian's Wall from coast to coast in northern England, seemed to best appreciate the limits of what a wall could achieve. From the outset, "Hadrian's Wall was not designed to withstand attack by a large and determined hostile army, for it was too long for the defenders to be strong at every point."[5] Rather, the wall functioned much like a border wall today. Its design was more about controlling the movement of people and goods than stopping it completely. From the outset, it was accompanied by a diplomatic presence, with the Roman army regularly crossing its line to engage with local tribes, building relationships to gather intelligence and to try to deter major attacks.[6]

The Romans knew Hadrian's Wall would not stop a strong enemy force, and thus the placement and design was about slowing down aggression or giving the Romans the opportunity to be proactive by developing relationships with those on the other side. Trade continued, information and materials were shared, and personal relationships were maintained by those living on both sides.[7] Hadrian's Wall thus was just one part of the overall strategy to maintain contrast between Roman territory and the tribes of the north. Controlling the interaction between both sides of the wall, instead of trying to stop it completely, was enough for the Romans, probably because they realized that there is a significant cost to improved insulation. Border walls do not do their jobs on their own; they need to be augmented by border personnel. As Adrian Goldsworthy writes of Hadrian's Wall, "Ultimately, its success rested less on the fortifications and barriers than on the soldiers who manned them."[8] This statement is true of all walls.

With Hadrian's Wall, the Romans did not try to prevent cultural equilibrium completely. They recognized that the resources required to prevent any interaction across the border were more than they were willing to invest. They seemed to accept that their society could function as desired despite the influence from the cultures on the other side. To relate to thermodynamics, if we think of Roman culture as "hot," Hadrian's Wall acted as an insulator; it slowed down the cooling from exposure to other cultures but did not stop it completely.

> But a boundary line, as any military expert will tell you, is also a potential battle line, for a boundary line marks off the territory of two opposed and potentially warring camps.
>
> —KEN WILBER[9]

Another famous wall that teaches us a lot about social equilibrium is the Great Wall of China. Walls have been going up between present-day China and Mongolia for at least two thousand years. Far from the restored stone wall that captures the imagination today, there are actually many walls, built of different materials and executed by many different dynasties, along this northern border.

The history of these Chinese walls is a lesson in why barriers designed to completely prevent the mingling of two sides is a bad idea. It's similar to trying to completely prevent two substances in direct contact from reaching thermal equilibrium—the necessary barrier requires too many resources to be practical.

First, walls are expensive. There is the maintenance, as well as provisioning for the people stationed at them. Second, people can go around or over walls, because walls have to end somewhere. The Chinese walls were an expression of political desire to set the location of the northern border, and as Julia Lovell explains in *The Great Wall*, they were not purely defensive structures.[10] Instead, they often pushed into foreign territory as a way of asserting claim. So, these walls were often not close to major centers, and they covered vast territory. Not only did they have to be staffed, they required that outposts and associated supply lines be maintained in order to provision them.

Right from the beginning there are stories about the essentially slave labor that was used to build the Chinese border walls and the horrible living conditions for those who staffed them. What good are walls without the loyalty of the troops stationed at them? Not much. The Great Wall was quite porous because "invaders could make detours around strong defenses until they found weaknesses and gaps,"[11] and it was often staffed by guards who made a better living accepting bribes from those wanting to cross.

Lovell describes the Ming dynasty attitude toward the Great Wall as "define, enclose, and exclude,"[12] which sums up the entire philosophy behind the Chinese border walls right from the beginning. On the one hand was the desire to keep the barbarians out. The nomads from the steppes of present-day Mongolia, the most famous of whom was Genghis Khan, were a constant threat to the Chinese people. But there was also a desire to keep Chinese culture in, to not pollute it with the ideas and sensibilities of others. The walls were thus also inward-looking, a way of maintaining "cultural superiority."

However, as Lovell describes, "it was not the case that border walls absolutely and immovably separated a culture of rice, silk, and poetry on the one side from a culture of horse milk, pelts, and war on the other."[13] There was a lot of intermingling. There were ethnic Chinese. They were invaded by barbarians. The barbarians adopted some Chinese ways. They became the new ethnic Chinese, who were in turn invaded by barbarians. This cycle played out multiple times over the centuries, influencing the development of Chinese culture. The more cultures mix, the more likely they are to reach cultural equilibrium; we tend not to regard people we share customs with as different.

Lovell tells the following story, which demonstrates the natural push for equilibrium and how hard it is to maintain contrast between two cultures who are in direct contact:

> In 307 BC—in the middle of the Warring States period—King Wuling of the northern state of Zhao started a court debate about fashion: should upper garments be buttoned to the left or down the middle? Behind this seemingly frivolous and innocuous question of style lay a strategic issue of huge political and cultural significance. King Wuling planned to swap the traditional Chinese gown for the side-buttoning tunic of the nomads, and the aristocratic Chinese chariot for their mounted archers. Embedded in the mooted change of dress was a revolution in worldview: an acceptance of the military superiority of the nomads and of the need to fight them on their own terms.[14]

Thus, the history of China is not the story of a culture that managed to completely insulate itself and remain "pure." Current Chinese culture is composed of influences and ideas that were exchanged along its borders.

Of all the walls in history, the Berlin Wall stands out as one that was erected to be an absolute, uncompromising barrier that was intended to prevent the mixing of two ideologies—to stop equilibrium. Walls don't just restrict physical movement; they can also shape and modify ideas and social norms.

The Berlin Wall was different from Hadrian's Wall and the Great Wall of China in that it was less a part of a military and diplomatic strategy and more a psychological barrier. It was not designed to facilitate interaction with potentially hostile tribes (like Hadrian's) or to claim territory and preserve culture (like China's).

The Berlin Wall tried to stop the movement of ideas as well as people. Soviet Communism and its East German counterpart depended on behavior-shaping propaganda and psychological controls, neither of which would work if challenged by outside economic or political ideas.

The Berlin Wall was built to stop every possible transfer from one side to the other. After World War II, when Germany was divided into East and West, Berlin became this little oasis of democracy behind the Iron Curtain of Communism. It was the only weak point in an otherwise formidable barrier between the ideas and politics of the Americans and the Soviets.

Occupied by Britain, the United States, France, and Russia after the war until 1961, Berlin still functioned as one city, which allowed for an escape route for those who wanted to leave Communist East Germany. As Frederick Taylor explains:

> Between 1945 and 1961, some two and a half million fled in this way, reducing [East Germany's] population by around 15 per cent. Ominously for the Communist regime, most emigrants were young and well qualified. The country was losing the cream of its educated professionals and skilled workers at a rate that risked making the Communist state totally unviable.
>
> During the summer of 1961, the exodus reached crucial levels. Every day, thousands of East Germans slipped into West Berlin and from there were flown to West Germany itself along the so-called "air corridors." The regime was not prepared to abandon the political and economic restrictions that fueled the hemorrhaging of its brightest and best.[15]

So they built a wall. And not just any wall—one with multiple layers of complexity and deterrents. In addition to the structure aboveground, subway tunnels, sewers, and anything that could give passage to the west was sealed off or modified so that human passage was thwarted.

The Berlin Wall never worked completely. People still crossed, albeit at huge risk, and some lost their lives in the attempt. But what is even more remarkable is that the Berlin Wall contributed to the very ideology it was trying to keep out. Effectively keeping the population prisoner only served to undermine the values of communism East Germany was trying to promote. The pressure built until one day, in November 1989, the wall was taken down by the very people it had been trying to keep apart.

The story of the Berlin Wall is a clear example of the inevitable force toward equilibrium. There was no way for the East German state to invest enough energy to prevent the social heat exchange and eventual equilibrium.

To keep two substances in direct contact from adjusting to the same temperature is difficult. It requires an insulator, and preventing any temperature change in the two substances is possible only with a constant investment of energy. The concept of equilibrium is a useful lens for understanding the inevitable fall of physical walls that humans have built around the globe. It is difficult to prevent two cultures in direct contact from sharing ideas and customs.

The Problem of Equilibrium

In *Twilight of the Idols*, Friedrich Nietzsche writes of politics, "Almost every party grasps that it is in the interest of its own self-preservation that the opposing party should not decay in strength."[16] This is pointing out that there is value in contrast. If all the forces are balanced, in a true state of equilibrium, there is no change, no growth, no movement. It is contrast that drives development.

We Don't Like Disorder

Maintaining order requires energy. Why put in that energy? Why extend ourselves to avoid the inevitable disorder of life? Using the second law of thermodynamics as a lens provides valuable insight into why reducing entropy is important.

Entropy can come across as too complicated or nonsensical, so some effort in coming up with an easy-to-use definition is well worth it. The simplest way to grasp the concept is to think of your residence. It would quickly turn into a mess without the constant effort of cleaning and tidying.

Murray Gell-Mann, a Nobel Prize–winning physicist, clarifies entropy in contexts such as organizing a pile of coins or the mixing of jelly and peanut butter in their containers. Why is it that if someone knocks the table the coins will get mixed up, or that despite their best efforts, your children inevitably get jelly into the peanut butter jar and vice versa? "The explanation is that there are more ways for [coins] to be mixed up than sorted. There are more ways for peanut butter and jelly to contaminate each other's containers than to remain completely pure. . . . To the extent that chance is operating, it is likely that a closed system that has some order will move toward disorder, which offers so many more possibilities."[17]

A simple example of entropy is life itself. There is a constant effort to maintain structure (avoid entropy) by consuming external energy (sunlight, food). In the process, life increases the entropy of (destroys) its environment and decreases entropy (builds or repairs) in the organism's body.

Another way to think of entropy is to imagine the game of broken telephone that you might have played when you were younger. A group of children sit around in a circle, and one child starts the game by whispering a sentence into the ear of the person next to them. The sentence gets transferred one child at a time until it has made its way around the circle. The final sentence is compared to the original, often with much hilarity. Something mundane like "Today is Wednesday" can turn into "I like scary movies." Because there are so many more options for change to occur, each repetition is more likely to drift from the original.

> Art is born out of as well as encapsulates the continuing battle between order and chaos. It seeks order or form, even when portraying anarchy.
>
> —JOHN YORKE[18]

Humans put a lot of effort into preventing disorder. If we look at society broadly, we notice that disorder flares up all the time. The structures we create nudge the natural disorder of life into order. Examples of this are laws, religions, social norms, customs, and the stories that explain and perpetuate them.

While the stories we tell are unimaginably diverse on the surface, if we go deeper, we can spot distinct patterns and structures that emerge every single time. The content may vary, but the form of the stories we tell is remarkably predictable. Fairy tales are one way we have combated disorder in our history. They offer explanations for occurrences that seem to have none, giving a structure to what we find hard to comprehend. Fairy tales also set out a common understanding that everyone can buy into, trying to slow down entropy by preemptively fitting the unexplainable into a systematic order.

The patterns in our fairy tales are so inescapable across time and cultures that it seems logical to suggest there must be a reason.

Soap operas may not seem to have much in common with Shakespeare, yet at the heart of every story is the drumroll moment—the turning point when everything changes and the characters must go on a journey to restore normality. As if we can slow down entropy by telling stories to reduce disorder.

Fairy tales these days are often associated with the Disney renditions most of us are familiar with. But the original compilations, such as those collected by the Grimm brothers, or the more original versions pulling from even older stories, like those by Hans Christian Andersen, offer a better view of how fairy tales can be understood as combating entropy.

In *Into the Woods*, John Yorke suggests that the way we tell stories is indicative of our desire to find order in the world. Stories are an attempt to tame the terrifying randomness that surrounds us. As we go through life, we are constantly absorbing chaotic information that we make sense of through narratives. Yorke writes, "Every act of perception is an attempt to impose order, to make sense of a chaotic universe. Storytelling, at one level, is a manifestation of this process."[19]

The core structure of the stories we tell can be described in a few different ways: equilibrium / disequilibrium / new equilibrium; journey there / journey back; someone is looking for something and someone or something is in their way; and so on. In more detailed terms, Yorke describes the archetypal story structure as follows:

- "Home" is threatened

- The protagonist suffers from some kind of flaw or problem

- The protagonist goes on a journey to find a cure or the key to the problem

- They find a cure or the key

- On the journey back they're forced to face up to the consequences of taking it

- They face some kind of literal or metaphorical death

- They're reborn as a new person, in full possession of the cure; in the process "home" is saved.

Fairy tales beat back the stress that disorder can cause by putting the world back in order. As Marina Warner argues in *Once Upon a Time: A Short History of Fairy Tale,* they convey a hope that order can come about even in the face of almost unexplainable acts.[20] Child abandonment and neglect, rape and death—fairy tales take away the randomness by putting these acts into a larger, explainable structure and offering insight on how to process them.

We are drawn to stories that make things feel a little less random, just as we are drawn to storytellers who seemingly simplify complexity. We are all aware of disorder and the natural uncertainty that follows it and are attracted to stories that reduce it.

By turning individual struggles into common experience, fairy tales put order into the disorder of "assault, cruelty, and injustice."[21] These stories do not feature gods or superheroes, and instead look at the everyday person as they navigate their ordinary lives. "The structures of wonder and magic open ways of recording experience while imagining a time when suffering will be over."[22] Namely, when disorder will be conquered.

There are no surprises in fairy tales. Not for the characters and not for us. We have heard the story before and know what will happen. However magical the world they depict, we have total faith in the structure of the story. That predictability is one means of providing order to things that would otherwise seem chaotic. What you learn about the world through fairy tales is to accept things that may not make obvious sense. Trust that there is order behind them, and by doing so slow down the entropy of life.

"The landscape of fairy tales is symbolic: 'The forest is where you are when your surroundings are not mastered.'"[23] Fairy tales provide a means of mastering your surroundings by presenting a way to understand your world, giving it some order, and helping you make your way through it.

While works that deviate from the archetypal narrative can be interesting, those that follow it most closely tend to enjoy the most commercial success. They just *feel* right. They are an escape from the chaotic real world. Unable to face meaninglessness, "in order to stay sane we must impose some kind of pattern."[24] This is what narratives achieve, and it's the same reason we craft them within our own lives. They give us a sense of a coherent identity.

It is interesting that fairy tales cross cultural and geographical boundaries. Similar stories occur in many places. Sometimes this is due to exchange via travel. The stories carried by wanderers were then modified and built on in their new homes easily because their structure had already occurred. Often, though, fairy tales in different cultures are very similar even when it's not believed they were shared through travel. They are a common cultural phenomenon. So it is understandable that they have a lasting, worldwide appeal.

Cinderella stories are a great example. The classic tale of a young woman living in unfortunate circumstances that suddenly change to remarkable fortune is found in many cultures. Variations include "Yeh-Shen" in China, "Cendrillon" in France, and "The Turkey Girl" in Native American Zuni culture.

The staying power of fairy tales "suggests that they must be addressing issues that have a significant social function."[25] By informing behavior in a similar way, fairy tales combat entropy and create a common understanding that most people can interact with.

Conclusion

Thermodynamics is the science of energy, heat, and work. It's the set of physical laws that govern how energy moves and changes in the universe. Chances are when you first came across the subject, it was dry, full of equations and abstract concepts. But the truth is thermodynamics is a useful intellectual framework for daily life. Not only can it reveal why your room gets messier over time, but it also explains why you should choose your friends wisely.

The first law of thermodynamics states that energy can neither be created nor destroyed, only transformed from one form to another. This means that every joule of energy in the universe, every bit of heat and work and motion is part of an unbroken chain stretching back to the big bang. When you hop on a flight that burns jet fuel, you're tapping into energy that was originally captured by plants millions of years ago and stored in chemical bonds until it was transformed into heat and motion.

But while energy is conserved, it's not always useful. That's where the second law of thermodynamics comes in. It states that in any closed system, entropy—a measure of disorder—increases over time. In other words, left on its own, the universe tends toward chaos. Your bedroom doesn't clean itself—it takes energy and effort to maintain order. Stars burn out, structures crumble, ice melts into water.

Entropy is the universe's tax on time. The constant battle against entropy is the driving force behind much of what we do. The constant struggle between order and disorder is the source of change and progress.

While engineers and scientists use thermodynamics to design engines or calculate the energy requirements of a system, we can use it as a framework for understanding the deep interconnectedness of everything. When you feel the warmth of the sun on your skin, you're experiencing the end result of a thermodynamic process that began in the heart of a star ninety-three million miles away. When you watch a campfire burn down to embers, you're witnessing the inexorable march of entropy in real time. Thermodynamics is the story of energy across time.

We're part of an energy story that stretches back to the dawn of time and reaches out to the farthest pockets of space. We can marvel at the fact that in a universe ruled by disorder, pockets of temporary order can emerge, whether it's a clean room, a planet, or a civilization. By understanding thermodynamics, we gain not just a technical toolbox but an appreciation for the beauty, complexity, and fragility of our very existence.

Inertia

Change requires force.

Nothing happens until
something moves.

—ALBERT EINSTEIN[1]

tarting something is hard, but so is stopping something. In physics, inertia refers to the resistance a physical object has to a change in its state of motion. Things at rest don't start moving on their own, and planets continue to circle the sun without a means of propulsion.

The phenomenon of inertia is the subject of Isaac Newton's first law of motion, which states, "An object at rest stays at rest and an object in motion stays in motion with the same speed and in the same direction unless acted upon by an unbalanced force." If a force—for example, friction—is not present, the object will continue as it was, moving with the same velocity or remaining at rest. Left to themselves, systems resist change. So too do people.

Galileo discovered the principles of inertia through an experiment by setting two inclined planes against each other, almost like a skateboard half-pipe, and then rolling a ball down one of them. The clever experiment made it easy to see that the smoother the surface, the closer the ball would come to reaching its initial height on the opposite plane, From this finding, he argued that any difference in initial and final height of the ball was due to the presence of friction, an opposing force.

In his book *Principles of Philosophy*, Descartes talks about inertia as well, stating that the first law of nature is that "each thing, as far as is in its power, always remains in the same state; and that consequently, when it is once moved, it always continues to move."[2]

Inertia is a useful model to try to understand some elements of our behavior, including our thinking patterns and habits. Our natural inclination to reject the new is in part normal resistance to the effort required to change. Keeping things as they are requires almost no effort and involves little uncertainty. We need force to effect change, and force requires effort. Inertia offers a lens to help us understand resistance to change and why we fail ourselves when we get complacent.

Inertia is the reason that starting something is harder than continuing. At a basic level, many brain studies have shown that the idea of multitasking is a myth. When we shift our focus from one input to another, we exert more energy and use more time to finish everything than if we would have completed one task before starting another.

Inertia also helps to explain why we continue bad habits and why it's hard to make systematic change. Many cities continue to rely on cars for short commutes instead of implementing an infrastructure to facilitate public transportation, walking, or cycling. Inertia is the reason we stay at jobs we hate, avoid meaningful conversations with people of different opinions, and almost never change the religion our parents imposed on us at birth. It is easier to stay on our current path, even if it's going in the wrong direction.

> For, like a mass in Newton's first law of motion, once our minds are set in a direction, they tend to continue in that direction unless acted on by some outside force.
>
> —LEONARD MLODINOW[3]

Momentum

Imagine a train pulling into a station and screeching to a halt. The driver doesn't press the brakes when they want to stop. They do it well in advance, allowing enough time for the full length of the train, weighing hundreds or even thousands of tons, to come to a standstill.

A train can't just stop moving as soon as the driver applies the brakes, because of momentum. The equation for calculating momentum is $p = mv$, where p is momentum, m is mass, and v is velocity. When something with mass is moving, it has momentum.

The greater the mass and the greater the velocity, the greater the momentum of an object. If you're out for a run, it takes a lot less effort for you to stop than it does for a train because you're lighter and slower. Doubling either the speed or the mass of an object will double its momentum.

Isaac Newton's second law of motion states that the acceleration of an object is the result of two factors: the forces acting upon it and its mass. This contrasts with the first law of motion, which states that an object will remain at its current velocity if the forces acting on it are all balanced. So, acceleration is the product of unbalanced forces.

Outside physics, we consider something to have momentum if it is progressing in a particular direction in such a way that it would take a weighty outside force to stop it or change its direction.[4]

Once an Idea Gets Rolling, It Can Be Hard to Stop

Why do some products hang around for centuries even when better and cheaper ones come on the market? Why do others burst onto the scene with so much promise, only to flame out quickly? We can use the lens of inertia to provide part of the answer to these questions.

Most of the time, our consumption patterns are based on habit, not conscious thought. We buy what we buy and have the preferences that we do because we've had them for a long time. When we go to the grocery store, we seldom invest the energy to apply critical thinking to the products we've bought dozens of times. The longer we've been buying something, the more ingrained this product is in our lives. Even if we find out it is unhealthy, we seldom switch immediately, if at all. We can understand why this happens by looking at Newton's second law, relating force to acceleration, which shows us that mass matters when it comes to inertia.

When a force acts on an object, the object accelerates in the direction of the force. If mass stays the same, increasing force will increase acceleration. If the force on an object remains constant, increasing mass will decrease acceleration. Heavier objects require more force to accelerate or slow them down than do lighter objects. Essentially, the greater the mass, the greater the inertia.

The relevance of mass has analogous application in our habits. While it's not a perfect parallel, you can often think of mass as duration when it comes to habits. The longer we've been doing something, the more it has become part of both our identity and our understanding of the world. Thus, the amount of effort required to change a habit is greater proportional to the length of time we've had it. What is true for the individual is also true for our larger so-cieties. The longer a product has been used by a society, the harder it is to change to a new one, even if there are obvious benefits. Let's look at two products, lead and absinthe, and compare their social inertia.

About two thousand years ago, Marcus Vitruvius Pollio wrote *On Architecture*, a wide-ranging series of books covering not only architecture but engineering, philosophy, and medicine. He had many suggestions and observations, one of which was, "Water ought by no means to be conducted in lead pipes, if we want to have it wholesome." Before we had gunpowder, compasses, or forks, we had strong indications that we shouldn't be exposing ourselves to a lot of lead.

No one really heeded his advice. Over the next millennia, lead was added to makeup, gasoline, and paint, and it was part of many manufacturing processes, such as printing. Concerns about its side effects kept cropping up as people continued to notice a high corre-lation between death and exposure to lead. Nonetheless, it was used to dilute wine, it made the pipes that carried drinking water, and it was added to face cream to help women achieve the paleness that was the social standard of beauty.

In 1910, Alice Hamilton was appointed to head a survey on in-dustrial illness in Illinois. Over the next few years, she became America's leading expert on industrial toxicology, providing defin-itive evidence of, among other things, the dangers of lead exposure in the workplace.[5] Despite this evidence, the American car com-pany General Motors proceeded with the creation of leaded fuel in the 1920s. Hamilton campaigned extensively against the introduc-tion of leaded fuel, and she and her colleagues provided an exten-sive overview of the toxicology of leaded gas and the dangers of lead-tainted exhaust.[6] And yet, fuel laced with lead wasn't banned in the USA until the 1980s.

Lead still crops up in other places despite all we know of its dangers. For example, it is added to paint to prevent cracking caused by changes in temperature. Leaded paint is still used in many countries today in homes and on toys even though nontoxic options are available at a similar price.

The story of lead can be contrasted with that of absinthe, whose rise and fall occurred within fifty years.

"Absinthe was made from a combination of plants and aromatics, including wormwood, aniseed, fennel and wild marjoram, which were first bruised and then soaked in alcohol and distilled, creating a bitter, pear-colored liqueur. . . . A measure would be placed in a glass, and was then diluted with ice-cold water poured through a sugar cube, turning the whole thing milky pale."[7] Starting in the 1860s, absinthe became a wildly popular aperitif—an alcoholic drink taken before dinner. "In the latter half of the nineteenth century whole districts of Paris were said to smell faintly herbal between 5 and 6 p.m., a time that became known as *l'heure verte* ('the green hour')."[8]

Fifty years later it was being compared to opium and considered a major social ill. Furthermore, "in France, doctors began to suspect that it was really a poisonous drug. . . . People were reporting hallucinations and permanent insanity."[9] Experiments were conducted, and animals sacrificed. Then, "in Switzerland, the final straw came in 1905, when a man called Jean Lanfray killed his pregnant wife and two young daughters, Rose and Blanche, after he had been drinking absinthe. The case was dubbed 'the absinthe murder' and the drink was outlawed completely in Switzerland three years later."[10] France followed in 1914.

Within fifty years absinthe was used, abused, and abandoned.

Interestingly, "subsequent tests have shown that much of the supposed proof of absinthe's inherently deleterious effects were nonsense."[11] It is no worse for you than any other alcohol of the same strength.

So, on the one hand, we have lead, proposed as poisonous for two thousand years and still in use; and on the other, absinthe, whose suspected effects caused it to be taken off the market within fifty years. Lead, now proven toxic, is still kicking around in consumer products. Absinthe, absolved of all responsibility, remains unobtainable in many liquor stores. Why the difference? Obviously, the reasons are complex, but the use of mental models is about the insight they provide. So, by using the lens of inertia, we can make some observations.

Mass matters. It is much easier to apply force to stop a light object versus a heavy one. Lead and absinthe had different societal masses. Lead performed several highly useful functions in multiple manufacturing processes. Absinthe got people drunk. Lead had been integrated into many other substances, and so there is also an incentive angle. The cost of containment and remedy for lead was extremely high, and people would have had to abstain from using products they found useful, not to mention the cost of retooling manufacturing systems that relied on lead. Absinthe stood on its own. Thus, it took far less effort to remove absinthe than it is taking to remove lead.

Once we consider a story true, it takes a great deal of force to change it. Data alone is rarely enough. This is part of the reason why the proof of something being harmful is not always enough to produce a change in behavior. The inertia of a product, a habit, or an idea increases the longer it is around. There are countless urban legends and popular myths that have persisted for a long time and have woven themselves into our understanding of the world, despite available evidence of their inaccuracy. Sometimes it can feel monumentally frustrating when reliable information doesn't seem to change an erroneous popular opinion. Using inertia as a lens helps us understand the dynamics that are involved and gives us some insights on how to tackle addressing the motion we want to change.

Escape Velocity

Escape velocity is the speed an object needs to break free from a planet's gravitational grip. In a sense, it is the ultimate triumph over inertia. For instance, when a rocket is taking off, it needs to reach an extremely high speed to get away from the strong gravitational influence of the Earth. As it moves farther away, it can slow down a bit. This is because the gravitational force pulling it back to Earth is no longer strong enough to overcome its kinetic energy. As the rocket gains altitude its fuel and kinetic energy are converted to gravitational potential energy. If the rocket can build enough velocity, it can escape the pull of Earth's gravity indefinitely even without further propulsion—this is referred to as the escape velocity and is equal to seven miles per second on the surface of the Earth. We can relate escape velocity to an idea that comes up later in the book, that of activation energy. How much effort do we need not only to overcome resistance, but to set an object on a new path?

The Inertia of Belief

> For the need to think can never be stilled by allegedly definite insights of "wise men"; it can be satisfied only through thinking, and the thoughts I had yesterday will satisfy this need today only to the extent that I want and am able to think them anew.
>
> —HANNAH ARENDT[12]

Inertia as a lens shows us that beliefs can become habits. Habits are entrenched behaviors, some of which are good, while others are bad.

In *Learning from the Octopus*, Rafe Sagarin writes that belief systems have an "enormous evolutionary inertia behind them,"[13] explaining that our capacity for belief has been one of our survival mechanisms and that this biological relevance helps explain why beliefs are so resistant to change. Thus, sometimes the inertia of our beliefs hinders us, such as when they make us blind to new opportunities. Or when we dismiss new information or ideas because they don't fit with what we think we know about the world. For example, the history of invention is a story of the dismissal of new ideas. From radio and the telephone to cars, airplanes, and laptop computers, many life-changing inventions were dismissed initially as irrelevant or useless. There are many stories of people who lost out on opportunities to develop and invest in these new technologies later lamenting their lack of foresight.

The flip side is that while we often look back and shake our heads at the lack of vision, it suggests that new ideas must overcome the inertia to displace existing ideas. And given that these technologies eventually did become an indispensable part of our world, there are obviously some visionaries whose beliefs were flexible enough to lend their support in combating the inertia.

Thus, the inertia of belief can also be a good thing. At the most basic level, when our beliefs persist, we don't have to relearn everything all the time. Furthermore, values with strong inertia can also help us persevere through obstacles and setbacks. This does not mean that we should hold on to our beliefs blindly, unwilling to update them once we become adults. Strong beliefs can stay strong while being flexible. In fact, if we continually refine and develop them based on new information and experiences, they can continue to support us through challenges.

Often the stories behind new theories and inventions show both aspects of the inertia of belief: the positive aspect that propels scientists and inventors to carry on in the face of rejection and ridicule, and the negative aspect that fuels those reactions.

The inertia of belief can make it difficult to cause real change in the world. But that same inertia can help those who are determined to cause change to hold on to their beliefs and push through. The story of nuclear physicist Lise Meitner demonstrates this dichotomy. She started off with the deck stacked against her in terms of the strong negative social beliefs that she had to navigate. In a more just world, she would not have had to do what she did, but her determination gave her the willingness to adapt to an unfair system.

Lise Meitner was born in Austria in 1878. At age twenty-three she was the first woman admitted to the University of Vienna's physics lectures and laboratories and went on to become the second woman to receive a PhD in physics at the university. In 1907 physicist Max Planck invited her to Berlin, where she worked for years as an unpaid research assistant.[14] During this time she met Otto Hahn, with whom she would collaborate professionally for decades, and together they discovered protactinium, the element with atomic number 91 on the periodic table. The university would not allow women to do independent research, so she and Hahn had to get creative to pursue their ideas. As described in her biography by Patricia Rife on the Jewish Women's Archive, "At first, she was an unpaid 'guest' under Hahn, but most people knew they were equals in their research team."[15] Officially though, her contributions were always minimized. As Ruth Lewin Sime describes in *Lise Meitner: A Life in Physics*, "In every publication Hahn was first author, to which Meitner apparently did not object, even though she had done much of the work."[16]

Despite the slights, Meitner maintained her friendship with Hahn for the rest of her life, even becoming godmother to his only child.

Eventually her work, the respect of her colleagues, and her growing contribution to radiation and nuclear physics led to her being asked to create and supervise the physics section of the Kaiser Wilhelm Institute for Chemistry. It was a position she held for twenty years. On being asked to establish the physics department, Meitner "took it as a sign of recognition, trust, and professional coming-of-age."[17] In 1919 she became a professor at the institute and thus was the first woman in Prussia with the title.

During the 1920s and early '30s, Meitner continued her work researching different aspects of physics. Any results achieved were the result of careful and patient work. She was the first person to observe and describe multiple transitions without the emission of radiation, and with colleague Kurt Philipp, she was "the first to identify positrons from a noncosmic source and to show, moreover, that positrons appear together with negative electrons in pairs."[18] Her accomplishments during this time put her in "the first rank of experimental physicists."[19] She began to see her teaching duties expanded as she climbed the academic hierarchy and received a series of prizes in recognition of her work.

In 1933 things began to change. That year the Nazi party decreed that Jewish academics were no longer allowed to be professors. Meitner continued her research but in 1938 fled Germany for Sweden with the assistance of legendary physicist Niels Bohr. During the war she worked in a seemingly more limited capacity at the Nobel Research Institute of Physics, living on a small research assistant's salary and feeling cut off from the work she had been doing in Berlin.[20]

However, it was during this time that Meitner made her most significant discovery. Hahn continued to communicate with her, detailing the results of his experiments and asking her to come up with the explanation for his results. Meitner began to ponder the data, and through an insight gained while discussing the matter with her physicist nephew, Otto Frisch, put together the first explanation of nuclear fission. Her work provided the first indication of the power contained in nuclear reactions and eventually led to, among other things, the making of the atomic bomb. It was Meitner's most significant contribution to physics.

Despite Meitner's work, Otto Hahn was the sole recipient of the 1944 Nobel Prize for the discovery of nuclear fission. Lise Meitner was nominated twenty-nine times for the Nobel Prize, including three times by Niels Bohr, but was never awarded the honor.[21]

We do not have to look hard to find beliefs with incredible inertia that Meitner had to fight against. First were cultural beliefs about women, what their capabilities were, and what their place in society was. At so many turns, Meitner had to navigate prejudices about women. On everything from receiving an education to her ability to conduct research in a lab, she had to work hard to overcome the inertia she faced.

In addition, being of Jewish descent in Nazi Germany meant having to deal with a mass of beliefs that had gained a frightening amount of momentum with incredible inertia. The political conditions in Germany were partly responsible for Otto Hahn's masking Meitner's contributions to the discovery of nuclear fission.

The remarkable aspect of Lise Meitner's story, however, is how her passion for physics propelled her through the challenges. First, it takes dedication to be a research scientist. Ruth Lewin Sime's accounts of Meitner's patience while conducting research suggests that she had total belief in her work. Not that there was a particular answer she was trying to prove, but that there was value in the scientific process itself. Thus, her beliefs were not a rigid dogma but a flexible understanding that grew through investigating and discovering new ideas. It was these beliefs that likely supported her when she had to take secondary position on papers she had done most of the work on, or when she had to work in subpar lab conditions for low pay.

Meitner achieved more than possibly any other woman working in physics at the time—not only the discoveries in experimental physics but also leading a department and earning widespread respect and prestige. She was treated as an equal within her field, and until the Nazis came to power, she enjoyed a position as the only female physics professor in Germany.

Meitner's beliefs in both physics and herself increased their inertia as her life went on, allowing her to respond to the challenges presented by the prejudice she encountered. Although she never won a Nobel, she was awarded many honorary doctorates and other prizes. In her later years she gave many talks to support women's progression in the sciences and continued her research until she was eighty-one. She was widely respected by colleagues all over the globe, and Sime writes that Meitner made friends for life wherever she went.

Meitner persevered in the sense that she continued to do what she loved despite the obstacles she faced. To other female scientists she said, "Remember that science can bring both joy and satisfaction to your life."[22]

Conclusion

Inertia is the stubborn resistance of the universe to change. It's the reason why objects at rest tend to stay at rest and objects in motion tend to stay in motion. You can think of inertia as the guardian of the status quo.

At its core, inertia is a property of mass. The more massive an object is, the more it resists changes to its state of motion. A feather, with its tiny mass, is easily blown about by the slightest breeze. A boulder, on the other hand, requires a powerful force to get it moving. This is why it takes more effort to push a heavy cart than a light one, more energy to launch a rocket than to toss a ball.

But inertia isn't just a physical phenomenon. It's an illuminating lens to see habits, beliefs, and our resistance to change. The longer we've held them, the larger the mass and the more force required to change them. The path of least resistance is always the status quo.

Getting started is the hardest part. Once something is moving in a direction, it's much easier to keep it in motion. But once something is in motion, it's hard to stop. This is why most self-help books about positive habits break things down into very small steps—to reduce the force required to overcome the status quo. For example, if you want to get in the habit of doing push-ups daily, start with one rather than with fifty. If you want to start a flossing habit, start with one tooth. After all, the bigger the mass—in this case the gap between where you are and where you want to be—the more effort required.

Inertia is both a challenge and an opportunity. Successful companies struggle with the inertia of their own success and the resistance to change that comes with size, complexity, and entrenched interests. Startups, on the other hand, can leverage their lack of inertia—their agility, their willingness to pivot and adapt—as a competitive advantage.

Momentum and inertia are closely related. While inertia is the tendency to resist change, momentum is the oomph an object has when it's moving. The more momentum something has, the harder it is to stop or redirect. The key is to pick the right direction and build momentum so inertia works to your advantage and carries you forward. This is the essence of the "flywheel" concept in business—the idea that success breeds success, that small wins can compound into big gains over time.

When you're fighting the status quo, remember the physics at play. Resistance is natural. Understand that it takes a sustained force in the right direction to build momentum in a new direction.

While the universe resists change, it always rewards those who dare to overcome that resistance.

Friction and Viscosity

Movement is a battle.

Insanity comes in two basic varieties: slow and fast. . . . Viscosity and velocity are opposites, yet they can look the same. Viscosity causes the stillness of disinclination; velocity causes the stillness of fascination. An observer can't tell if a person is silent and still because inner life has stalled, or because inner life is transfixingly busy.

—SUSANNA KAYSEN[1]

F riction is a force that must be overcome to achieve an outcome. There is always something getting in the way and trying to slow us down.

While we can never eliminate the forces that impede our progress, we can work to minimize them. Like a smooth surface provides less challenge to a rolling ball, or how water is easier for a human to swim through than it is for a krill, shaping our environment to reduce the challenges of opposing forces is a key to improving productivity.

Friction is a force that opposes the movement of objects that are in contact with each other, such as the wheels of a pair of roller skates moving across the ground. For objects to move, they must overcome friction that pushes in the opposite direction. This requires extra energy, which produces heat and sound. Smooth surfaces cause less friction than rough ones, which explains why walking on pavement is much easier and less tiring than walking on gravel. There are no frictionless surfaces, only surfaces with less or more resistance.

All objects experience friction. There are two key types of friction: kinetic and static. Kinetic friction occurs when two objects are sliding past each other. This explains why an object in motion, without consistent forces pushing it forward, will come to a halt.

For example, if you place a book on a table and give it a push, it will move a bit and then stop. The kinetic friction absorbs the energy you transfer to the book in the push. Static friction, on the other hand, occurs when an object is stationary; it's what prevents it from moving.

Although scientists have been examining friction for about six hundred years, there are still gaps in our understanding. Despite some of its mysterious qualities, friction remains a useful mental model because it captures how our environment can impede our movement.

Viscosity, which can be seen as the partner of friction, is the "measure of how hard it is for one layer of fluid to slide over another layer."[2] If a liquid is hard to move, it is more viscous. If it is more viscous, there is more resistance.

Viscosity isn't usually an issue for humans in our day-to-day lives. We mostly deal with gravity and inertia, although viscosity is always present. But for small particles, gravity and inertia become a nonissue compared to viscosity. So if you make things bigger, viscosity is less relevant.

A tiny plankton moving in the ocean is going to have to struggle through the viscous water and will stop coasting forward almost as soon as it stops moving. For a whale, on the other hand, the viscosity of the water hardly registers. Its size means it can push water out of the way with ease and capitalize on other forces, such as inertia, to keep forward motion.

There are two important aspects to using friction and viscosity as a model. First, what is easy in one environment might be harder in another. For instance, what we can accomplish in times of peace is different than what we can accomplish in times of war. Second, we also learn that the main forces relevant to a particular situation depend on the scale you are operating at.

Surface Tension

"Viscosity matters when something small is moving through a single fluid . . . surface tension, its partner in the world of the small, matters at the place where two different fluids touch."[3] The story of the measuring of surface tension is the story of an individual who persisted: one woman working in a society that made it almost impossible for a woman to move in the environment of scientific study. Agnes Pockels wanted to study physics, but at the end of the nineteenth century in Germany, women were not allowed into the universities.[4] Her younger brother became a physicist, sharing his textbooks and, throughout his life, advances in the discipline.

At home, taking care of aging parents, she maintained her curiosity and passion as best she could in the limited setting. She developed a simple tool called the Pockels trough, which "was able to measure the surface tension of water under the influence of different surface concentrations of the oils and soaps she worked with."[5] She went on to publish several papers on surface tension, essentially forming the base of the research on the concept, without ever receiving formal training or education in science. Her tool and her research were built upon by others, who went on to receive awards like the Nobel Prize. But her accomplishments are more remarkable when we consider the high viscosity of the environment in which she succeeded.

Slowing the Flow

Everything that moves has to move through something, including information. Why does some information get disseminated quickly, whereas other times it gets bogged down and seems to go nowhere?

The answer often has a lot less to do with the content of the information than with the environment it moves through. To understand just how much a communications environment can be manipulated to affect the pace of information exchange, let's look at Soviet Russia. By the 1980s the Soviets had created a high-viscosity communications environment that made it hard for information to flow through it. Like a goldfish trying to swim through honey, people had an unrelentingly difficult time trying to communicate information to those who might need it.

During the Cold War era, the Soviets amplified forces that negatively impacted the free flow of individual bits of information, potentially because it's easier to control things that are moving slower. The viscous information environment they created may have been useful to the state for maintaining control, but it also caused the broad scope of the Chernobyl disaster.

During and after the explosion at the Chernobyl nuclear power plant in 1986, there was a lack of information getting to those affected, from citizens to supporting government departments to other countries. A lot of information was out there, but it had a hard time flowing to those who needed it because of the structure of the Soviet system.

In *Chernobyl: The History of a Nuclear Catastrophe*, Serhii Plokhy describes the entire scope of the disaster. He explains that the leadership of the Soviet Union was characterized by an approach of burying the past instead of learning from it. Their complicated bureaucracy created an environment that made it very hard for correct information to get to those who needed it. This was manifested in censorship, the criminalization of sharing certain information, regular domestic spying, and a total lack of empowerment of the people on the ground.

Chernobyl was not the first nuclear accident in the Soviet Union. However, it was illegal for anyone to officially report on or discuss any that had happened previously, notably the multiple accidents at the nuclear power plant in Leningrad, as if by not acknowledging something, the Soviets could pretend it out of existence.[6] Because information about previous issues was suppressed, there were no lessons learned that fed into the design of the Chernobyl plant or its procedures.

After the accident at Chernobyl, the pattern of zero communication continued, with nothing being reported within the Soviet Union or to the foreign press. There were secret resolutions, and everything was classified. One consequence of this approach was that the people immediately affected—those who lived in the surrounding area—had no idea what was happening or how to protect themselves. "Intercity telephone networks had been cut, and the engineers and workers at the nuclear plant had been prohibited from sharing news of what had happened with their friends or relatives."[7] Information control was more important than the lives of people.

How does a situation like this come to be? There are a lot of aspects to consider, as a highly viscous information environment is not created by one factor alone.

To start, there was the Soviet preoccupation with image. They didn't want to look bad to their citizens or the West, as they believed this would weaken the Communist state. They insisted things go on as usual, including the large May Day parade in nearby Kiev, which exposed thousands to high levels of radiation. The Soviets accused the Western media of spreading rumors about Chernobyl and kept repeating in official reports "that everything was fine, and that the party was in control."[8]

Additionally, the Soviet mentality within the political structure was characterized by fear and a lack of accountability. Problems were pushed up the chain, because no one wanted to take responsibility and make a decision and thus have to deal with the potential consequences of being wrong and embarrassing the government. But at the same time, "the protocol was to bully subordinates into submission and then demand the fulfillment of unrealistic production quotas."[9] People couldn't safely say, "No, we can't get that done in the time frame you are asking for." With no one wanting to communicate negative information up the chain, and erroneous information being pushed down the chain, building operations like those at Chernobyl cut corners to meet unrealistic deadlines.

Chernobyl itself was built on shaky foundations with questionable reactors, and with safety standards that would never have cut it in North America or Western Europe. No one in the Soviet Union seemed to want to hear accurate assessments of problems or projects. Thus, the information that moved up and down the chain was often completely fabricated. Essentially there was high viscosity for true information, whereas false information faced a low-viscosity medium. Similar to fluid hitting a boundary with different viscosities, false information was disseminated further because it flowed easier.

Finally, the Soviet leadership "was still deeply grounded in the Soviet tradition of secrecy and neglect for the immediate well-being of the people while allegedly staying focused on the greater good and a better future."[10] In the aftermath of the Chernobyl accident, this attitude manifested as a total lack of information sharing with those affected. Radiation levels increased while the residents of nearby Pripyat had weddings and played in the streets. Even though radiation levels were damagingly high, it took days for evacuations to start. And even then, nothing true was communicated, with residents being told they would be back in their homes in three days. The Pripyat hospital, in the town where all Chernobyl workers lived, "was equipped to deal with almost anything but radioactive poisoning."[11] Because whether Chernobyl ever had problems or not, the Soviet leadership had already decided that radioactivity was never going to be an issue.

And even though Chernobyl is in the Ukraine, the Ukrainian leadership often found out what was going on from Moscow.

All these elements combined to create a highly viscous information environment that made it near impossible to speak the truth of what was happening or to communicate it to anyone. As Plokhy describes, "The immediate cause of the Chernobyl accident was a turbine test that went wrong. . . . Immediately after the accident, as panic spread, the authoritarian Soviet regime imposed control over the flow of information, endangering millions of people at home and abroad and leading to innumerable cases of radiation poisoning that could otherwise have been avoided."[12]

What is interesting is that their approach ultimately undermined Soviet goals. Many people felt betrayed by their government and pushed relentlessly for details about the accident. As these started to trickle out, outrage was displayed by many Ukrainians, which helped to fuel the Ukrainian push for independence from Moscow. Creating greater viscosity for information flow may seem like a way to control people and protect them from difficult information, but it easily backfires. If people get an inkling something is hidden from them, they'll push as hard as possible to find it. If they succeed, they'll pay far more attention to it than they would have done otherwise. The negative consequences that result from a lack of information sharing in situations like Chernobyl often undermine the control that a government was trying to exert in the first place.

Trickle-Up Innovation

How else can the lens of opposing forces like we find in the friction and viscosity model be useful? One area is organizational effectiveness. If we think of an organization, we can appreciate that the forces that influence innovation are different for the executive team and the frontline worker. So if the goal is to encourage more innovation on the front lines, then you need to pay attention to what encourages and limits movement in *that* environment, not in the C-suite.

The Ford Model T left two legacies: the iconic image of the beginning of the automobile age, and the mass-production system. For Ford, and later GM, mass-production systems were not designed to incorporate the potential for innovation at the level of the factory worker. Essentially, "the workers on the shop floor were simply interchangeable parts of the production system."[13] Massive amounts of inventory were kept on the floor, and problems were not fixed until the end of the line. Workers were not there to address problems or improve the system. They were just there to perform their repetitive task, leaving any rework or problem-solving to specialists.

In the 1940s, Toyota, the Japanese car company, was struggling to survive after the war. Japanese government expectations were that financial support and success meant exports, which meant being internationally competitive.

Studying the mass-production system of the North American car manufacturers, Toyota knew it wouldn't work for them. They didn't have the initial capacity to get a machine of that size functioning. But they noticed something else. Mass production generated a lot of waste, was inefficient because it deferred the addressing of mistakes to the end of the line, where they were most costly to fix, and took an exceptionally long time to change when a new production model of car came out. Toyota development guru Taiichi Ohno thought there was room for improvement. One of his insights was to focus on the environment of the frontline worker.

He saw that output could be significantly affected by reducing the friction happening at that level. "If workers failed to anticipate problems before they occurred and didn't take the initiative to devise solutions, the work of the whole factory could easily come to a halt."[14] Therefore, getting more effective output from the shop-floor worker was not about speeding up performance or setting higher quotas. It was about creating a smoother environment that empowered workers to engage with their work.

If we want people to innovate and take initiative in real time at the ground level, then the organizational culture and structure must be one in which it is supported and safe to do so. What creates an environment with low friction for the workers, so they are better able to move to create positive change?

One of the things that Ohno noticed in the mass production system was that "none of the specialists beyond the assembly worker was actually adding any value to the car. What's more, Ohno thought that assembly workers could probably do most of the functions of the specialists and do them much better because of their direct acquaintance with conditions on the line."[15] A first step was to change the behavior on the line by including responsibilities like minor repairs and quality checking. Every worker was given the ability to stop the line to fix a problem.

As James P. Womack, Daniel T. Jones, and Daniel Roos explain in *The Machine That Changed the World,* "In striking contrast to the mass production plant, where stopping the line was the responsibility of the senior line manager, Ohno placed a cord above every work station and instructed workers to stop the whole assembly line immediately if a problem emerged that they couldn't fix. Then the whole team would come over to work on the problem."[16] Pulling this "Andon cord" created a lot of immediate friction—like going from water to cement in a second—but allowed for mistakes on the line to be addressed immediately. Furthermore, the day was arranged so that time was set aside for workers to share ideas on how to improve process. All of these changes were about reducing the friction of the worker environment in the long term.

The result of the changes to the assembly line was a system that produced cars that needed less rework at the end. So even though "every worker can stop the line ... the line is almost never stopped, because problems are solved in advance and the same problem never occurs twice."[17] The culmination of these tangible changes made to the factory-worker environment resulted in improved car quality, production efficiency, and worker morale.

Morale is critical to an environment that fosters innovation. In order to take risks, people need to feel supported. Toyota fostered an environment on the factory floor that emphasized communication and collaboration. Workers helped each other solve problems and could switch their focus with ease depending on what the situation called for. The system developed by Ohno encouraged them to be knowledgeable about the entire process and get curious about finding solutions and efficiencies. The resulting process is called "lean" and is summed up in the following: "It transfers the maximum number of tasks and responsibilities to those workers actually adding value to the car on the line, and it has in place a system for detecting defects that quickly traces every problem, once discovered, to its ultimate cause."[18] Paying attention to the environment of workers is a way for organizations to metaphorically keep their feet on the ground. By "touching the territory," they can empower the people closest to the problem and reduce the friction in their organization.

Changes have to be supported up to the top, and everyone needs to recognize that the forces at higher levels, which push for things like strategy or visions, are not as relevant at the working level. It's all fine and nice to put out messages of where a company wants to go, but it needs to make sure that the environment doesn't have such high friction that everyone feels like they are trying to move a cement wall to get there.

Toyota designed an environment that "provides workers with the skills they need to control their work environment and the continuing challenge of making the work go more smoothly. While the mass-production plant is often filled with mind-numbing stress, as workers struggle to assemble unmanufacturable products and have no way to improve their working environment, lean production offers a creative tension in which workers have many ways to address challenges."[19] ("Unmanufacturable" here refers to having to put together components that have flaws and will require rework at the end.)

In lean manufacturing, the environment is designed and continually improved to encourage workers to take initiative and innovate. Using the lens of friction, we can see that what impacts the environment of a factory worker is not the same as what shapes the environment of the executive. If you want to change a situation, you must appreciate the forces that are strongest in that particular environment.

Conclusion

Friction and viscosity are the sand in the gears of the universe, the invisible hands that slow the motion of all things.

Friction is the grip between surfaces in contact, the roughness that resists sliding. Viscosity is the thickness of fluids, the internal friction that makes liquids sluggish and syrupy. Together, they are the great moderators of motion.

Think of the last time you tried to slide a heavy piece of furniture across the floor. The resistance you felt, the effort required to overcome the grip of the surface—that was friction at work. Or consider the slow, thick pour of honey from a jar, the way it clings and drips in slow threads. That's the viscosity of the fluid resisting the force of gravity, the internal friction that makes the honey flow like molasses rather than water.

While friction is the enemy of efficiency, it's also necessary for traction. Without it, we couldn't walk or drive, couldn't hold tools or tie knots. Viscosity too is a double-edged sword. In pipelines and hydraulic systems, high viscosity means higher pumping costs, slower flows, and greater strain on equipment. But viscosity is also what makes oil a good lubricant, what allows paints and coatings to spread evenly and adhere to surfaces.

Friction and viscosity are powerful metaphors for the forces of resistance in every domain of life. In human relationships, friction is the conflict and tension that arises from differing goals, personalities, or beliefs. It's the interpersonal roughness that can generate heat and wear, but also the traction that allows us to influence and connect with others.

While often hidden, friction and viscosity work against us whenever we try to do something. To overcome resistance, we often default to using more force when simply reducing the friction or viscosity will do. However, doing both is more effective than either in isolation.

Friction and viscosity can also be wielded as weapons. Rather than try to catch up to the competition with more effort, you might want to explore slowing them down by adding resistance through increased regulation, bureaucracy, or other clever ideas.

In the end, reducing resistance is often easier than adding force.

Velocity

Direction over speed.

If a man does not know to what port he is steering, no wind is favorable to him.

—SENECA[1]

Most people assume speed and velocity are the same thing. They are not. Understanding the difference helps increase productivity, simplify focus, and improve results. Speed is the distance traveled over time. Velocity measures displacement over time. The important distinction is that velocity has both speed and direction.

Velocity moves you toward a goal. Speed does not. If you are in a race and you run in a circle, you might move with a lot of speed, but you're not closer to your destination. Progress matters more than activity.

The concept that underpins using velocity as a model is displacement in a direction. If we take a step forward, we have velocity. If we run in place, we just have speed. Thus, our progress in a given area is not about how fast we are moving now but is best measured by how far we've moved relative to where we started. To get to a goal, we cannot just focus on being fast but also need to be aware of the direction we want to go.

We calculate velocity by dividing the change in distance by the change in time. Something has a constant velocity if it is moving at a consistent speed in a straight line without changing direction. Usually a constant velocity in the right direction is the most effective strategy to get where you want to go. Too many changes in direction and you can end up going in circles.

Kinetic and Potential Energy

Picture yourself throwing a ball up into the air and then watching it fall back to the ground. Its flight involves two types of energy: kinetic and potential.

As the ball flies through the air, it has kinetic energy. This energy is the energy from motion. It comes from the energy you transferred when you pushed it with your hand, thereby exerting an unbalanced force upon it. When the ball falls, it transfers the kinetic energy to the ground. Kinetic energy is a function of velocity.

When the ball is up in the air, it has the potential energy of its position. This energy is considered stored and exists as a result of the force, gravity, that pushes it toward the ground. The higher it is, the greater the potential energy. Potential energy may be gravitational or elastic, due to an object being either raised or stretched.

The kinetic energy of an object is relative to what the other objects are doing in the environment. The ball will have more kinetic energy relative to your friend sitting in a lawn chair watching you throw it but will have almost none relative to the dog that is chasing after it.

Potential energy, on the other hand, is completely independent of the movement of other objects in the environment. When you throw that ball in the air, you can calculate the potential energy regardless of how fast or slow anything else around you is moving.

Faster to the Goal

Napoleon became famous for his emphasis on speed toward a goal in the context of his military campaigns. "'The strength of the army', he stated, 'like power in mechanics, is the product of multiplying the mass by the velocity.'"[2] His desire to move faster in his planned direction helped him win many battles and changed how enemies were able to respond. His rewriting of battle tactics to achieve velocity ultimately influenced military strategy. This speed was literal—he moved his troops at an unprecedented pace. But the speed was toward a goal. Faster troop movement was a part of his overall strategy.

We can understand how Napoleon's ability to move his troops faster contributed to his successes when we look at his Italian campaign, which was early in his career and exemplified the velocity-based approach that continued throughout his life. As Adam Zamoyski explains in *Napoleon: A Life*, when he was just twenty-six, Napoleon led a campaign in Italy against the Austrians. It was his first as the commander in chief of an army and was actually his first independent command in the field. He went into the Italian campaign as an unknown quantity in the French Republic and came out as a celebrated leader and defender of France. He achieved this by employing new and unexpected tactics, many inspired by the principle of velocity.

Napoleon made velocity one of his core principles of battle. In Italy, his army was neither the strongest nor the best trained, and thus superior movement was a battle tactic. "Bonaparte needed to keep up the momentum so that neither of his opponents had time to regroup and strike back."[3] The effects of investing in velocity weakened the enemy by not giving them time to adjust. Moving fast toward his objectives actually obviated potential obstacles, because the Austrians didn't have time to put any up.

The pace of his troops was relentless. Even barefoot or poorly clothed, they would move fast. There are records of one division covering nearly fifty miles in thirty-six hours. Another stretch of four days saw his troops fight three battles and cover fifty-six miles. In *Napoleon: A Life*, Andrew Roberts writes: "The sheer tempo of the operations ensured that he always kept the initiative, bowling unstoppably along a narrow valley gorge replete with places where the Austrians should have been able to slow or halt him."[4]

Part of what allowed him to move fast while on this campaign was "a profound study of the history and geography of Italy before he ever set foot there [and] his willingness to experiment with others' ideas."[5] He developed expertise of the territory, which gave him flexibility, and he chose his path so as to maintain as constant a velocity as possible.

In order to move with velocity, Napoleon also needed to get others to move at the same pace. He was very involved in the lives and welfare of his troops, partly to inspire them to push themselves to meet the tempo he wanted to move at. He employed various tactics to achieve this. First, "his treatment of the troops under his command had been designed from the start not only to make them more effective as fighting men but also to turn them into *his* men."[6] By "giving them victory . . . and talking to the men as equals,"[7] he boosted their self-esteem and made them feel they were achieving what other men and armies could not. They admired Napoleon and completely bought into his vision. Velocity became a group goal. They all wanted to move quickly, seeing it as integral to victory.

Second, he issued clear and simple instructions. Not only did he come up with brilliant battlefield strategies, but he seemed to instinctively understand that in order for a strategy to work, it must be communicated in a way that could be understood and executed. The more time people spend decoding complex instructions, the slower they will move in the direction you need them to go. And since strategy can often get lost in movement and in the complexity of battle, he knew that clear communication would encourage velocity.

In trying to increase your velocity, it's important to recognize and account for the factors that can limit it. For Napoleon, there were limitations on how fast he could move. Some were within his control, such as camp followers, of which he seriously reduced the number; others were outside his control, such as weather. But part of the reason he could move faster was that the existence and condition of roads had improved during the previous century.

Napoleon's tempo also depended on supply requirements keeping pace. But where he could jettison baggage or weight, he did. His troops "didn't sleep in tents at night because the armies marched so rapidly they could not have carted with them all the requisite baggage."[8] Frequently his "army had advanced so far that it was running out of supplies."[9] Thus, "one of the reasons he maintained such a fluid campaign was that he had no resources for anything else."[10]

Our understanding of velocity is incomplete if we don't comprehend what it is not. For Napoleon, increasing the pace of engagement to improve his velocity worked numerous times in many of his campaigns, but it proved to have limits. Direction at all costs actually undermined his ability to achieve military success in some cases. Napoleon's impatience during one battle of the Italian campaign, at Cosseria, "cost the French at least 600 and possibly as many as 1,000 casualties."[11] And nowhere was the limitation of emphasis on velocity more evident than his foray into Russia in 1812.

The distance from Paris to Moscow is about 1,550 miles. This is more than twice the distance from Paris to Rome or Paris to

Vienna. It was farther than Napoleon had ever gone in a military campaign by far, and one he embarked on with one of the largest armies the world had seen. He employed his usual tactics to accomplish his goal of taking Moscow, which was understandable for two reasons. One, they had worked before. Two, the maintenance of such a large force so far from home was both exceptionally costly and difficult. The campaign also needed a quick resolution because they did not have the supplies and necessary infrastructure for a long campaign through many months of a Russian winter.

However, one of the complexities of velocity is that, because direction is paramount, size sometimes compromises our velocity. The bigger we are, the harder it is to adjust our direction.

For Napoleon, on his way to Moscow, the tactics of speed ultimately undermined his velocity. Because he gave up so much in order to go fast, he didn't have the resources to adjust when the route to Russia became treacherous for both his army and his objectives. Writing about the campaign, General Carl von Clausewitz notes that Napoleon lost around one half of his army before Smolensk, and many more before Moscow.[12] Disease, starvation, and thirst all culled the ranks of both the soldiers and the horses. And that was just on the way there.

Napoleon got to Moscow, but with ninety thousand men instead of the at least four hundred thousand he started with. Clausewitz suggests that "with more precaution and better regulations as to subsistence, with more careful consideration of the direction of his marches, which would have prevented the unnecessary and enormous accumulation of masses on one and the same road, he would have obviated the starvation which attended his advance from its outset and have preserved his army in a more effective condition."[13]

The goal was not to reach Moscow. The goal was to occupy Russia and force them into agreement about French superiority. And here Napoleon failed. He did not have the manpower to follow the Russians farther into their territory, and he had no plans to attend to his army in retreat.

In this sense, Napoleon's planning was inadequate, which resulted in much speed but in little real territory covered. His initial planning was insufficient for the distance and terrain he planned to cover, preventing him from being able to adjust and adapt to the conditions he encountered and the evolving Russian strategy. Going back to the starting line is never fun. It's even less fun when you end up with less than you started with the last time. Despite covering so many kilometers, Napoleon ended up back where he started, only with fewer troops and a reputational hit. If anything, this increased his velocity in another direction, toward the day when France no longer respected or wanted his leadership.

In your own life, if you think of the ground you need to cover to achieve your goal, the speed at which you move in that direction is not the only factor, because time is not the only component of success. When someone says they'd like to be debt-free by age forty, they can increase the speed in that direction by making certain financial choices. There are, however, certain implications. They probably want to be debt-free while maintaining their important relationships, not committing any crimes, and being healthy enough at the end to enjoy it. Figuring out how to improve your velocity must take into account the full scope of what you want the arrival at your destination to look like. Better to go in the right direction slowly than in the wrong direction with speed.

Eye on the Prize

A snapshot of the career decisions of Mae West is another lesson in direction over speed.

Early in her career, West realized that she needed more control over what she was appearing in if she wanted to achieve the success she desired. So she put effort into the other components of a production, beyond acting. "The transition from struggling performer to creator, producer, and star of her own scripts came slowly, and required a major mobilization; getting there took concentrated energy, belief in her own abilities, sweat, and well-worked connections."[14]

West seemed to be totally devoted to her goals. She turned down scripts she thought were a step backward or portrayed women in a way that didn't complement the image she was creating. She reworked her roles until they were completely her own, until they couldn't have been played by anyone other than Mae West:

> She went out very little. In the classic age of the speakeasy, a place she made much use of in her stage material, she was hardly ever reported to be in one or photographed there. She figured rarely in the gossip columns except for obvious publicity purposes. She did not frequent nightclubs or premieres, except her own. The reason seems to be that when not actually onstage, she was working. West was a writer.[15]

West wrote, cowrote, or significantly modified almost everything she appeared in. She came up with the classic one-liners for which she is still famous—like "Goodness had nothing to do with it, dearie," and "When caught between two evils, I generally like to take the one I never tried."

Starting on the stage, then moving into film, she was one of the few actresses at the time who worked and were successful outside the Hollywood studio system. She kept control of her persona and thus her career. In 1935 she earned more than any other female in the world, and the most in total earnings in the United States second only to media tycoon William Randolph Hearst. She approached her career focused on the long game. She knew the direction she was headed and made decisions to increase her velocity in that direction.

Conclusion

Velocity is the great differentiator, the measure that distinguishes the stagnant from the swift.

In the discipline of physics, velocity is a fundamental quantity, a key variable in the equations that describe the behavior of everything from subatomic particles to galaxies. It's the v in the formulas of motion, the arrow that points the way from here to there.

Velocity is also a metaphor for life. Consider it the rate at which we learn and grow, the speed at which we innovate and create, and the focus with which we pursue our goals.

Velocity challenges us to think about what we can do to put ourselves on the right trajectory, to find a balance between mass and speed to move in the direction of our goals. The ability to set a direction, improve your tactics, and adjust to new information becomes paramount.

Velocity isn't just about raw speed. Direction matters just as much. A car moving at high speed in circles goes nowhere, while a slow and steady walk in a straight line can cross continents.

Velocity is progress. Sometimes progress comes from more force and sometimes progress comes from removing friction. Once you have a destination, you can improve your velocity by working harder and eliminating things that aren't contributing toward reaching that goal.

Leverage

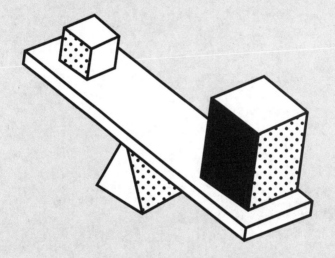

Enough to move the world.

Design by humans
tends to be spare,
over optimized,
and have the
opposite attribute
of redundancy,
that is, leverage.

—ATTRIBUTED TO

NASSIM NICHOLAS TALEB

L everage is achieving results significantly greater than the force you put in. Isn't this what we all want in life?

Think of written language: a way to leverage what people have learned in the past so that we don't have to relearn everything from scratch with each new generation. Or consider standardization of processes, which gives companies leverage over people by making them easier to replace. Levers are everywhere, once you start looking for them.

People who simply think that working hard is the path to financial wealth are mistaken. Leveraging your judgment requires opportunity and hard work. But once you have judgment, you want to continue to leverage it in order to decrease the amount of effort needed to achieve your goals.

A good place to begin understanding the concept of leverage is the etymology of the word. We can trace its origins back to the Proto-Indo-European "legwh," which described something light, agile, or easy. From this, the Latin "levare" formed, referring to something that was "not heavy." But the word was absorbed into English in the fourteenth century from Old French, where "levier" referred to raising something. In essence, "leverage" refers to making something light by raising it in a specific manner—using a lever.

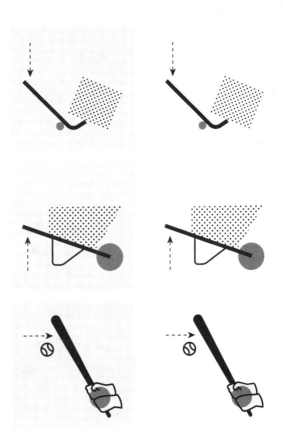

There are three main types of physical levers:

1. Force/fulcrum/weight, such as using a crowbar to open a door.

2. Fulcrum/weight/force, such as a wheelbarrow.

3. Fulcrum/force/weight, like a baseball bat. This third one is a bit counterintuitive, because you have to put in more energy than you would just lifting the weight, and we usually use le-

vers for the opposite reason. However, you get the weight to move a longer distance in return.

Archimedes is credited with establishing the concept of leverage more than two thousand years ago. He famously stated that given a lever long enough, and enough distance, he could lift the earth.

However, the Peripatetic school, the followers of Aristotle, wrote of levers before the birth of Archimedes. In *Mechanica*, a work believed to have been written by members of this school of thought, they state:

> For since under the impulse of the same weight the greater radius from the center moves the more rapidly, and there are three elements in the lever, the fulcrum, that is the cord or center, and the two weights, the one which causes the movement, and the one that is moved: now the ratio of the weight moved to the weight moving it is the inverse ratio of the distances from the center. Now the greater the distance from the fulcrum, the more easily it will move.[1]

Used to great effect for thousands of years, levers enable the gain of disproportionate strength. For example, the ancient Egyptians used levers to lift stones weighing up to one hundred tons in order to build the pyramids and obelisks. Many of humanity's tools, used for centuries all over the world, incorporate leverage—scissors, pliers, door handles, wheelbarrows, fishing rods, and more. Levers are one of our simplest, yet greatest, inventions.

Leverage unleashes the potential of what we can do. When we all had sticks, the variation in productivity wasn't much. Small changes in individual performance didn't have significant absolute impacts. It wasn't until we developed tools that allowed us to leverage small changes in individual performance that we started to see a lot of variation in productivity. To take that further, if technology leverages variation in individual performance, then we can expect the gap between the most productive and least productive people in a society to increase over time.

Understanding Where You Have Leverage

Levers provide leverage. In human interactions, these levers are not purely physical, but instead items or ideas that have a shared, common value. Leverage itself is amoral—neither good nor bad. When the term "leverage" comes up in day-to-day conversation, it sometimes has a negative connotation—as if having it allows you to manipulate a situation to your advantage. Leverage is not, however, about manipulation. It's about influence. Think of negotiations, in which having leverage increases the chances that you will get your desired outcome. We are taught that by applying pressure in the right place you make it attractive for the other party to move in your direction; it often doesn't take much force if the leverage is substantial enough. And really, the best way to have leverage in any deal is to not need the deal at all.

Knowing how much pressure to apply in any given situation is critical. Too much pressure breaks the metaphorical lever or takes you out of win-win. No one wants to be forced to do something, and if they are, they won't think kindly of you. Too little pressure and you might not achieve your objective. Leverage should be applied with conscious thought as to when it's helping you achieve your aims and when it's hurting your ability to do so.

Roger J. Volkema, in his book aptly titled *Leverage*, explains two of the principles of leverage in negotiations. The first is that leverage in human interactions is based on perceptions; the second is that it is a social or relational construct. What this means is that for something to be leverage, everyone has to have roughly the same perception of its value, and this is going to be dependent on social context. It isn't any good to say, "I'm going to give you this box if you agree to my terms," if the other person doesn't associate any value with that box. Furthermore, the power of leverage changes. You cease to have leverage if the other party walks away from the exchange.

Leverage is not a binary—something you either have or don't have. Some people may use their leverage to get X. Some people may have the same leverage and use it to get X, Y, and Z. In order to use leverage to maximize your return, you need to figure out its potential and wield it wisely.

Applying Leverage Where It Counts

In a situation of true leverage, the lever, not the application of force, does most of the work. When it comes to leverage, we want to know three things:

1. How do I know when I have it?

2. Where and when should I apply it?

3. How do I keep it?

If we can figure these out, we can have significant power over the forces acting against us.

Reading any history seems to suggest that humans naturally grasp the principles of leverage. Attaining and holding on to power seems to be a species pastime, and leverage crops up as much as solitary force. Conquering may often be about sheer numbers or, increasingly, asymmetry in technology, but no matter the path to victory, most conquerors extract ongoing leverage over the conquered. They do this through the distribution of land and holdings, payments and reparations, and sometimes marriage contracts (which are used less today but shaped, for example, the borders in most of Western Europe for centuries). These acts themselves, meant to protect and insulate the conquerors from the conquered, often sow the seeds of future destruction.

We can learn a lot about leverage by looking at someone who had no access to solitary force and who had to rely completely on leverage to attain and maintain power: Eleanor of Aquitaine. Queen of France and then England in the twelfth century, she achieved a remarkable amount of power and influence through leverage.

Eleanor was born to the Duke of Aquitaine, ruler of a territorial principality in what is now France. At the time, rulers of duchies in France were at least as powerful as the King of France, who really only ruled over a small territory around Paris. Aquitaine was a large and prosperous territory during Eleanor's life, encompassing rich farmland, a dozen ports that facilitated both local and overseas trade, and an important manufacturing center for helmets. The towns were thriving, business was booming, and the activities of the region provided the ruling family with a lot of money.[2] These factors meant that the ruler of the duchy wielded considerable power in the region.

Due to the death of her brother, and because Aquitaine custom allowed women to inherit, Eleanor became ruler of the duchy.[3] The ability of a woman to inherit a duchy was not consistent across the region. Ralph V. Turner explains in *Eleanor of Aquitaine* that "Once a part of the ancient Roman province of Gaul, Aquitaine still preserved in Eleanor's childhood customs surviving from Roman rule that guaranteed women greater freedom than those in northern Europe enjoyed."[4] An unofficial east-west line ran through France, with Aquitaine being in the south and Paris being in the north. Therefore, Eleanor's expectations of her right to rule were not consistent with those of all her contemporaries.

We can think of Aquitaine as Eleanor's lever, the tool she used to move kings. Through her marriages to two kings, and as the mother of three more, Eleanor used Aquitaine to wield an exceptional amount of influence for a woman in the Middle Ages.

To even be the Duchess of Aquitaine, Eleanor first had a little bit of luck: the fact that a woman could inherit, and that even in marriage it would always be her property and not her husband's. The power accorded to aristocratic women was beginning to change, and a couple hundred years later such clear ownership by a woman in Aquitaine would have been less likely. So Eleanor's leverage was initially obtained by the circumstances of her birth.

However, she aimed to use her inheritance to the fullest. She saw herself as a queen-duchess, descended from the Carolingian rulers, and was determined to take a visible leadership role. Turner writes that "a major aspect of her nature was a pursuit of power,"[5] an attitude out of step with the role women were expected to play in the Middle Ages. Being the Duchess of Aquitaine automatically came with some leverage, a small amount that could have easily been deployed and spent making a good marriage. Eleanor was exceptional because throughout her life she used her birthright to try to achieve increasing power and influence over the affairs of France and England. She used Aquitaine to give herself a voice and role in the affairs of the time, to a degree and impact that was extremely rare for a woman in the Middle Ages.

By the usual customs of the time, when Eleanor married, her

husband would govern Aquitaine, but the territory itself would always belong to her. Thus, in order to keep influence in and over her territory, she had to keep influence over her husband. She first married Louis, who became King of France. Her father had made her future father-in-law her protector and charged him with seeing to her marriage. The ailing French king chose his son Louis for Eleanor, and less than a month after her marriage, Eleanor became Queen of France.

Ralph Turner writes that "the marriage of Eleanor and Louis VII would prove to be a trial for both, bringing the couple little happiness."[6] Furthermore, Louis VII was focused on religious conflicts and devoted his time and money to unsuccessful Crusades instead of focusing on consolidating his power in France. After many years, Eleanor chose to exit that marriage. In part, she left Louis because she felt that he could not help her effectively keep control over Aquitaine, which was "a confusing collection of a dozen or so counties."[7] Keeping the duchy together required firm control and constant maintenance, which Louis was too distracted by his other pursuits to provide. When her marriage to Louis ended, she retained ownership of Aquitaine. She married Henry, Duke of Normandy—who became Henry II, King of England—because she likely hoped that he had a forceful enough personality to help her exercise leadership in Aquitaine.

Ownership and control are different things. All indications were that Henry might be able to govern the large, rebellious area much better than Louis. "In an act almost unheard of in her time, Eleanor acted independently without consulting her kin or other counselors."[8] It was probably the value and prestige of Aquitaine that sold Henry on the marriage—it was a large territory that generated a sizable income for its ruler. Also, being large, it had a population that could be drawn on to help fight battles elsewhere.

Despite her unhappiness and disappointment, it was a bold and risky move to push for the annulment of her marriage to the King of France. Without the security of marriage, Eleanor and her lands would be vulnerable. So why do it? One of the reasons was that Aquitaine and her legacy there were extremely important to her. "As she grew up, she absorbed her dynasty's sense of its dignity as successors to Carolingian royalty,"[9] and she devoted her life to preserving the legacy of her ancestors. Knowing that she had to rely on a husband to actually govern, Eleanor chose the future Henry II of England, who she believed had a better chance of maintaining control of the territory. Aquitaine would cease to be valuable if she no longer had control over it.

Many years later, in an effort to preserve Aquitaine as a separate entity from the English and French crowns, Eleanor named her son Richard as Duke of Aquitaine. There was a lot of custom behind this, as he was the second son, and thus it was normal for him to inherit the property of his mother. But Eleanor also invested a lot in her relationship with Richard, most significantly backing him in his fight with his father for the English crown, so that she could maintain some degree of control over what happened to and in the duchy.

She did not, however, rely solely on her relationships with her husbands and son to maintain influence. Throughout her life, Eleanor spent much time in Aquitaine. She developed relationships with the nobles, the church representatives, and the people. She financially supported many building projects, such as the abbey at Fontevraud, and took an interest in seemingly small affairs, settling disputes among the minor nobles in Aquitaine. Neither her husband Henry nor her son Richard were well regarded by the people of Aquitaine, and fights and rebellions were always breaking out, as the perception was that the kings of England were simply using Aquitaine to further their own royal interests. Especially in her later years, Eleanor sought to undo, or at least mitigate, the effects of the harsh rule of her husband and son.[10] Consequently, she attained and maintained significant influence in her territory, in no small part because she chose to live there and become active in the politics of the region.

The story of Henry and his sons is legendary. The stuff of plays and movies, their hatred of each other, distrust, and disloyalty brought total disarray to Western Europe. The family indulged in constant fighting and rebellion over who would become king. Eleanor supported her sons against their father and ended up a prisoner of her husband for fifteen years.

Territories are not objects. They are dynamic spaces filled with people interacting in complex systems. With all their fighting, Henry and his sons never seemed to comprehend what Eleanor intuitively understood: land can only be used as leverage if the people living in it are supportive of your leadership. Leading requires followers.

As the empire her husband Henry built, combining English territory and large swaths of what is now France, started to collapse due to the total dysfunction of the family, Eleanor began to be concerned about her legacy. She wanted Aquitaine to continue to be ruled by her offspring, carrying the line of leadership forward, and "she was resolutely opposed to seeing it lose its separate identity, absorbed into the domains of either of her two husbands."[11]

After Richard died, Eleanor's son John ascended to the throne of England. He turned out not to be the best leader, angering many of his subjects and managing to forever compromise royal authority in England by signing the Magna Carta, but in terms of preserving the family legacy, he was the best she had. All of her other sons had died. So "Eleanor traversed her duchy . . . issuing charters confirming properties and privileges in an attempt to win her subjects over to John's side."[12] She was in her seventies at this time, and it was important to her to pass on the leverage that was Aquitaine to her son. This she accomplished before she died in 1204, at the remarkable age of eighty.

What are some of the ideas about leverage we can learn from Eleanor of Aquitaine's story? First, don't sell yourself short and underestimate the value of your leverage. It seems that right from the beginning, Eleanor was clear about the value of Aquitaine to both the French and English kings. She knew that the resources the region provided could significantly augment the power of whichever monarch controlled it.

Second, keep other people wanting what you have. For leverage to exist, all parties must perceive its value. Throughout her life, Eleanor worked to maintain the value of Aquitaine. She invested money and time there in building infrastructure and reducing conflict. She knew that if Aquitaine became too unruly, it wouldn't be attractive to a monarch seeking to augment their kingdom. Furthermore, she seemed to understand that a prosperous Aquitaine would continue to give the region leverage in geopolitical affairs after her death.

Third, understand when you can use your leverage and when you can't. Eleanor used her leverage to have choice in marriage, to influence leadership and succession in England and France, to carve out independence from her husbands, and to build her own legacy. She also seemed to know, however, when the resources and power of Aquitaine were not enough to change her situation. Perhaps the best example of her awareness of the limitations of her leverage was when she was imprisoned by her husband Henry for fifteen years. She could not use Aquitaine to give anyone enough power to free her, so she did not sacrifice her territory in a wasted effort to escape.

The Dark Side of Leverage

When wielded smartly, leverage can help you achieve better outcomes. And who doesn't want that? However, just because you have leverage doesn't mean you should employ it. As we will see, there is a darker side to leverage, namely when it is employed to the maximum all the time.

When leverage becomes entrenched systematically, it acts more like the application of tyranny. This has happened more than a few times in history, including in the twentieth-century coal company towns in West Virginia.

When technological development allowed coal to be easily transported out of the West Virginia hills, coal operators bought up extensive land in the state. Coal became the most significant economic resource in the state by far. Coal operations required workers, and these miners lived in company towns. With no other industries or big cities nearby to offer alternatives, coal operators used their initial leverage to give themselves an exceptional amount of control over the lives of both their workers and the state in which the companies operated.

The company towns were effectively isolated from the rules and norms that prevailed in the rest of the country. Inhabitants did not own their houses or the land they were built on and could be kicked out with no notice. Workers were paid in "coal scrip," a proprietary currency unique to each operation that could only be spent in the company store. There was no mayor or local political officials to represent the residents. Information was controlled.

Coal-scrip wages could only be spent in the company store, with each store being unique to each mining operation.

Any media the company didn't approve of was banned, and the postmaster, a company employee, could read all incoming and outgoing mail.[13]

The issue of coal scrip in particular was a significant point of leverage. As David Corbin explains in *Life, Work, and Rebellion in the Coal Fields,* not only did it require that workers buy all their goods from the company store, but it allowed the coal operators to completely control the value of the work being performed. Wages were essentially recouped depending on the needs of the company, because the company store, being a monopoly, could charge whatever it wanted. In this way too, any wage increases were immediately negated by corresponding price increases in the store.[14]

This control exercised by a company operator over the town inhabitants gave the company access to further points of leverage. Ballots for state elections were inspected by mine guards, so miners effectively had to vote for the interests of the company, and coal companies controlled county court and jury appointments. This leverage was used to exploit loopholes in safety, child labor, compensation, and criminal laws, or even to disregard the laws altogether. In 1913, "a U.S. congressman from Wisconsin toured the coal fields of West Virginia and reported that 'one cannot imagine the power of the mining companies. . . . It elects senators and judges. It owns both the Republican and Democratic parties in the state. All laws are made to suit the mine owners. All the judges are elected through their influence, even up to the judges of the Supreme Court.'"[15]

How can one act against this kind of exceptional leverage? Often, it's only through widespread collective action that aggregates small amounts of power until enough is pooled so that there exists counter-leverage. Think strikes and unions. One person walking out on the job may not change much, but if everyone does, significantly more leverage is available to be exercised. Eventually, after brutal labor disputes, the miners of West Virginia formed and participated in unions.

Before that, however, individuals still had some basic degree of leverage. They could choose to walk away, exercising their ability to be geographically mobile. And many coal workers and their families supplemented their coal scrip income through cash from farming, gardening, and selling homemade alcohol, which gave them a small measure of independence from the coal companies. The leverage you have may not always be the leverage you want, but chances are, if you look, you will find you have some somewhere.

Conclusion

Leverage is the force multiplier of the world, the principle that allows the small to move the large and the few to influence the many. It's the idea that a little input, strategically applied, can yield outsize outputs.

At its core, leverage is about the amplification of effort. Think of a crowbar prying open a stubborn lid, or a pulley system hoisting a heavy load. In each case, the tool or mechanism allows its user to exert force in a way that multiplies their natural strength and capacity.

But leverage isn't just useful in physics. Rather, it's a principle that applies across our lives.

Leverage is often lurking in the background of nonlinear outcomes. Consider the author who took the ideas in their head, put them in a book, and sold millions of copies, or the Wall Street trader who made a single decision that resulted in billions. Or even the CEO who directs the people working for them.

In the realm of personal development, leverage is about identifying the key habits, skills, and relationships that will have the greatest impact on your life and work. It's about focusing your energy on the critical few rather than the trivial many, about finding the points of maximum leverage where small changes can cascade into massive results.

An example of personal leverage is an employee who learns to use AI to amplify their impact on the organization far beyond their experience or effort. While labor is still a form of leverage, that labor can often be done by chips. In this sense, the person who can leverage technology can compete in a way never before imaginable.

But leverage is not without its risks and responsibilities. Just as a small action can have an outsize positive impact, so too can it have negative consequences. If you borrow too much money against your house and it turns out to be less valuable than assumed or interest rates change, the amplifying effect of leverage can quickly wipe you out.

Good ideas taken too far often cause unanticipated consequences. Wielding leverage to maximum effect all the time, as the West Virginia mine owners did, sows the seeds of ongoing unrest that undermine one's ability to be truly effective. No one wants to feel exploited, and those who are never give their loyalty or their best work.

The key, then, is to use leverage wisely and judiciously by understanding the systems you want to influence and considering the potential second- and third-order effects of your actions.

Leverage is a tool, not a toy, and like any tool, it requires skill, judgment, and respect.

CHEMISTRY

Science and everyday life cannot and should not be separated.

—ROSALIND FRANKLIN[1]

Activation Energy

Get to the end.

There's at least one time when it's ok to lie to yourself: to get the activation energy required to start a new project.

—PAUL GRAHAM[1]

Activation energy is needed for everything from getting up in the morning to revolutions. It's the ingredient that starts a reaction, breaking apart the current state of affairs and transforming it into something new. When we have enough activation energy, we have the power to finish a reaction, achieving a sustainable result. We know the amount of activation energy is correct when enough new connections form that it becomes impossible to revert to the way we were.

In chemistry, activation energy is the minimal amount of energy that must be delivered to a chemical system to initiate a reaction, breaking bonds so that new ones can form. Molecules must collide to react, and movement speeds up when temperature increases. Consider a match. If you gently rub it against the striking strip on the side of the matchbox, nothing happens. There isn't enough force to initiate a reaction. Striking the match against the striking strip with some force crosses the activation energy threshold and initiates a chemical reaction that lights the match.

All chemical reactions have a required activation energy, but there is a range. We start with an increase in temperature, which leads to an increase in molecular velocity, resulting in an increase in the frequency of molecular collisions. The more collisions, the more chances of having sufficient energy to produce a reaction.

Energy and Climate

The concept of activation energy comes in large part from the Swedish chemist Svante Arrhenius (1859–1927). He proposed the Arrhenius equation, which calculates the relationship between temperature and reaction rates. In the simplest terms, the equation shows us that higher temperatures lead to faster reaction rates because the molecules of the reactants involved have more energy. They move around more, having more collisions with greater force. Arrhenius realized that reactions cannot happen without a minimum level of activation energy. Oddly, no one had codified this intuitive idea before. People have known for millennia that higher temperatures make things happen faster—hence food kept somewhere cool lasts longer than food left out in the sun. For physical chemists, the Arrhenius equation is of great importance, because it helps calculate the amount of activation energy required for different reactions to occur at the desired rate.

Naturally, then, reactions requiring greater activation energy usually proceed slower. The inputted energy, usually in the form of heat, breaks the bonds of the reactant molecules and increases their speed, thereby increasing their rate of collision. The state in between the initial and final stages of chemical reactions is the high-energy, unstable transition state. Because the transition state is unstable, the molecules don't stay there long—they quickly proceed to the next step of the chemical reaction without requiring any further input of energy.

Without an initial input of sufficient energy, however, the molecules stay the same and a reaction does not occur. In some cases, this is positive, as without the requirement for activation energy our world would be a chemically unstable place. For example, we would be at serious risk if propane combustion occurred spontaneously at room temperature or if the hydrogen and oxygen in air had sufficient activation energy to yield water.

Activation energy is part of our daily lives. We heat eggs to re-form bonds into a cooked product. We boil water to make our tea, re-forming some of the molecules into a gas in the process.

One of the most important aspects of activation energy is that you need enough of it to power a reaction through to its conclusion. We all know that one sheet of newspaper won't start a fire in our fireplace. It looks like a real fire for about ten seconds. Then it burns out, and we're left staring at the minimally charred logs we've stacked in the grate.

What we need is enough paper to get those logs burning. We pile it in. We add kindling, smaller pieces of wood that will sustain the reaction until the big pieces really take off. We touch the match to the paper in a few different places. And we monitor and adjust the logs for optimal exposure to the flames and sufficient oxygen flow until the reaction takes hold and things are burning nicely.

Sustaining significant change requires the same effort. You need to plan for not only the initial flame, but all the energy required to get and sustain the fire you want.

Finishing What You Start

In trying to achieve lasting change, forming new bonds is critical. If the new bonds don't form, the reaction will not complete and the old whatever will return. The activation energy you employ must move re-formation of bonds along to such an extent that it becomes hard, if not impossible, to revert to the way things were. Successful reactions demand a new way of doing things.

The bigger and more challenging an action is, the more activation energy required. And it's important to remember that the buildup to doing something is part of the activation energy required—this buildup includes everything on the camel, not just the straw.

Figuring out the right amount of activation energy is pertinent to quitting some addictions. It's not just the moment you decide to quit, it's everything that had to happen, every crisis you had to face, for you to enact that decision. As to how much activation energy will be required for you to finally stop the negative behavior and build new bonds that are completely different, you need enough to propel the action through the breaking of your current bonds that facilitate the addiction. Usually it requires more energy than you think to break the habit, but once you've broken it, it becomes much easier to maintain the new state.

Evaluating both your internal and external environments to identify the situations and suggestions that compel you to reengage in the addiction is an important step. These are triggers, and they require energy to resist, and so you must try to change them up.

Otherwise, with no new structure to replace the old one, the old bonds will re-form.

Change that doesn't last is easy. Where a lot of people miss the mark on what is required to produce real change is figuring out the initial investment of energy needed to not only start the reaction but to finish it. When we don't put in enough activation energy, we fail to produce the results we want. After enough attempts, this failure is discouraging. We think we are doomed to fail or the situation is impossible to change. We rarely consider if we are putting in enough effort to support the formation of a new structure when the old one breaks apart.

The reason why so many revolutions fail is that it takes a completely different set of skills to fight than to govern. Most revolutions focus on the energy needed to break apart the existing structure. In most cases the energy requirement to start change is not insignificant: physical strength in terms of weapons and ideological strength in terms of support from a significant amount of people. If you were planning a revolution, these two requirements are likely the areas you would focus on. Who needs to be removed, and where are your opportunities to facilitate that? How much firepower and how many supporters do you need? The activation energy required to start the reaction must take leadership changes and weapons capacity into account. But the model of activation energy suggests that you can't stop there, because removing the leadership is not the full reaction. Revolutions are aimed at changing the structure of a society, so the planning must involve the steps needed to make that happen.

Therefore, you also must anticipate what's required to form a new structure once you break the old one apart. How do you keep the support of the people? What can you put in place that will allow your revolutionary goals to cement themselves? And how long will it take? Everything you need to do, right to the end of your goals, is the real activation energy required to finish the reaction. Success isn't going to happen overnight. Plan for the amount of energy required to see you through to the end. Let's look at an example of an actual revolution to explore the idea of creating sustained change.

Burkina Faso is a small, landlocked country in western Africa. Formerly a French colony, it became independent from France in 1960. Then called Upper Volta, it nonetheless was dependent on French support. Thomas Sankara was a revolutionary in Upper Volta in the 1980s. He was born and raised there and grew up solidly middle class in a country that was quite poor, doing military service that took him around his country. He witnessed firsthand the detrimental effects of the existing political leadership on his country. He developed into a revolutionary, motivated by the suffering and corruption he saw and what he believed was the vulnerability created by his country's dependence on the West.[2] He helped stage a successful coup, changed the name of the country, and then led it for four years. His story, and the story of those years in Burkina Faso, teaches us a lot about the effort required to sustain change.

Sankara recognized that bringing down the existing government would not be enough to implement sweeping changes, including increasing literacy and the availability of education and health services. As Ernest Harsch chronicles in *Thomas Sankara: An African Revolutionary*, Sankara did not join earlier coups because he didn't see them as being able to address the systemic corruption and inequality in Burkina Faso. Sankara, and the junior officers in the military who supported him, wanted to wait until they were "strong enough to decisively influence events."[3]

We can think of Sankara as planning his revolution by determining how much activation energy is required to see a reaction through to its end. In any revolution, it is not enough to take apart the current system because in the absence of anything to replace it, the same problems, such as corruption and disenfranchisement, are likely to reassert themselves. There were multiple revolution examples from the twentieth century Sankara could have studied, from Cuba to Chile, to provide insight into the preparation required to build a new political, economic, and social infrastructure.

In addition, Sankara obviously learned from the ongoing political unrest in his country. From 1960 to 1982 there were multiple coups and power changes. Tensions between military and civilian leadership, as well as pressures ranging from labor unions to droughts, led to social unrest and power struggles. Sankara eventually joined a coup that had widespread popular support and became president of Burkina Faso from 1983 to 1987. His four years as leader were spent trying to lay out enough kindling and light enough flames that eventually the fire of his vision would become self-sustaining. "Sankara . . . did not waste time. He soon outlined the broad sweep of his revolutionary vision: an overhauled state to serve the interests of all citizens; the elimination of ignorance, illness, and exploitation; and the development of a more productive economy to reduce hunger and improve living conditions."[4]

He empowered local leaders to take on his vision and pushed hard for the equality of women in Burkina Faso society by outlawing female genital mutilation and forced marriage, and by being the first African leader to appoint women to major cabinet positions. Health clinics and schools were built at a rapid pace all over the country, most often by volunteers inspired by his sincerity in wanting to genuinely transform Burkinabe society to the betterment of all. He instituted a successful nationwide literacy campaign and mass vaccinations.

All of these initiatives were part of the activation energy required to build a new social and political system. Sankara wanted to build a country that was self-reliant, and he rejected foreign aid on the opinion that "he who feeds you, controls you."[5] He organized extensive land redistribution to peasant farmers and more than doubled the annual wheat production in three years. Sankara tried to inspire those around him to buy into and work toward building the new structure. "Those who worked with the president learned that by aiming for the seemingly unattainable, they were able to accomplish much more than they had ever dreamed—they could push the boundaries of what was possible."[6]

Sankara tried to put practices in place as if his new system was already mature and the manifestation of all these changes was guaranteed. He took a gamble. Part of the activation energy required for a successful reaction is that you have to be determined to see it through to the end. You must be committed to your reaction.

Sankara put in reforms "to encourage Burkinabe to become more responsible for managing land in a rational way and for preserving the environment more generally. 'One cannot imagine the development of agriculture and an increase in its productivity without a program for the regeneration and conservation of nature,' he said."[7] This was 1985, and sustainability wasn't yet an issue of importance in North America. Thomas Sankara, however, was trying to position Burkina Faso as if the country was at the beginning of a great developmental flourishing. He owned his vision.

He may have been right in many ways about the activation energy needed to create and sustain a new, stable system. The efforts he put forth, the people he engaged, the staggering improvements he led in four years are testament that he really did try to get the requirements right. However, what he seems to have misjudged was how much of that activation energy had to be provided by the people themselves.

As with any sweeping political change, not everyone buys in right away. Change often scares people. It's only natural to try and preserve the status quo. Not surprisingly, there was some opposition to Sankara's new policies. His reaction was to repress it instead of addressing frustrations by modifying his plans or compromising with other political groups. He instituted tribunals that tried people for crimes without credible evidence, and "when the nation's schoolteachers went on strike, [he] dismissed all of them."[8] Reactions like these undermined his long-term goals; it's hard to improve education without teachers. They also caused loss of support for his leadership.

The problem with having an uncompromising stance was it didn't give people who might have been skeptical the chance to find common ground. In Burkina Faso, "Sankara was so committed to achieving his ideals he was unwilling to give them enough time to ripen in his people."[9] Without widespread commitment by a population, it is hard to make significant political and social changes in a country.

Sankara didn't get the time to possibly course-correct. He was assassinated in 1987, and the reactions he started were not yet stable enough to continue on their own. Burkina Faso was taken over by the old order, who valued corruption and concentrated wealth in the hands of a few.

In reaching for goals that were beyond the dreams of most, Sankara expended enough activation energy to have a very interesting, although not likely planned, success: a legacy. As Harsch explains, "So what was left of Sankara's revolution? The most obvious answer is: the memory of the man, and the ideas he so passionately defended."[10]

His legacy continues today. "Whether at anniversary commemorations or on other occasions, it has not been uncommon to see young people across West Africa wearing Sankara T-shirts. Activists can readily find his words . . . and musicians from Mali, Senegal, and Burkina Faso have released popular songs and videos sampling passages from Sankara's speeches."[11] In Senegal, youths go to rallies wearing T-shirts with Sankara's image and the words "I'm still here."

Sankara likely would have preferred to have many more years to try to carry out his vision, but it does show that investing energy in change can sometimes produce surprising reactions. Ultimately there wasn't enough energy for him to produce a stable, prosperous Burkina Faso, but "because he embodied and defended causes that resonate today among the world's oppressed,"[12] he was able to produce a stable legacy. And that is quite remarkable.

Putting the Brakes on Backsliding

What is the activation energy required to go from being a poor country to being a rich one? What is required to achieve sustainable economic development to a level that a downturn will not put you back to the beginning?

In the book *How Asia Works*, Joe Studwell examines the underpinnings of the success of the economies of Japan, South Korea, and Taiwan, and the failures of Indonesia, the Philippines, and Thailand. All these countries have experienced periods of intense growth, but only the first three were able to turn that growth into a sustainable system that could weather downturns and challenges. The key to activation energy is to evaluate how much of it you need to see the reaction through to its conclusion. At what point have you gone far enough that you can't go back?

Studwell argues that there were "three critical interventions" that Japan, South Korea, and Taiwan undertook to achieve sustainable economic development. They first maximized output from agriculture; next, each country directed investment and entrepreneurs toward manufacturing; and finally, all had financial policies that supported both of these things. Thus, these three countries applied an integrated approach that "changed the structures of their economies in a manner that made it all but impossible to return to an earlier stage of development."[13]

As Studwell explains, "the vehicle for the change was a series of land reform programs . . . to take available agricultural land and to divide it up on an equal basis (once variation in land quality was allowed for) among the farming population. This, backed by government support for rural credit and marketing institutions, agronomic training and other support services, created a new type of market."[14] Once these agricultural policies were firmly established and their productivity manifested in economic improvement, the governments of Japan, South Korea, and Taiwan set up policies aimed at boosting manufacturing. In order to create long-term productivity in the manufacturing sector, firms were rewarded for their success as exporters. Firms that didn't measure up to this global competition were culled.

Financial policy in Japan, South Korea, and Taiwan was designed to support the agricultural and manufacturing policies. In summary, "Finance policy in northeast Asia recognized the need to support small, high-yield farms in order to maximize aggregate farm output rather than maximizing returns on cash invested via larger, 'capitalist' farms. And finance policy recognized the need in industry to defer profits until an adequate industrial learning process had taken place. In other words, financial policy frequently accepted low near-term returns on industrial investments in order to build industries capable of producing high returns in the future."[15]

Conversely, the Asian countries that were developing at the same time but did not follow these agricultural interventions had long periods of impressive growth, but they were unable to sustain it. With no real land reform in Indonesia, the Philippines, and Thailand, agricultural output was dampened because landlords made more money renting plots than making investments to increase yields, and families had no incentive to maximize the outputs on land they didn't own. In terms of manufacturing, these countries allowed firms to focus solely on the easier sell to domestic markets, which removed the incentives for knowledge transfer and technological development. And, of course, financial policy in each country supported these approaches of no land reform and little to no exports, focusing instead on consumer lending. Studwell explains, "The best banking returns in the East Asian region are produced in the region's most backward countries—the Philippines, Indonesia and Thailand."[16] Short-term focus on banking profits did not create sustainable growth reactions in these developing countries.

Therefore, when times were good, growth was possible, but when financial crisis hit, those that had not substantially transformed their economies were unable to deal with the challenges. Growth stalled in Thailand, Indonesia, and the Philippines, and the populations went back to being poor. Their policies did not have enough activation energy to complete their economic development.

To be clear, it wasn't all smooth sailing for Japan, South Korea, and Taiwan when they started to implement their policy changes. Some businesses were winners and became internationally popular, like Toyota and Nikon, but there were also losers. Some international relations were strained. There was no overnight success, and the general population had to sacrifice short-term returns for the long-term national interest. However, managing the difficulties is part of getting to the finish line of a reaction.

The point here is not that there is a prescription for the exact amount of activation energy needed to fundamentally transform a nation's economy. As Studwell explains, "different economics [are] appropriate to different stages of development."[17] Instead, recognize that reactions do have an activation energy, and you have a greater chance of success when you consider what is needed to bring about not just the start, but the conclusion of a reaction.

The arguments Studwell sets out are not about how countries can maintain healthy development but are rather an idea of how to "become rich in the first place."[18] Land reforms and protectionism in developing industry are not long-term policy positions—they are instead short-term components of the activation energy required to bring about sustainable growth. In making the case for effective development in Japan, South Korea, and Taiwan, Studwell writes, "There is no significant economy that has developed successfully through policies of free trade and deregulation from the get-go. What has always been required is proactive interventions—the most effective of them in agriculture and manufacturing—that foster early accumulation of capital and technological learning."[19]

Conclusion

Activation energy is the spark that ignites the fire of change, the initial burst of effort required to kick-start a reaction or transformation. It's the metaphorical push that gets the boulder rolling down the hill, the investment of energy needed to overcome inertia and set a process in motion.

In chemistry, activation energy is the minimum energy that must be input for a reaction to occur. It's the hurdle molecules must overcome to break their bonds and form new ones, the energetic barrier separating the reactants from the products.

But activation energy isn't just a chemical concept. It's a principle that applies to any system where change is possible but not automatic. In personal growth, activation energy is the effort required to break old habits and form new ones. In innovation, it's the investment needed to turn an idea into reality.

The key is to recognize activation energy for what it is: a necessary upfront cost, not a permanent obstacle. Once things are moving, momentum takes over. Once the reaction starts, it becomes self-sustaining.

Catalysts

Change agent.

Catalysis . . . is to chemical reactions what civil engineering is to the Alps: you do not need to cross the mountain passes to get to the Mediterranean, you can pass through the Simplon Tunnel.

—LARS ÖHRSTRÖM[1]

C atalysts accelerate change. While they cannot, on their own, make a reaction happen that would normally not, they can significantly reduce the time required for change to occur.

Success can act as a catalyst for failure, just as failure can be a catalyst for success. If success leads to a loss of focus or complacency, it accumulates into failure if left unaddressed. A failure, on the other hand, can be a catalyst to explore why something didn't work and change the approach to get a better outcome.

Finding the right catalyst is critical. No single substance increases the rate of all reactions. Because different reactions have different activation energies, there are many different catalysts. The final important feature of catalysts is that they are not consumed by the reaction. They can be removed and used again, making them extremely useful.

The mechanisms through which catalysts work are relatively simple in theory: they create alternative pathways for the reaction to occur, which means more of the reactant particles have enough energy. The reaction is then faster, safer, and, in industrial contexts, cheaper.

Catalysts are everywhere, even if they might not be obvious. Many everyday products—including bread, paper, yogurt, and detergent—are manufactured with help from catalysts. Inside our bodies, catalysts facilitate processes ranging from movement to digestion.

A common example of catalysts making our lives easier is in the catalytic converters of diesel- or gasoline-fueled cars. Exhaust fumes from these cars contain toxic products, including carbon monoxide. Released into the atmosphere, the products have myriad harmful effects, including exacerbating respiratory conditions. To minimize this, catalytic converters contain catalysts that turn exhaust fumes into less harmful gases.

Human experimentation with catalysts dates back to early uses of yeast for alcohol creation, and the employment of catalysts in the combination of fats with alkali substances for the production of soap. Serious study began in the eighteenth century with the work of Elizabeth Fulhame. Through extensive experimentation, Fulhame discovered that most oxidation reactions cannot occur in the absence of water. She also noted that the water involved appeared to be regenerated and was not used up in the process. Fulhame is an extraordinary figure in the history of science, in part for the forward-thinking nature of her work and in part for being one of the first women to make a substantial contribution to a field. For the latter reason, many of her peers refused to accept her work. Time has shown her to be correct, and the impact of her discoveries is hard to overstate.

Several decades later, chemist Jöns Jacob Berzelius coined the term "catalysis" and syndicated the work of numerous earlier researchers into a coherent theory. By the end of the nineteenth century, researchers had a workable understanding of catalysts, which Wilhelm Ostwald defined as substances that speed up reactions. Ostwald believed that there was no chemical reaction that could not be improved through catalysts.

When the industrial revolution began, people soon realized the potential for using catalysts in manufacturing, with a number of patents filed. Financial gain proved to be a powerful incentive for those researching catalysis, which is probably why there were so many advancements in a relatively short time.

Catalysts are the unsung heroes of the many processes that they make faster, cheaper, and safer.

The First Internet

Catalysts are not required for a reaction to occur, but they make things easier. Having them means that there are more possible starting conditions for reactions. Like all models from the physical world, they are value neutral. Catalysts can just as easily speed up the occurrence of negative reactions as of positive ones.

Once you start looking for catalysts, you see them everywhere—like the printing press, which significantly sped up the learning process. If obtaining knowledge is thought of as a reaction, then prior to the printing press this reaction required comparatively huge activation energy to get started.

Handwritten books were rare and the purview of a very small section of society. Getting access to them was complicated—you needed the time and the means to seek them out. In order to learn, scholars would have to wander from scriptorium to scriptorium, hunting down one of Aristotle's or Euclid's works. In addition, they couldn't rely on the integrity of what they were reading—hand copying lent itself to errors and embellishment, and books were sometimes erased so the parchment could be reused. For medieval scholars, the older a manuscript was, the more likely it was to be accurate.[2]

The printing press acted as a catalyst to accelerate the process of obtaining knowledge by creating a repeatable process for copying knowledge: books. These books were cheaper and faster to make than the old manuscripts, and thus were more widely available.

Knowledge now required less time and money to obtain—effectively lowering the activation energy. The printing press increased knowledge because it broadened the conditions in which the reaction could occur. There were more pathways to learning and for accessing information.

Unexpected Consequences

Social catalysts can take on unexpected forms. Consider the Black Death, which swept the world for several centuries, peaking in the fourteenth century. The epidemic was tragic, wiping out hundreds of millions of people. Yet it also proved to be a powerful catalyst for social, religious, economic, and cultural change. Though we can't know if these changes would have happened anyway, and it is only the distance of time that enables us to find anything positive in it, it seems that the Black Death was the beginning of many elements of the society we now live in.

The precise origins of the Black Death are unlikely to ever be known, but we do know how it spread. Animals, in particular rats, carried fleas infected with the plague bacteria when they climbed aboard ships sailing around the world. The fleas then jumped onto humans, bit them, and infected them with the Black Death. In the 1340s, the trading routes that were bringing Europe new wealth and opportunities brought it something more sinister. With no knowledge of what was causing this devastating disease, people continued to move and trade, spreading the plague farther and farther afield.

As time progressed and more and more people died, society

began to change. Old systems of labor collapsed with so few people left to work. Workers could demand more money because they were less replaceable. As wages rose, rents fell as landlords realized, to their chagrin, that they possessed more land than there was demand for. Survivors were considerably better off, and increased social mobility enabled even the poorest people to rise in society and earn more money. New industries bloomed to meet their needs, as those who once struggled to survive now had disposable income. Land became cheap and labor became expensive. With fewer workers, people developed labor-saving technology to make farming more efficient. The overall effect was a restructuring of society to be more equal.

While the Christian Church had long dominated society, the Black Death weakened its grip for two reasons: people found it difficult to reconcile the tragedy they saw with religious teachings, and the numbers of priests and religious leaders shrunk. Those in religious orders died in the same numbers as anyone else. In the cultural gap created, new ideas emerged and led to the Renaissance. While European culture had stagnated for centuries, the weakening of the Church enabled dramatic advancements in science and significant changes in the topics pursued in literature and poetry. People did not become less religious, and the Church remained at the heart of society, but with changing sensibilities.

The Black Death may have led to improved conditions for women, who began to enter the workforce in new ways, particularly in industries such as brewing. Women also began marrying later in life.

Medicine also changed. After making only minor improvements for centuries and relying on humoral theory, doctors realized that old ideas surrounding the human body were incorrect, and they moved toward research based on observation.

The Black Death was a catalyst for change in almost every area of society. Although these changes may have happened anyway, the epidemic sped them up. As Peter Frankopan writes in *The Silk Roads*, "And yet, despite the horror it caused, the plague turned out to be the catalyst for social and economic change that was so profound that far from marking the death of Europe, it served as its making."[3] The changes were not evenly distributed, and not all of the survivors enjoyed the same benefits. By and large, however, the Europe that emerged from the tragedy was an entirely different place. As populations recovered, European society continued to evolve. Although the immediate economic gains faded, some of the new structures were there to stay.

Catalysts lead to change. The right catalyst makes an endeavor that once seemed impossible simple. It need not only be about wide, systemic changes, like those just described. There are many smaller catalysts that we encounter in our everyday lives. Getting out of breath while walking up a flight of stairs might be the catalyst for someone to start exercising. Reaching a significant birthday might prompt someone to make a career change. A health scare may push someone to improve their habits. For many people, unpleasant events, such as getting fired or rejected, prove to be catalysts for tremendous personal growth.

Autocatalysis

When the outputs of a reaction are the same catalysts needed to start it, the reaction becomes self-sustaining and accelerates on its own. This is called "autocatalysis." While it doesn't go on forever, often there is a good window of time when you get a huge boost.

Autocatalysis reinforces itself and can be positive or negative. Ingestion of chemicals to alter your mood often becomes autocatalytic. The more you take them, the more they cause the feelings you are trying to avoid. A good night's sleep, on the other hand, can also be autocatalytic, as the increase in focus, mental clarity, and emotional regulation becomes the input into wanting another good night of sleep.

In terms of harnessing the power of catalysts, producing an autocatalytic reaction is the gold standard. How many things in life do we wish could continue on their own for an extended period of time, without constantly needing the input of our energy?

The Comfort of a King

The endorsement of the rich, famous, or respected can act as a catalyst in the evolution of cultural norms. Society evolves. Over time, we change our sensibilities and preferences, our notions of acceptable behavior, even our concepts of what it means to be human. The forces that influence these changes come from a variety of sources.

Innovations in technology allow for different means of organization, whose effects ripple through society, or geopolitical changes that require different functions from citizens and thus serve to create new perceptions of roles in society. Sometimes these developments stagnate, not having enough energy to produce systemic change. Other times, seemingly innocuous changes are embraced by opinion leaders, who become, in effect, catalysts speeding up the adoption of the changes in society.

Louis XV of France was just such a person. Going into the eighteenth century in France, and Europe in general, homes were decorated to show off one's wealth and possessions. They weren't private sanctuaries but rather public displays of status. By the mid-eighteenth century the home as a public space had changed. Homes began to be designed for comfort and intimacy. We went from straight-backed wooden chairs to padded sofas, and public privies to private flush toilets.[4] It was incredible, and now most of us couldn't conceive of going back. Thus, we all owe a small debt to Louis XV for embracing the desire to have a comfortable home.

Part of the change to seeing the home as a private space was a result of larger social changes that were occurring. The upper classes were moving around less due to more stable political situations. Technological advancement was booming, leading to a new look at things like indoor plumbing and central heating. And, perhaps most important, the Enlightenment was developing, placing emphasis on individual liberty and the sharing of knowledge and ideas. One of the products of these changes was that the French royalty no longer wanted to be uncomfortable at the palace.

During his reign, Louis XV transformed Versailles from an uncomfortable and public space to a place that reflected the desire of individuals to live somewhere they could also enjoy. He created almost a parallel palace of interior rooms where he, his family, and close confidants could exist outside the public eye. He replaced wooden footstools with legions of sofas and armchairs and made it perfectly acceptable for intimate acquaintances to sit in the presence of the king. In his private rooms he was just Louis. He installed indoor plumbing and flush toilets in their own private rooms. For the first time, guests at Versailles didn't have to relieve themselves in the hallways. Bedrooms were no longer places where anyone could wander through. Rooms were smaller and had specific functions. In short, Louis XV put in place many aspects of the modern home.[5]

Importantly, Louis didn't invent any of these things. He was greatly influenced by the sensibilities of his father's mistress, the Marquise de Montespan, who started some of the changes at Versailles, and his own mistress, the Marquise de Pompadour, who embraced the notions of comfort and privacy. They, in turn, were influenced by the changes and developments happening in society around them.[6]

Therefore, it is quite possible that the widespread acceptance of the standards of comfort and privacy would have come to pass anyway. But, as Joan DeJean writes in *The Age of Comfort*, "The invention of modern comfort was a vast, and vastly costly, enterprise, one that transformed first the look of royal residences and then the cityscape of Paris, and did so, furthermore, in fast-forward mode, so rapidly that contemporaries kept repeating that it was all happening as if by magic."[7]

Early adoption by Louis XV and the royalty made comfort desirable and cheaper. The more people who wanted comfort, the more who bought into it, the more the prices lowered. This created a feedback loop in which comfortable elements for the home became accessible to more and more people. Louis XV helped to make comfort both socially acceptable and financially affordable.

Developments in technology often act as catalysts for social changes.

Conclusion

Catalysts are the unsung heroes of chemical reactions, the silent partners that accelerate change. By decreasing the amount of time required to cause change, they also make reactions possible that might not have occurred otherwise.

In chemistry, a catalyst is a substance that increases the rate of a reaction without being permanently altered itself. But catalysts aren't just chemical curiosities, they're a powerful metaphor for the forces that drive change and growth.

In business, a catalyst might be a new technology that opens fresh possibilities, or a visionary leader who inspires a team to new heights. In your personal life, a catalyst could be a life-changing book, a transformative experience, or a mentor who sees your potential and helps you realize it. Of course, while we benefit from others acting as our catalysts, we can be catalysts ourselves—helping others find the activation energy they need to thrive.

Alloying

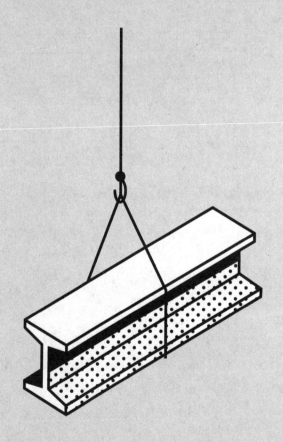

Greater than the sum of its parts.

Innovation is taking two things that already exist and putting them together in a new way.

—ATTRIBUTED TO TOM FRESTON

Alloying combines components in specific combinations to produce a substance that can achieve something the individual elements cannot. An alloy is a mixture, either in solution or in compound, of two or more metals, or a metal and a nonmetal. Alloying, then, describes the process of creating an alloy. Alloying synthesizes a product with unique properties, such as greater strength, anticorrosion, service life, and general performance.

Alloying has greatly impacted the lives of humans. The Sumerians, for example, developed bronze, made of 90 percent copper and 10 percent tin, which made the resulting material harder and more chemically resistant than either pure copper or pure tin. Creating tools and weapons from bronze instead of copper allowed them to rule over their neighbors. Bronze was also effectively used by Asians during the Bronze Age. Copper mines in Asia produced a different quality of bronze than those found in other parts of the world. For this reason, they were able to make better musical instruments, mirrors, tools, and weapons during that time.

In the same way that copper and tin produce bronze, the right combination of skills in the same person can produce unexpected results. Marrying a relentless work ethic with extreme reliability and willingness to learn works better over the long term than any of them acting alone.

Another important alloy in history is steel, which is still the most widely produced metal. The combination of iron and carbon results in steel, which is much harder than pure iron. The hardness of steel led to improved agricultural tools and weapons. The addition of metals such as magnesium, nickel, and chromium to carbon steel lends various characteristics to the alloy. These additives give the steel different properties, such as stainlessness, and wear or corrosion resistance.

Not every combination of elements produces a better, more useful alloy, but when you find one that works, the results accomplish something previously out of reach. "In the first 4,000 years or so of steel making, the early chemists and metallurgists had no real idea what they were doing and thus found it very difficult to optimize their processes. Add to this difficulty the large and very diverse selection of iron ores found in nature—frequently with phosphorus and silicon atoms causing a nuisance—and you may appreciate some of the complexity of the problem. Simply copying a successful procedure might not give a satisfactory product with iron ore from another mine."[1] However, they kept at it, giving themselves and their societies new opportunities for growth and development. With a successful alloy, one plus one can truly equal ten. The application of this model is relevant to everything from building teams to knowledge.

Medicine is one field in which the concept of alloying comes into play. Sometimes, a combination of two or more drugs can have a greater benefit than each drug individually. For example, chemotherapy drugs can be so toxic that they are almost certain to produce potentially fatal side effects. But combining them with a drug that reduces the impact of the side effects can make the treatment effective. In other cases, a chemotherapy drug may be designed only to target a particular biochemical pathway. If the drug is used in isolation, the cancer cells may simply develop resistance and use alternate pathways, rendering it useless. Combining drugs that target different pathways leads to a drastically higher chance of destroying a tumor or halting its growth.

In our lives, we often have one significant skill but don't have the other skills necessary to get the most out of it. We need to partner with those who do, forming an alloy that is greater than the sum of its parts. When we're building something from scratch, we need to consider both the raw materials and how they mix together. A team in which everyone has good ideas and nothing else won't be as strong as a team that also includes someone who has an eye for which ideas are worth pursuing and the skills to make them a reality.

How Two Men Beat an Army

Working together and combining skills can give two people greater abilities than either one has alone. The War of 1812, between the British and the American republic, was fought along the border of what is now Canada and the United States. The British were trying to protect the remainder of their North American interests after having lost to the Americans in the War of Independence. The Americans were looking to ideally get the British out of North America completely or at least obtain a bargaining chip for their ongoing negotiations regarding British naval behavior. Canada was of interest on account of abundant resources and a small settled population.

The British, however, were embroiled in war with France, and so their North American territory was imperial priority number two. Therefore, only a fraction of their potential resources was devoted to stopping the Americans. It was apparent to those on the ground in Canada that some creative thinking was required.

The Americans thought taking Canada would be the equivalent of taking a walk. The land was vast, and the people willing to defend it were few in comparison. They were not expecting much of a challenge. So it was to their great surprise that the critical position of Fort Detroit was surrendered to the British without any actual fighting. How this came to pass was because of two men who were able to achieve together what they could not as individuals.

Tecumseh was a Shawnee chief and leader of a Native American confederacy. His "consuming passion was the establishment of a native state on American territory."[2] His war was not the one of 1812, but a separate effort to secure native territory. Major General Isaac Brock had spent his career with the British army, and although he would have preferred a posting in France to one in Canada, he staunchly defended British interests there. As James Laxer writes in *Tecumseh and Brock: The War of 1812*, "their backgrounds and life experience could not have been more different."[3]

When the Americans declared war, these two men realized that an alliance with each other gave them an improved chance of success. For Brock, Tecumseh brought experienced warriors and an extensive knowledge of the territory. For Tecumseh, an alliance with the British was important to check American control of land on the continent. In Brock, he also found an ally for his goal of a native state. "Tecumseh and Brock understood each other. Together, they could do what neither could do alone."[4] Both men felt that the upper hand would be gained by going on the offensive. So they set their sights on Fort Detroit.

Working together to employ a brilliant psychological assault on the American fort, they managed to take it without any actual fighting. Brock and Tecumseh coordinated their efforts to give the impression there were thousands more Native Americans waiting to fight at Fort Detroit than there were. Brock played on the fear of Native Americans held by the American commander of the fort, and Tecumseh used his men to provide a calculated visual manipulation. When the Americans rode out with the white flag, neither side had lost any men.

The capture of Fort Detroit in an almost completely bloodless battle took the Americans by surprise. "During the battle for Detroit, Tecumseh and Brock reinforced each other's strengths, marrying the speed and flexibility of the native force to the firepower and solidity of the British regulars. That potent combination proved lethal for the cumbersome Americans and their shaky commanders. The consequence was a victory that should not have been won."[5]

Both men would continue to fight for what they believed in, and those causes would claim the lives of both within a year. The British succeeded in keeping the Americans out of Canadian territory, building on the successful tactics at Fort Detroit. When the end of the war was negotiated, and with neither Tecumseh nor Brock present, British support for Native American territory in America was not included in the treaty.

Knowledge, the Ultimate Alloy

When we reflect on our knowledge, we recognize that it has component parts. At the very least, we can easily appreciate that there is knowledge we have gained from direct experience and knowledge we have gained from theory, like that from books. Knowledge about when a stove is hot is often gained firsthand in our early years, but how that heat is produced is something we later learn in a science textbook.

Furthermore, most of us appreciate that to learn only from others, or to credit only that which is gained from direct experience, would be functionally useless. A scenario in which you could learn from only one or the other would not produce the alloy we call knowledge. Theoretical learning cannot prepare you to understand all the nuances of your particular life, such as your partner or the dynamics of your team. And if you relied solely on your own experiences to learn, you would be condemned to repeat the mistakes of others, which is extremely ineffective. Theory and experience together create knowledge, and each serves to augment and advance the capabilities of the other. Experience can trigger the updating of theory, and the validation or application of theory can trigger new experiences.

The alloy that is knowledge can further be conceptualized with more complexity. Aristotle discussed five components of knowledge. "They are what we today would call science or scientific knowledge (*episteme*), art or craft knowledge (*techne*), prudence or practical knowledge (*phronesis*), intellect or intuitive apprehension (*nous*) and wisdom (*sophia*)."[6] These components of knowledge were not mutually exclusive; they reflect the understanding of how much knowledge we bring to bear on any given situation. When driving, we understand the rules of the road and how to operate the machine. We further understand how road conditions are likely to impact our drive, in terms of both vehicle handling and travel time. We also factor in how other drivers are likely to respond in the variety of circumstances we could possibly face as we progress to our destination. The sources of our knowledge are varied.

To really explain knowledge as an alloy, something that is strengthened when we mix certain components in, we can look at the life of Leonardo da Vinci. In Walter Isaacson's account, he explains that Leonardo was able to conceive of things in an extraordinary way, leading him to discover or validate concepts that were often hundreds of years ahead of his time.[7]

Leonardo was curious; he wanted to know how the world worked and why. He also possessed and honed the skill of intense observation, studying birds and plant stems for hours, or making extensive notes and drawings on eddies of water and optics. He would observe a phenomenon, make a guess as to the principles behind it, and seek to validate those through further observation. Leonardo was willing to challenge accepted truths, seeking to understand them by questioning them. "His lack of reverence for authority and his willingness to challenge received wisdom would lead him to craft an empirical approach for understanding nature that foreshadowed the scientific method developed more than a century later by Bacon and Galileo."[8]

He was mainly self-taught, having had almost no formal schooling, but he recognized the value of learning from the experiences of others. A quote from one of his journals reads, "Get the master of arithmetic to show you how to square a triangle.... Ask Benedetto Protinari by what means they walk on the ice in Flanders ... Get a master of hydraulics to tell you how to repair a lock, canal and mill in the Lombard manner."[9] These notes suggest that no one has the time to do everything, and the alloy that is our knowledge must contain what we can learn from others.

Leonardo also readily combined knowledge from different disciplines, his understanding of nature informing his art, or his theatrical experiences pushing him to understand more about optics.

His interdisciplinary approach strengthened his knowledge by giving it a varied practicality and usefulness. "Thus, Leonardo became a disciple of both experience and received wisdom. More important, he came to see that the progress of science came from a dialogue between the two. That in turn helped him realize that knowledge also came from a related dialogue: that between experiment and theory."[10]

In building our knowledge, the environment we are in plays a huge part, as it is the source of our experiences. For this component, Leonardo was lucky, because he was born at a time and place that valued the mixing of ideas from different disciplines. In fifteenth-century Florence there were others who brought multidisciplinary thinking to design and creativity. "This mixing of ideas from different disciplines became the norm as people of diverse talents intermingled. Silk makers worked with goldbeaters to create enchanted fashions. Architects and artists developed the science of perspective. Shops became studios. Merchants became financiers. Artisans became artists."[11] There is a role for discussion and communication in developing one's knowledge. Sharing knowledge is a part of how you test it, seeing how much stronger your alloy really is after you've added some new information.

Imagination can drive curiosity, as was the case for Leonardo, and it is an important component of the knowledge alloy. Imagining what can be drives you to validate what actually exists and then to apply the investigative rigor to see if you can bridge the two. Leonardo was exemplary in this respect. "His uncanny ability to engage in the dialogue between experience and theory made him a prime example of how acute observations, fanatic curiosity, experimental testing, a willingness to question dogma, and the ability to discern patterns across disciplines can lead to great leaps in human understanding."[12] We start with what we get in terms of genetics and environment, but at a certain point we take over control of what we can become. Understanding that knowledge is an alloy of experience and theory that can be further strengthened with elements of curiosity, imagination, and sharing gives us the ability to develop it as a true source of power in our lives.

Disproportional Wear and Tear

What works for one part of the system doesn't necessarily work for all of it. In a mechanical system, when one part is subjected to significantly more wear and tear, it makes sense to coat it with a strong alloy that will minimize the damage in proportion to the wear and tear on the rest of the system. You don't want to have to stop production for the frequent replacement of just one bit.

Leonardo also played a role in the development of an alloy in the original, chemical sense. He "was also the first person to record the best mix of metals to produce an alloy that reduces friction. It should be 'three parts of copper and seven of tin, melted together,' which was similar to the alloy he was using to make mirrors. 'Leonardo's formula gives a perfectly working anti-friction composition,' wrote Ladislao Reti, the historian of technology who played a role in discovering and publishing the Madrid Codices of Leonardo's work in 1965. Once again, Leonardo was about three centuries ahead of his time. The first anti-friction alloy is usually credited to the American inventor Isaac Babbitt, who patented an alloy containing copper, tin, and antimony in 1839."[13]

Conclusion

Alloying is the art of mixing elements to create something greater than the sum of its parts. While our intuition tells us that pure substances are best, alloying shows us that this is not always true. One plus one can equal ten. By blending ingredients in precise proportions, metallurgists can create materials with bespoke properties—the lightness of aluminum with the strength of steel, the corrosion resistance of chromium with the affordability of iron.

But alloying isn't just about physical properties. It's a metaphor for the power of diversity and combination in all walks of life. Within teams, alloying is the mixing of different skills, perspectives, and personalities to create a group that's more creative, adaptable, and resilient than any individual could be alone. In ideas, it's the blending of concepts from different fields to spark innovation and insight.

In people, alloying is the combination of skills that makes them unstoppable. Consider a person possessing deep engineering skills with an ability to explain ideas clearly. Surely they are more valuable than someone with just the engineering skills. Now add empathy, humility, resilience, and drive. This person becomes incredibly rare.

The key to successful alloying is knowing which elements to combine and in what proportions. Too little of one ingredient and you don't get the desired effect; too much and you might end up with something brittle or unstable. The art lies in finding the sweet spot, the golden ratio where the whole becomes more than the sum of its parts.

BIOLOGY

A totally blind process can
by definition lead to anything;
it can even lead to vision
itself.

—JACQUES MONOD[1]

Evolution Part One: Natural Selection and Extinction

Adapt or die.

Organisms in nature have survived and thrived for billions of years because they have one powerful trait at their disposal—they are adaptive.

—RAFE SAGARIN[1]

E volution is a powerful mental model because it explains success and failure, the relationship between the environment and the individual, and why you had better plan for constant change. There are so many valuable applications of this concept, we have broken it down into two chapters.

The first, "Evolution Part One," looks at natural selection and extinction. We show how environmental pressures shape groups, spurring them to evolve or die out. The second chapter goes into more detail on ways to adapt to the inevitable changes we face. Evolution as a mental model can be summed up as "adapt or die." We think, however, it is important to understand not only how we can adapt but what it is we are responding to when we do.

Looking at natural selection and extinction together pushes us to consider the parameters that we must evolve in. We either respond to the changing demands of our environment, or we die out. Natural selection further teaches us that optimization for our environment is an ongoing and dangerous process. We are constantly trying to obtain advantages that will increase our chances of survival and help us avoid extinction as a species.

The word "selection" can be confusing because its common usage implies choice: I'm selecting this over that. In reality, the concept means that the more favorable a trait is for a particular environment, the higher the chance of that organism living long enough to procreate. Biologist Geerat J. Vermeij describes it as "nonrandom elimination."

Charles Darwin spent decades studying the natural world, and he was one of the first to make the observation that nature played a significant role in shaping all organisms. As each generation contends with its environment, the struggle for the resources needed for survival means that any traits that promote survival will likely get passed on. Thus, over time, the frequency of traits within a population changes as a response to environmental conditions. This is the definition of natural selection.

Natural selection "is very much about advantages here and now, not in the distant future. Traits conferring long-term advantages emerge because they also work well in the lives of individuals and produce positive feedbacks."[2] For a mutation to be successful, it can't negatively impact an organism's ability to survive at that time. For example, slow zebras are the ones who are eaten by the lions. The faster ones survive and reproduce. Over time, the entire zebra population becomes faster. A key element of natural selection, then, is that the beneficial traits that are selected by the environment increase the survival potential of the species. We can also apply an inversion lens, demonstrating that any adaptive response that is not useful will be selected against. As Rafe Sagarin goes on to note, natural selection "is an incredibly simple process requiring just three simple elements—variation between individuals, environmental conditions that favor (or select) certain variants over others, and a means to reproduce those variants that are better suited to the environment."[3]

There are many ways to be successful in any given environment. It is not only the most successful trait that will reproduce in successive populations but the entire upper echelon of successful traits. We can imagine that it's not only the faster zebras who will be more likely to reproduce but also zebras that have a more powerful kick or better eyesight.

One of the key elements to selecting for positive traits is that they have to be repeatable. Either the genetic mutation or the learning must be able to be passed on to the next generation. If adaptive behaviors can be used and developed in a successive series of situations to increase the fitness of the individual and the species, those behaviors will be selected for.

> New circumstances tend to be calamitous for an economic unit if they are either very large or very rare relative to the size and lifespan of that unit.
>
> —GEERAT VERMEIJ[4]

Every biological behavior and feature exists for the same reason: to survive long enough to reproduce and therefore avoid extinction. All living things are out to ensure the survival of their species. Organisms must adapt to survive.

The vast majority of the species that have existed on earth since life first emerged are now extinct. In biology, extinction is defined as the moment when the last member of a species dies. For example, the last passenger pigeon, Martha, died in captivity in 1914. But the point where there is no possibility of a species surviving tends to occur earlier, when its population density is below the threshold necessary to keep it away from extinction, a set of circumstances known as Allee effects.[5] A species may also become extinct in the wild when the only survivors are in captivity and would be unlikely to repopulate their natural habitat if released. With too few individuals remaining, breeding may be impossible. This may occur because a species has died out by itself, or it may be the result of the activity of another species, as was the case with passenger pigeons. Once numbering in the billions, this species was entirely wiped out by human hunting within a few decades.

We can't ever identify the precise cause of an extinction. The influences are always complex and unique to the situation. Often, we can only infer causes from outcomes. In addition, extinctions are not always rapid. Sometimes they take place in increments over millennia. We do, however, know the most common causes.

One cause is competition. A species may die out because it must compete with a better-adapted rival. Two species requiring the exact same resources cannot coexist in the same area. The successful introduction of alien species sometimes leads to the extinction of native ones. Unable to adapt fast enough, the native species is deprived of the resources it needs. Another cause, and one of the most common, is a change in environment. This could be due to climate change, deforestation, a volcanic eruption, or anything significantly disruptive.

To confuse matters, extinctions don't occur in isolation. Ecosystems are full of complex, nonlinear interdependencies. When one species dies out, it may take others with it. Sometimes, the interrelationships are straightforward. If a prey species goes extinct, it's logical for its main predator to do likewise if it lacks alternatives. Or the interrelationship may be less direct. If a predator goes extinct, its prey may be able to breed in greater numbers. This can put a strain on its own prey and drive this prey to extinction. Thus, we cannot predict the outcome of an extinction.

A further issue with classifying extinction is that it means we must be able to classify a distinct species. It can be hard to define what constitutes a species. If a dog interbreeds with a coyote, for example, is that a new species? We are far from identifying or even discovering all the species on this planet. Many have gone extinct without us ever knowing they existed in the first place. There are an estimated ten million distinct species, of which fewer than 20 percent[6] have been catalogued.[7]

In any system, it's natural for parts to continually wear and need replacing. This is true of ecosystems. Extinctions are a ubiquitous feature of life on earth, as a sort of meta–natural selection. The same selection process that applies to individuals also applies to species as a whole. The catch is that the very evolutionary process that ensures a species' survival can also be its downfall. Natural selection within a stable environment tends to be a process of refinement. A species will become more and more attuned to the precise adaptations it needs to survive. This is ideal in reliable conditions, but it can mean a species lacks the resilience it needs to survive any changes. So, while the best-adapted organisms may be the strongest during normal conditions, they may struggle to survive volatility. Generalist species are far more resilient than specialists. A rat or a cockroach can survive almost anywhere, a panda less so.

One of the main ways species guard against extinction is by having a lot of offspring, fast. The population can quickly restock after events like a new disease. Species that breed slowly are more vulnerable, although they can find ways around it, as humans have done.

While extinction is an extreme event, it's often normal for large numbers of a species to die out. Deer and elk starve in large numbers on a regular basis. Once the population in an area gets too big, there isn't enough food available. The periodic mass starvations end up benefiting the species. As brutal as this is, it's necessary for the whole species to endure.[8]

Extinctions happen all the time. This is when species are continually dying out but at a steady pace and from a range of causes. By contrast, a mass extinction occurs when a lot of species disappear in one go. It tends to be the result of a single cause, such as a sudden change in climate conditions, like those caused by a meteor.

Thus, natural selection and extinction are two very important concepts from evolution. Together they explain why and how organisms respond to changing environments and what happens when the responses fail. These same principles can be used to look at the development and progression of nonliving things and to better understand why certain social or cultural artifacts change and thrive while others fall out of favor or disappear altogether.

> So how does a business survive in constantly changing environments? When change hits, a common response is denial or trying to adapt with a business model that no longer works. We can influence the outcome of changing environments more rapidly by first recognizing that we actually need to survive and then moving to survive with new ideas.
>
> —ROBERTA BONDAR[9]

The Evolution of Language

Why do some customs, products, and social norms thrive, while others disappear from the landscape? Natural selection is a lens we can apply to understand how environmental pressures promote certain changes, leading to growth and dominance. And why the same process penalizes those populations that are unable to meet those pressures.

A fascinating example to illustrate the constant interaction between environment and species that leads to evolution is the way some languages grow and become global, while others go extinct.

Over human history, there have been thousands of languages used by humans to communicate. Some of these never spread beyond narrow regional dialects used only by a small group of people. Others spread far beyond their original environment to be used by people in all areas of the world. Languages are, in a sense, subject to the pressures of natural selection, which means they can also die out if they aren't well suited to their environment.

French is one of the successful languages. It evolved from the Latin spoken in the region of present-day France and can be classified as a romance language. The roots of the language that became modern French had remarkable adaptability. As it evolved, French picked up words from many of the different languages it came into contact with, so that even today it retains words that have origins in Norse, Gaulish, Frankish, Arabic, Spanish, and Italian.

Environmental pressures on languages predominantly come in the form of geopolitical changes. Shifts in power result in shifts in language usage. Jean-Benoit Nadeau and Julie Barlow explain in *The Story of French*, "Three main events pushed the language from one phase to the next: the fall of the Roman Empire, the conquest of England, and the rise of Paris as a center of power."[10] Early French responded to these changes by mutating—picking up words from other languages—which helped it survive by keeping it useful.

For centuries, the development of the French language was a series of successful adaptations. Use of the language spread all over Europe through conquest and invasion, and thus speaking it was desirable. It became the only real common language of the region.

French was used as the language of administration, and gradually "people who wanted power knew they needed French."[11] The mutations it picked up spread throughout the population, reproducing as more and more people began teaching French to their children as their mother tongue.

The spread of French meant that the language faced more complex environmental pressures. It began to settle into the modern version of the language in response to these pressures. First, "by the twelfth century, writers from the regions around Paris ... were making a conscious effort to eliminate dialectical characteristics in their writing so they could be understood by a larger number of people."[12] Second, as it became the pan-European language of business, its grammar, spelling, and precise meanings had to be set so as to avoid disputes based on interpretation. Finally, the growing popularity of printed materials pressured the language to commit to rules and standards, as well as concise characters to save on cost.

French was able to adapt accordingly. Gothic characters were replaced with Roman ones, and dissemination of printed French materials helped communicate and solidify a common understanding of the language. French speakers furthered its use by creating dictionaries and grammar that increased utility. "Because it was defined, French in the seventeenth and eighteenth centuries was regarded as easier to learn."[13] These measures served to create accessibility. The easier it is to learn a language, the more appeal there is in making the attempt.

When geopolitics shifted and colonialism became the goal of many European countries, French again was able to adapt and infiltrate new ecosystems. It continued to incorporate words from other languages confronted in new territories, thereby showing flexibility, which encouraged uptake. As Nadeau and Barlow explain, many French explorers and missionaries understood that communication was a key to relationship building and so taught French and correspondingly learned native languages all over the globe. When colonialism ended, French was often the only common language in an area that had multiple local dialects.

French, however, does not have a perfect record of adaptation. In many ways the language, although global, was heavily influenced by the culture of France. One of the impacts of this situation, for example, was that some cultural prejudices worked against the evolution of French in the colonial era. "An important segment of the [French] elite was simply not interested in questions of industry, science, technology, money or markets—issues that were vital to the development of a trading empire. The French Academy, of course, completely ignored scientific and technical vocabulary (as well as new vocabulary from the colonies)."[14] The bias of French culture limited the language. You aren't going to use a language to try to communicate your ideas if it has no words for the elements you need to express.

French eventually overcame the lack of words in scientific and technical fields and contributed many inventions and innovations to the world. But the point is that in order for languages to evolve, they must have the flexibility to adapt. Any measures that try to constrain flexibility risk the language becoming unusable and eventually extinct.

To this day France responds to the pressures on its language created by the global prominence of English (and Mandarin and Spanish) by trying to make it easy for people to learn French. "French lexicographers do their spring cleaning regularly so that the language doesn't hold on to words it doesn't need."[15] And more significantly, there are French schools all over the globe. Many are part of the private Alliance Française, and others are run by the

Letters evolve, and so do languages.

French government, but the vast majority are open to anyone who wants to learn the language.

Other concentrations of French speakers, such as those in North America and Africa, actively promote the use of French through language laws and cultural associations. Mandating usage is one way of keeping a language alive.

Evolution can be threatening if you can glimpse some of it happening. The changes you observe can suggest that your own fitness may be lacking and that the products of the evolution of your species will be unrecognizable. The evolution of language faces a similar challenge—will it still be French if the language evolves in such a way as to be incomprehensible to contemporary speakers?

Part of the tension in French is about trying to resolve the conflicting pressures placed on the language by changes in the environment. Nadeau and Barlow write that entire tenses have been dropped from usage, and slang is being adopted at a rate that makes it hard for dictionaries to keep up. Some people react by fighting to keep the language "pure" and consistent with centuries-old usage. They advocate a top-down approach to language development. Others accept changes and innovations and view them as a source of creativity and a way of staying relevant.[16] The lens of evolution and natural selection suggests that trying to freeze a language, or trying to maintain tight control on its evolution, is the exact wrong reaction in terms of preventing extinction. If a language cannot adapt, it will cease to be useful. If it ceases to be useful, it will go extinct.

The story of the evolution of French can be contrasted with that of Latin. Latin is perhaps the best-known dead language. The debate over what makes a dead language and whether any particular language falls in that category is endless. By the strictest definition, a language is dead only when no living people speak it. The more typical definition is when a language is no longer native to any community who would speak it as their mother tongue.

Latin originated in Rome, then spread across Europe and Africa as the Romans took over the surrounding areas. The oldest surviving example of written Latin dates back to the seventh century BCE. According to legend, Rome was founded about half a century earlier. In an era when most people spent their entire lives close to where they were born and had little reason to interact much with anyone outside their own community, Italy was home to numerous minor languages, of which Latin was just one. It was pure luck that Latin ended up taking on such significance. By most estimates, Latin ceased to be anyone's mother tongue and diverged entirely into separate languages by the seventh century CE.[17] While geopolitical changes after the fall of the Roman Empire strengthened French, they gradually killed Latin.

This doesn't mean no one knows the language or that it is not in use in any manner. Latin remains the official language of Vatican City and has a significant role in Catholicism, often used in writing by officials. It's used in some traditional, ceremonial situations, like the graduation ceremonies at Oxford University in England.

In addition, a significant portion of the technical terminology used in medicine, epistemology, taxonomy, law, and other fields is Latin. This is partly tradition and partly to give these fields a universal language to facilitate ease of communication across borders. Some schools still offer Latin classes, and many people still choose to study it. For scholars who study old texts, a knowledge of Latin is useful so they don't need to rely on translations, which may be subjective. For these reasons, Latin is unlikely to disappear altogether. But the fact that it is not spoken as a native language puts it into the dead category.

Just as a species that goes extinct can have descendant species that survive, incorporating some of its traits, dead languages can be the ancestors of living ones. Latin formed the basis of many of the existing languages in nations that once fell under the Roman Empire, including Italian, French, Portuguese, Romanian, and Spanish.

The main reason Latin fell out of use is its complexity. Learning Latin is far more arduous than learning any of the languages it spawned, as there are numerous ways to modify each word depending on the context. The selection pressures on languages tend to push them toward whatever form is easiest to learn. A language is well adapted to its environment if people can learn it and if they have a strong enough reason to learn it. Much like in everyday use, we often contract words or drop syllables to make our speech easier, Latin evolved into a simpler form known as Vulgar Latin. Because no central authority existed to codify and define the proper use of Latin, its simpler form diverged in different parts of what was once the Roman Empire, becoming a range of different languages. As humans, we have a tendency to minimize energy output, which gives us a preference for languages that are easy to use and understand. That doesn't mean the simplest languages become the most popular. But it does mean that in the absence of formal, enforced standards, languages drift toward greater ease of use. This is part of what happened to Latin; it wasn't best suited to its environment. In addition, there were no laws requiring the use of Latin in particular areas. French, by comparison, was more formalized, with defined standards for its usage. Being easier to learn likewise gave it an advantage in surviving long-term.

Beyond the languages that have direct links to its structure and grammar, other languages use Latin words or ones derived from them. It's estimated that more than 60 percent of English words are derived from Latin or Greek. For instance, "antique" and "ancient" come from "antiqua," meaning "old." Likewise, French uses numerous words of Latin origin, like "agir" (to act) which comes from "agere," and "bouteille" (bottle) which comes from "butticula." Thus, although Latin is a dead language, it has had a lasting and widespread influence on many languages that are still in use and spoken by millions of people.

The contrast between French and Latin shows us how languages are subject to the pressures of natural selection. Languages also need to evolve to survive in a changing environment, or they decline in use and eventually go extinct.

Conclusion

Natural selection is the hidden hand that selects the fittest from a never-ending pile of genetic variation, while extinction is the hammer that shatters the unfit and clears the way for variations to arise.

In biology, natural selection is the process by which traits that enhance survival and reproduction become more common in successive generations of a population. It's the invisible hand that guides the adaptations of the living world, favoring those creatures that are best suited to their environments and pruning back those that fall short.

But for every winner in the great game of natural selection, there are countless losers. Extinction is the fate awaiting those species that fail to adapt, that find themselves outpaced by changing circumstances or outcompeted by more successful forms. The evolutionary end.

Without the possibility of extinction, there would be no imperative to evolve to our changing environment. And without the sculpting hand of natural selection, the unfit and ill-adapted would consume scarce resources.

These principles apply far beyond the realm of biology. In business, in technology, in ideas, we see the same relentless winnowing of the unfit and the elevation of the adaptive. The companies that thrive are those that can navigate the shifting landscape of consumer demand and technological change, while those that stagnate are swept away by the tides of creative destruction.

On a personal level, we are all subject to the pressures of selection and the risk of extinction. Our skills, our knowledge, our ways of thinking must constantly evolve to keep pace with an ever-changing world. Those who consistently adapt are the ones who thrive in the long run.

Above all, remember that in the great game of life, there are no permanent victories—only the ceaseless striving to stay one step ahead.

Evolution Part Two: Adaptation Rate and the Red Queen Effect

Getting better all the time.

Adaptation is as good as it has to be; it need not be the best that could be designed. Adaptation depends on context.

—GEERAT VERMEIJ[1]

W e have to deal with the environment we are in, not the one we wish we were in. Adaptations are successful relative to their performance in a specific environment, relative to the pressure and competition the organisms face. We don't have to be objectively best, just better than those we are competing against. "In other words, living things do only as well as they have to rather than optimize."[2]

"Adaptation" refers to both the trait that is useful and the process of change it undergoes as it is passed on. It functions as both a noun and a verb. Adaptations start as genetic variations that occur in the right time and place to be useful. "Adaptability controls the sweet spot between reaction and prediction, providing an inherent ability to respond efficiently to a wide range of potential challenges, not just to those that are known or anticipated."[3]

The story of the peppered moth in Britain is a textbook example of adaptive change to specific environmental pressures. While normally the moths were very light, there were nonetheless variations that resulted in dark coloring. However, against the normal backdrop of their environment, the dark moths stood out and were quickly eaten—at least at first. However, during the industrial revolution, what was once a negative trait became a positive one.

When blankets of sooty pollution were covering everything for miles, the lighter moths now stood out and became an easy target for their predators. The dark variants became far more successful at camouflaging in the dark soot and were therefore better able to survive and produce significantly more offspring.

Gene mutation confers an advantage that increases the frequency of that mutation in the population. Mutations are constantly being tested in the environment. It's interesting that now, with more efforts at pollution control due to the deleterious effects of smog, the lighter moth is making a comeback.

Populations of organisms adapt in response to changes in both the organic and nonorganic environment. Less sunlight or warmer temperatures influence the process of adaptation, as do changes in the other organisms that occupy the same environment. Predators adapt to changes in prey, and they also adapt to changes in their competitors. When it comes to adapting to environmental change, "nature is limited to the raw materials at hand, and there's only so much you can do with them." One consequence is that there might be the same solution for different problems in different species.[4]

Adaptations can arise in multiple places, basically simultaneously. Consider that "humans had earned a living by hunting and gathering wild foods for 10,000 generations, but in just a few, brief millennia, food production sprung up across the globe. It happened separately in at least a dozen places."[5] Which brings up the full context of the word "adaptation." There are genetic mutations that allow for direct adaptation, then there are the mutations that allow for learning and thus adaptation on a much shorter timescale.

Identifying Opportunities to Adapt

> Adaptation requires leaving or being forced from your comfort zone and into a place where you observe and experience new threats to your security.
>
> —RAFE SAGARIN[6]

When we think about World War II, most of us know that France was occupied by the Germans early on. The Nazis rolled into Paris in the spring of 1940, and not until D-Day, four years later, did the Allies get a toe back in the country. The French toiled under the Vichy government for the rest of the war, and some supported the Allied effort through a small but potent resistance. Have you ever asked why France fell so fast?

It's interesting to think about. After all, when the Treaty of Versailles concluded World War I, it was the Germans, not the French, whose military was greatly reduced. Despite this, the French continued to be anxious about future German aggression. They maintained their military. They built the Maginot Line as a defensive structure in eastern France. They strategized on how to protect their country. They bought tanks and kept up drills and vowed they would not suffer a repeat of World War I.

Germany was in an entirely different situation. After the First World War, the country "was left, as even the Allies admitted, with something closer to a police force than an army. When the promise of reductions in all armies failed to materialize in later years, it added to British unease about the German treaty, and to German resentment. With an army of 100,000 men and a navy of 15,000, and with no air force, tanks, armored cars, heavy guns, dirigibles, or submarines, Germany was to be put in a position where it could not wage an aggressive war."[7]

Germany's munitions were destroyed, and the country was not allowed to import anything that could be used as "war material." They couldn't have cadets' and veterans' societies and "couldn't do anything of a military nature."[8] Further, they were ordered to pay huge sums of money to the Allies, reducing their ability to rearm. Of course, later events showed that the Germans ignored many of the terms, and the Treaty of Versailles has been widely criticized for creating the conditions that led to World War II. However, the point here is that given the circumstances leading up to 1939, it is by no means obvious why the Germans were so successful in invading France.

At the outbreak of the war, France had 110 divisions, "of which no less than 65 were active divisions." The Germans, on the other hand, "had 98 divisions, 36 of which were untrained and unorganized." Explaining the technical capacity of each military in 1939, B. H. Liddell Hart says, "On the surface, it would appear that the French had ample superiority to crush the German forces in the west."[9] So why didn't they even come close?

Warfare in 1939 had many new components. It was a changed environment to which the French had not adapted. They hadn't undergone the selective pressures needed to be prepared for the German army.

The Treaty of Versailles had, in a sense, been about maintaining the adaptive status quo. The hints World War I gave that warfare had fundamentally changed and thus required new thinking were largely ignored by the leaders of Europe. In France there was both "an incomprehension of the new idea of warfare, and official resistance to it."[10] The French were twenty years out of date in their thinking. They had modern equipment but "lacked modern organization."[11] And they had not invested in airpower to support their ground troops.

On the human timescale, adaptability is about recognizing when the way you have done things in the past is becoming less and less successful in a changing environment. It requires you to innovate, like mutations in the evolution timescale, to see if you can come up with ideas that will improve your chances of success.

In the 1930s, the French prepared themselves for a war they had already fought. Hart writes, "The French High Command still regarded tanks through 1918 eyes—as servants of the infantry, or else as reconnaissance troops to supplement cavalry. Under the spell of this old-fashioned way of thought they had delayed organizing their tanks in armored divisions—unlike the Germans."[12]

To be fair, the Germans had not fully worked out how to succeed in this new environment either. It wasn't like they had perfected which adaptations were going to work the best. They were "still far from being a really efficient and modernly designed force. . . . At the same time the German High Command had, rather hesitatingly, recognized the new theory of high speed warfare and was willing to give it a try."[13] And it was this willingness to adapt, even in only a few individuals at first, that was one of the reasons they were so successful in the early part of the campaign.

As with genetic mutations, improved fitness doesn't require everyone to adapt at the same time. At the outset of the war many in the German High Command were remarkably similar to the French in how they thought the invasion would play out in terms of tactics and timing. There were just a few more Germans in positions of sufficient power who were willing to try new tactics. One of the more notable of these is General Heinz Guderian. Hart writes, "The

Battle of France is one of history's most striking examples of the decisive effect of a new idea, carried out by a dynamic executant."[14]

Hart's explanation of Guderian's actions is a chronicle of adaptation in action. "Guderian has related how, before the war, his imagination was fired by the idea of deep strategic penetration by independent armored forces—a long-range tank drive to cut the main arteries of the opposing army far back behind its front. A tank enthusiast, he grasped the potentialities of this idea, arising from that new current of military thought in Britain after the First World War. . . . When war came Guderian seized the chance to carry it out despite the doubts of his superiors."[15]

Guderian's adaptations took him right through the French defenses, giving him an unobstructed path to the English Channel. It was his series of actions that the Germans built on to complete the occupation of France a year later. Guderian led an adaptive German response to the changes in the warfare environment. Like the color of the peppered moth, the changes were successful only in a very specific environment. The German responses to other environmental conditions were significantly less beneficial and contributed to their eventually losing the war and returning France to the French.

Long Live the Red Queen

The Red Queen effect is a compelling principle of evolutionary biology and vivid image to help understand the pressures that all organisms face just in surviving.

The least fit of a species dies first. You can't stop adapting because no one around you is stopping. If you do, your competitive position declines, bringing your survival into question. Every living thing is constantly on the lookout for opportunity, the place to accrue advantage, and thus adaptation is also driven as a response to changes in those with whom we share our environment. Staying the same as we are often means falling behind.

The Red Queen effect was first used in the context of evolutionary biology by Leigh Van Valen in 1973. In his research, he noticed something interesting: that at no point was a species protected from extinction. Evolution is an ongoing process, and all species must continually respond to pressures in their environment or die off. What's more, constant adaptation is something that everyone is doing all the time. Hence the use of the Lewis Carroll character from *Alice's Adventures in Wonderland*. The Red Queen tells Alice, "Now, *here*, you see, it takes all the running you can do, to keep in the same place."[16]

At the biological level, organisms don't choose to adapt. A leopard doesn't sit up one day and say, "Wow, the antelope are getting faster. I need to do something about that." Rather, the increased speed of the prey means that only the fastest predators will get food and live long enough to reproduce. Thus, over time, the average speed of the predator species increases. The pressures on both the predator and prey are constant, which is what produces the Red Queen effect.

However, this principle applies to the much smaller timescale of our lives as well. And, importantly, we can choose to do something about it. There are so many humans on the planet that even if only 20 percent were trying to move ahead, it's enough that they wouldn't leave much behind for the rest of us. There are enough people trying to get smarter, better, and more of the limited resources that are available, that it puts direct pressure on everyone to keep up.

> If feedback is positive, or reinforcing, cause and effect together unleash a runaway process with all the characteristics of an arms race. If negative, or stabilizing and self-limiting, feedback acts as a brake, muting change and damping fluctuations.
>
> —GEERAT VERMEIJ[17]

The Red Queen effect is often applied to business strategy and human conflict. These two areas bookend the spectrum of the use of this model. Applied to business, it is an argument against complacency. As noted, the originator of the hypothesis, Leigh Van Valen, observed that longevity does not protect species from extinction. No matter how long a species has survived, a failure to adapt can result in extinction. There is no plateau a species can reach when it gets to say, "OK, the hard work is done. I can coast now, getting by on what I have." Because all species are continually adapting, the pressure is constant.

The same dynamic exists in business. Your competitors are always working to get ahead, and thus you must as well. Your customers' needs are always changing, and you need to be able to identify and meet these. Considering the actions of your competitors and the desires of your customers is part of the core, daily functions that your business must always perform.

Some organisms exist within an aggressive Red Queen effect, which is the situation for many bacteria, while for others, like cockroaches, the pace is less intense. It is possible that high capacity in both flexibility and learning can slow one's particular experience of the effect. Overall, when applied in business, this principle can promote an environment where there is an infinite capacity for innovation.

At the other end of the spectrum we may apply the Red Queen effect to human conflict. As in an arms race, in which one side invests resources to outdo the other, eventually the cost of the resources is immense, but no advantage is gained. An arms race points to the limits of using the Red Queen effect as a model. In some scenarios, namely those in which there is an end to beneficial adaptation, it is better to look at changing parts of the environment in which you are trying to survive instead of trying to keep up in a race that is undermining your overall ability to adapt. Actions that put the existence of an individual or a species in danger are not the goal of adaptation and not supported by the Red Queen effect.

Vestigial Structures

Natural selection happens in imperceptible increments over vast periods of time. That means sometimes we can see traces of its path.

It's a misconception that organisms are perfectly formed and adapted to their environments. We can see the traces of natural selection, a slow and imperfect process, in vestigial structures. These are traits that are present in a species or some members of a species but no longer have any function or value. Vestigial structures may be present only during the embryonic stage or they may be a permanent feature. In the past, they served an important purpose that helped a species survive.

For example, flightless birds such as ostriches usually have small, useless wings that are leftover from the ones that once gave them flight. The human goose bump reaction to stress or fear is a vestigial response, based on how our ancestors would have fluffed up their fur to look bigger when confronted with a predator. Some snakes have the remnants of a pelvis from the time when they had legs, as do whales.[18] The presence or absence of pelvic remains is one way we classify snake species. Pigs have useless toes raised off the ground. The parasite responsible for malaria contains the vestiges of a chloroplast in its single cell. Moles have skin-covered, de-evolved eyes hidden beneath their fur, despite being blind.[19]

So why don't vestigial structures just go away? It all comes down to natural selection. An organism's traits are selected for or against by natural selection only if they have any impact on its chances of survival. If a vestigial structure confers no benefit but causes no harm, there is no reason for it to disappear. Getting goose bumps during a horror movie isn't likely to reduce an individual's chances of reproducing, nor does it require enough energy to be a meaningful hindrance. So goose bumps will probably stick around for a good while longer unless random mutations eliminate the response or it becomes detrimental.

Even when vestigial structures do go away, it happens gradually over many generations. At a certain point, they cease to be relevant to the process of natural selection. There are even instances when further shrinking or eliminating a vestigial structure would be more detrimental than leaving it in a diminished form, so it remains. For them to disappear completely may require overall structural changes in an organism that are not feasible, or not important enough to exert selective pressure. Scientists are always learning more, and sometimes a feature that seems to serve no purpose has one we haven't discovered yet. Vestigial structures can be helpful for learning about evolution and determining if species have a common ancestor.

> Success is measured by persistence.
>
> —GEERAT VERMEIJ[20]

One of the interesting problems for humans is that the pressures we face from each other are not isolated and often require a complex response. We are not just trying to run faster than an antelope. We are trying to be better in so many ways that we often feel like we are failing at everything. So we burn out or we give up.

However, like velocity, the "speed of adaptation is not the same thing as effective adaptation. . . . The point is that what matters is not the speed of adaptation, but what problems it helps you solve and what problems arise as a result of an enemy's adaptations."[21]

First of all, the principle of adaptation is that it is useful. Useful adaptations are well suited to life, and they increase your ability to be successful in that life. They have to improve your function. Also, adaptations come with trade-offs. Increasing your fitness in one way will mean a decrease in fitness in other areas. Humans have big brains. A benefit is unmatched problem-solving ability. We can survive in a wide variety of situations for which we have no direct experience. The trade-off? The bodies that house these big brains can't be fully grown inside the womb. So we are vulnerable for many years after birth.

Adaptations are further constrained by the fact that an organism must be viable at all stages of the adaptation process. What this means on the human life timescale is that if you are compromising your physical health or your sanity, you are not adapting. You are instead weakening your ability to successfully respond to changes in your environment.

Adaptations are about being successful in your environment, so it becomes critical to define success. For animals it means living long enough to pass on your genetics and, depending on your species, getting your young through the early vulnerable stages. Mammals, in particular, don't just need to have offspring but need to teach them how to successfully navigate their environment.

But beyond our biology, there is no universal definition of success that all humans would agree upon. For some it's about power and recognition, for others it's about the freedom of choice, and others still would emphasize spiritual enlightenment and peace. However, a fundamental component of success must be that it involves benefit. You gain when you succeed. Anything that compromises your ability to succeed is not justified by this model. Running as fast as you can to stay in place is not a euphemism for sixteen-hour workdays. It should not be the reason you don't see your children or used to justify ignoring the needs of your body and soul.

> No innovation comes into existence perfectly hewn. Error is thus necessary for the generation of variation.
>
> —GEERAT VERMEIJ[22]

Don't Reinvent the Wheel, Repurpose It

There is a lot of opportunity that already exists in your world. You don't have to start from scratch with adaptation. In evolutionary biology, making use of things you already have is sometimes referred to as an exaptation.

The term "exaptation" was first proposed by Stephen Jay Gould and Elisabeth Vrba in 1982 to make the point that a trait's current use does not necessarily explain its historical origin.[23] In other words, just because A is used for B by species C does not necessarily mean that species C evolved A for the purpose of doing B. It may very well be the case that B is something that this species learned to do after the adaptation of A.

For example, although today most birds use their feathers to fly, it would be incorrect to say that this means feathers emerged in these birds specifically for flight. In fact, feathers first emerged in dinosaurs for the purposes of insulation or attracting mates, not flight. Natural selection selected for dinosaurs that had feathers because they better allowed them to survive and reproduce. This is the adaptation: Feathers first provided heat and attractiveness. Later on, feathers also became useful for flight as observed in the modern bird. Once the structure was present, the function of flying became possible. The structure did not emerge for the purposes of flying, but it was repurposed to support this new use. It was an exaptation.

There are many other examples of exaptation in the animal world. All of them demonstrate that exaptations are useful to survival because they expand our options in responding to changing environmental conditions. Pandas have a bone, the radial sesamoid, that allows them to easily manipulate bamboo stems, their primary source of food. Most mammals and reptiles have this same bone, yet none eat bamboo or otherwise use the bone to assist in feeding. The bone is available to all of them, but only the panda needs it. Should the environment put certain kinds of pressure on the other species requiring them to adapt their feeding habits, this bone is available as an exaptation that would aid in survival.

In other words, structures that arise for the purposes of fulfilling an associated function, like echolocation in bats, are adaptations, while structures that arise and are then used for a function other than the one they originally performed, like feathers in birds, are exaptations. The distinction between adaptation and exaptation is not always a clear one, which is why we put them together as a model. What we can get out of this overlap is insight into repurposing already acquired skills and knowledge.

The Surprising Evolution of the Self-Playing Piano

About twelve hundred years ago in Baghdad there lived three brothers: Muhammad, Ahmad, and al-Hasan, collectively known as the Banu Musa. They were scholars who wrote many books on topics such as mathematics and astronomy. One of their most fascinating works was *The Book of Ingenious Devices*. This book was a catalog of machines, including a self-trimming lamp, an automatic flute player, and a programmable machine.[25] This last was "the Instrument Which Plays by Itself," a detailed design for a hydraulic organ that played music notes triggered by small divots in a pinned cylinder. Thus, a human did not interact with the machine directly; instead, they "programmed" the machine via the instructions on the cylinder.

In *Wonderland: How Play Made the Modern World,* Steven Johnson traces the technology of the musical machine devised by the Banu Musa through music boxes and mechanical toys and player pianos, and shows how the innovations generated in the pursuit of this entertainment were the foundation of the frequency-hopping technology so essential to our wireless age in the form of cellular phones, Bluetooth, and wi-fi.[26]

How did the technology make this leap?

In 1940, near the beginning of World War II, the Battle of the Atlantic was raging. German submarines were sinking boats with regularity, resulting in a devastating loss of both military and civilian life. Hedy Lamarr, Hollywood actress, and George Antheil, composer, teamed up to try to do something about it. Their goal was to invent a remote-controlled torpedo to attack German submarines.[27] One of the main challenges was the vulnerability of the frequency used to control the torpedo. Using one frequency meant that it could be easily discovered and jammed. They needed to find a way for the remote controller and the torpedo to "frequency hop" in synchrony. This way it would be near impossible to find, and the Allies could direct their torpedo without interference.

When faced with a challenge, where does one look for inspiration? Usually you start with concepts you already understand and materials you already have. This is the essence of exaptation.

Lamarr and Antheil were faced with the challenge of synchronizing the movement of frequencies. Antheil looked into his current store of knowledge and realized he'd faced a similar challenge before—trying to synchronize the musical notes of multiple player pianos in a composition of his called the *Ballet Mécanique.* "This is where Antheil's experience . . . supplied the missing element that completed Lamarr's invention. . . . He proposed a control system whereby the instruction for frequencies were encoded in two perforated ribbons. Where the holes in the piano roll signaled a musical note, the holes in the ribbons signaled a frequency change."[28]

What was invented or learned for one purpose stays available to be used for entirely different functions. "For almost a thousand years we had that meta-tool [programmability] in our collective toolbox, and we did nothing with it other than play music."[29] And then we branched out with this tool. We started programming textile looms, torpedoes, and computers. Programmability in all the functions in which we use it today has become indispensable, and we can pretty much guarantee this wasn't what the Banu Musa had in mind when they came up with that original ingenious device.

> Inventions are almost never solitary, isolated creatures; they depend on other inventions that complete them, or endow them with new applications that their original inventors never considered.
>
> —STEVEN JOHNSON[30]

Innovation without a Plan

Exaptations in evolution do not necessarily have to be new uses from current adaptations—traits that already have a purpose. They can develop from bits lying around that were started for no particular use at all, which has a parallel in technology. Sometimes people invent things solely for the sake of the invention. They don't have a fundamental social use or business model in mind. There are far more patents than things we use on a regular basis. Sometimes, those isolated inventions provide a foundation for innovations that were not at all anticipated.

What we learn from exaptation is that we don't always know the value of something at the outset, and there doesn't always have to be a justification for doing everything.

> We must not forget that when radium was discovered no one knew that it would prove useful in hospitals. The work was one of pure science. And this is a proof that scientific work must not be considered from the point of view of the direct usefulness of it. It must be done for itself, for the beauty of science, and then there is always the chance that a scientific discovery may become like the radium a benefit for humanity.
>
> —MARIE CURIE[31]

Sometimes things that have no apparent purpose at the outset can later be co-opted into use. Having to know the benefit of everything before you begin leads to missed opportunities. No one has a crystal ball—you can't anticipate all that will be required or have use as our global environment changes.

The history of commercial products is littered with exaptations. Bubble Wrap was invented in 1957 by Alfred W. Fielding and Marc Chavannes when they sealed two shower curtains together and captured bubbles of air on the inside. Obvious use? No. They first tried to sell it as wallpaper, but there were no takers. Then they tried marketing it as greenhouse insulation, but this failed. Finally, the company took it to IBM as a way to protect all their new business computers while in transit. The usage took off and the product developed into the Bubble Wrap we have today.[32]

Time and place also matter for exaptation. A use that might be perfect in one country might seem irrelevant in another. Or a product marketed at one point in history may fall flat but succeed at another time. If they'd tried marketing Bubble Wrap as wallpaper in the 1970s, when wacky wallpaper and plastic clothing were a trend, it might have taken off. Exaptation is all about context. If birds hadn't faced environmental pressures to fly, feathers may have remained as a form of insulation or evolved to serve a different function.

There's also Play-Doh. It had a twenty-year career as wallpaper cleaner in the days when coal was the primary home fuel. Using coal turned the walls sooty, and the substance that became Play-Doh was used to remove that soot. But then coal began to be replaced by heating systems based on electricity or natural gas, and Play-Doh wasn't needed anymore to clean walls. Developed by Cleo McVicker and his close relatives Noah and Joseph, Play-Doh was a product without a future. But McVicker's sister-in-law, a teacher, had been using Play-Doh as a craft medium in her primary classes. She convinced him to investigate marketing it as a child's toy. It was fun and nontoxic, and it lasted awhile if sealed properly in between uses. McVicker got prime product placement with the children's show *Captain Kangaroo*, and sales exploded, making it one of the most popular children's products of all time.[33]

Or there is the story of Botox. It's a toxin, a "naturally occurring by-product of the microorganism that causes botulism, a potentially lethal paralytic disease caused by eating contaminated preserved food."[34] The bacteria have likely been around a long time and have killed a lot of people. It wasn't until the nineteenth century that the anaerobic bacteria that cause botulism were isolated and identified.

In the 1970s, a form of the toxin was used to treat eye disorders, including uncontrollable blinking and crossed eyes. By the 1980s it was "widely applied by both ophthalmologists and neurologists as a remedy for . . . facial, eyelid, and limb spasms." In 1987, Jean Carruthers, an ophthalmologist, inadvertently discovered cosmetic uses for Botox when a patient mentioned how her eye treatments were relaxing her face. It took a few more years for Botox to hit the mainstream, but it eventually achieved widespread cosmetic application.

Thus, what exaptation is fundamentally about is flexibility. We cannot know the exact pressures we will face in the future. So what we need is a box of diverse tools that can be used and combined in almost a limitless number of ways to meet the challenges we face. Some of these pieces will never have any use, and some will be complete game changers. But no one can divine this ahead of time. Survival of a business often depends on being able to change quickly. You can't do that if you have to start from a blank slate every time environmental pressures push you to develop and innovate.

It also teaches us that as individuals we must not underestimate the options we have at our disposal. Too often we get stuck in "functional fixedness," a mindset in which we see in things only their intended use, rather than their potential use. A fork doesn't have to be just a tool to put food in your mouth. It could also be a hook, tack, or hair detangler. It may be combined with other household objects to fulfill even more purposes. As the saying goes: do what you can, with what you've got, where you are. In fact, one of the tests used to measure creativity by psychologists is to ask people to come up with as many uses as possible for an everyday object like a brick. The more exaptations someone can envision, the more creative they're considered.

The knowledge we've accrued, the lessons we've learned, are all available to us at any given moment to forge new paths in the environments we are in. The most amazing part of this concept is that it happens on two levels. There is the conscious one, in which you look around at what you have and actively seek out what you can repurpose. But these abilities also manifest on an unconscious level. Like the bird, who did not say, "Hey, maybe I can use these feathers to fly," but instead had feathers that influenced its behavior in situations they were not originally selected for, we too navigate our world differently the more knowledge and skills we can draw on in any given situation.

Conclusion

There's no such thing as a permanent lead. No matter how well a species adapts to its environment, it must keep running just to stay in place. Complacency will kill you.

The Red Queen effect is a consequence of the never-ending arms race between predator and prey, between parasite and host, between competitor and competitor. As one species evolves a new adaptation others evolve countermeasures, leading to a constant escalation. The faster you adapt the faster your rivals must adapt in response, and vice versa.

This has profound implications for the pace of evolution. In a static environment, natural selection might favor a leisurely pace of change. But in a world of constant one-upmanship, where your competitors are always nipping at your heels, the premium is on speed. The species that thrive are those that can adapt quickly, that can turn the evolutionary crank faster than their rivals.

But the Red Queen effect isn't just about biological evolution. In any competitive domain—business, technology, even ideas—the same principle applies. Companies must continually innovate to stay ahead of their rivals. Technologies must evolve at a breakneck pace to avoid obsolescence. Ideas must adapt and grow to maintain their relevance.

The key is to recognize that adaptation isn't a onetime event but a continuous process. It's not about reaching a finish line but about maintaining a lead in an endless race. Those who rest on their laurels, who become complacent in their success, are quickly overtaken by hungrier, more agile competitors.

But there is a catch when it comes to people. Once we gain an advantage, we want to hold on to it at all costs, and if we're not careful, this can slow the pace of adaptation. Before long, our competitors catch up or find innovative ways to neutralize our strength. Sustained success comes from being flexible enough to change, to let go of what worked in the past and to focus on what you need to thrive in the future.

In a world of constant change, standing still is the quickest path to extinction. Victory goes to those who can continuously adapt.

Competition

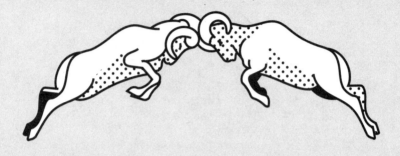

COMPETITION IS A DRIVING FORCE OF THE BIOLOGICAL WORLD. ALL living things are out to survive and breed as much as possible. This puts them in competition for finite resources like food, status, territory, and mates. This may be between whole species or individuals. The fight for resources is a zero-sum game.[35] The more one individual receives, the less there is for others. So competition is inherently harmful to the losers. If a species cannot attain the resources it needs, it will go extinct. The availability of resources dictates the type and intensity of competition. The scarcer the resource, the more aggressive the competition.

Intraspecific competition occurs within species when members fight for the same resource.[36] For example, male zebras engage in vicious fights over females. The urge to spread their genes is so strong that losers may die in the process. Male zebras will also kill the offspring of rivals. Interspecific competition occurs between species. If they live in the same area and need the same resources, they're forced to compete. Trees in a forest compete to grow the tallest and get the most sunlight. All species are constantly engaged in both types of competition.

The distinction is not as clear-cut as it might seem. Everything a species does impacts others within the same ecosystem. Competition can be direct or indirect. If living things must actively fight each other for a resource, it's direct. If there is no confrontation, it's indirect.

We cannot understand any of the biological mental models without also considering competition. It's the reason the natural world is so diverse. As Darwin recognized, all life is a struggle for survival.[37] Species that are able to fight for the resources they need to survive and reproduce are the successful ones. The type and intensity of competition is dictated by the availability of resources. The scarcer a resource is within a region, the more aggressively organisms must compete for it. When resources are more abundant, competition may be less intense. This, however, typically allows a species to breed until its numbers reach a level at which individuals are forced to compete.

Competition doesn't just occur in biology. It's also the driving force behind many human systems. The upside of competition is that it forces improvements. Competition is an important concept in business. Companies are constantly fighting for market share. This process is beneficial for consumers, because it forces companies to keep prices low and quality high whenever possible. Monopolies—in which one company dominates an entire market and customers have no other option—are discouraged because they allow for abuse and create stagnation.

Ecosystem

Everything is connected.

Some systems . . .
are very sensitive to
their starting conditions,
so that a tiny difference
in the initial push you
give them causes a big
difference in where they
end up, and there is
feedback, so that what
a system does affects
its own behavior.

—JOHN GRIBBIN[1]

In biology, an ecosystem encompasses a community of interacting species and their nonliving environment. All components play a part in determining the characteristics, from the type of soil to the amount of sun or water available. Some animals cooperate, others compete, and changes in any component can affect both the fitness of individual species and the health of the entire system.

When you learn about ecosystems, you gain insight into how diverse components interact in defined environments in a way that promotes the continued existence of the system. Individual species may gain and lose, and the system itself may be exposed to challenges that it must adapt to and recover from, but the web of interaction that has developed supports the holistic functioning of the system.

An Interconnected Web

The key point to understand about ecosystems is that they are systems. The different parts don't exist in isolation; they interact and interconnect in myriad ways. If we intervene in them, we can't expect the outcomes to be predictable. We need to look at them as a whole and respect that it's sometimes better to leave them alone than to try improving them. But we often suffer from intervention bias, the desire to always do something instead of leaving things alone, when it comes to ecosystems. We forget that they've evolved to manage quite well if we let them get on with it.

For instance, in areas that are prone to forest fires, the local fire department may attempt to put out every single fire they hear about as soon as possible, regardless of size. The problem is that fire is a natural part of these ecosystems. It is only humans that view naturally occurring fires as a problem. As destructive as wildfires can be, they also have ecological benefits. Burning dead plants releases the nutrients they contain back into the soil, helping to fertilize the next generation of plants. Fires cut through the thickest areas of plants, letting sunlight reach new areas. They wipe out alien species and diseased plants.[2]

Perhaps most important, regular small fires burn up accumulating plant matter. If humans intervene and put these out, larger amounts of fuel build up and pave the way for fires that are beyond the scope of what the ecosystem can handle. Often, the harder we try to control ecosystems, the harder they fight back.[3]

Likewise, our efforts to save endangered species from extinction often focus on interventions, rather than on preserving the natural ecosystems they need to survive. Take the case of elephants. African elephants are currently considered vulnerable, not endangered, but it is believed they may end up extinct in a matter of years if current rates of poaching and habitat destruction continue.[4] Asian elephants are classed as critically endangered.[5]

The best thing we can do for elephants is to preserve their habitats, allowing them to live and breed naturally. But much of the effort to save elephants from extinction is focused on captive breeding programs, especially artificial insemination. While this works and is safer than other methods of captive breeding, elephant artificial insemination is a classic case of us failing to recognize and support the value of ecosystems.[6] It is incredibly expensive and produces results that are far more limited than if we were to hypothetically use the same funds to preserve elephant habitat.[7] In addition, artificial insemination only produces more captive elephants, which are deprived of the space they need to roam and the social ties they would otherwise enjoy. They have much higher infant mortality rates than wild elephants, and a substantial number die from conditions related to their limited space for movement.[8]

Ecosystems are not just about their individual parts. Sometimes we're so focused on trying to reinvent and improve upon them that we forget they're quite capable of self-organizing.

> Economic systems are, of course, complex structures, in which the pattern of interactions resembles a web. This means that the dominant party in one interaction may well be the subordinate in another. Control thus diffuses through the ecosystem, generally from entities with high energy demands to those with more modest requirements. The ability to adapt to, or at least to accommodate, the power structure remains the ticket to success for all players—dominants and subordinates alike—regardless of how much influence an entity wields.
>
> —GEERAT VERMEIJ[9]

There is no size restriction on ecosystems. Isolated puddles in rocks have their own ecosystems, but so too does the ocean. Matter and energy move across ecosystems. Animals migrate, pollen blows around, and water can transport a variety of species or materials to other systems. Very few ecosystems are completely closed. Long-distance migration of many species ties ecosystems together.

Organisms within an ecosystem have varying degrees of importance for the maintenance of that system. Some are foundational to its survival. These are known as keystone species: organisms that would cause an ecosystem to completely change or collapse altogether if they were not present. Without them, new and possibly destructive organisms could take over the same niche. The term comes from zoologist Robert T. Paine, who compared them to the special stone known as a keystone, which is used at the top of an arch to ensure its structural stability. Without the keystone, the arch would collapse. It is a small component, but everything else depends on it. Keystone species can be hard to identify, as they may be present only in low numbers or may not be highly visible species. We can only know for sure that an organism is a keystone if its numbers drop and we see the second-order effects of that.

It is common for keystone species to be predators (organisms that eat other, usually smaller, organisms), as they play a crucial role in maintaining the numbers of their prey. Predators tend to be present in relatively small numbers compared to their prey. In other cases, herbivores (organisms that eat plants) are important for maintaining the levels of certain plants, thereby keeping the habitat in a favorable state for other organisms. Some species can have reciprocal relationships (see the chapter on Reciprocity), wherein the loss or reduction of one would harm the other and the effects would ripple out to the rest of the ecosystem. So, in general, the value of keystone species is dependent on their ability either to provide what other species need to survive or to control population levels.

An example of a keystone species is the sea otter, which lives in kelp forests. Sea otters eat sea urchins, which in turn eat kelp. If there are enough sea otters in the ecosystem, they prevent the numbers of sea urchins from getting too high. Without the sea otters, all the kelp would get eaten, which would eventually also lead to the demise of the urchins. In addition, kelp plays a valuable role in removing carbon dioxide from the atmosphere, benefiting the environment as a whole, and supporting a wide variety of other species. Without the sea otters, the ecosystem could not survive. No other predator in the same habitat could fill the same niche as the sea otter. If their numbers drop too low, it could have a genuine impact on global climate change.[10]

Finally, ecosystems aren't static. The internal dynamics are constantly changing as the system adjusts to and recovers from disturbances. Some ecosystems are robust, others more fragile. Some have a high capacity for resistance, which is the tendency of a system to remain close to its equilibrium state. It takes a significant disturbance to affect these ones. Resistance is contrasted with sensitivity, describing those systems for whom very weak disturbances can have a profound effect.

Also measurable is a system's resilience, which is the speed with which it recovers after a disturbance. The strength of an ecosystem is thus better considered in more than one dimension. Sensitive systems with very high resiliency can be just as strong as highly resistant systems that have trouble bouncing back.

This is why the ecosystem is such a useful mental model. The parallels with human organization are clear. Our family units tend to function as their own system, and so can our teams at work. But we are also part of the larger ecosystems of our cities or organizations, and people can move across ecosystems with ease, bringing change and challenge.

The Law of the Minimum

The law of the minimum states that the yield of a crop will always be dictated by the essential nutrient that is available at the lowest level. No matter how abundant the other essential nutrients are, being deficient in one will always limit the crop's growth. If the level of that nutrient is increased, another will become the limiting factor. One way to envision this is as a bucket with a hole through which water leaks out. The bucket cannot fill to the brim as a result. The deficient nutrient is the hole in the bucket.

The law comes from botanist Carl Sprengel, who formulated it in the 1820s. Biochemist Justus von Liebig later popularized the concept, an important one for farmers to understand. When the price of a particular fertilizer increases, some farmers are tempted to use less of it and more of cheaper nutrients. But this stunts the growth of their crops, as the other nutrients do not compensate for the deficient one.

It is not necessarily what is available that matters. What is scarce can be paramount too. We can see this in our own lives as well. If you skimp on sleep to have more time, tiredness then becomes the limiting factor to your productivity, not time.

In manufacturing, a bottleneck is a similar concept. A factory process can only move as fast as the slowest step. Likewise, in mathematics we refer to multiplying by zero, which is akin to the law of the minimum: put a zero at the end of a multiplicative calculation and it cancels out the numbers before it, no matter how high.

> Over time, closed systems produce fewer and fewer innovations, because closed systems, by definition, are based on certain increasingly unchallengeable fundamental principles.
>
> —GARY HART[11]

Trade Ecosystems

Examining the silver trade between China and Spain in the sixteenth century brings out many of the nuances of ecosystems, demonstrating how there are limits to their organization and infrastructure and how more is accomplished when you work within them.

The first lesson comes from the results of China trying to maintain a closed trading system. For various reasons, over a long period the imperial government did not want to trade with other countries. Fearing a weakening of power or thinking that there was not much to bother trading for, the government in Beijing banned all trade.

Trade with China, however, didn't stop; it was just done in a different way. No policies, customs, duties, or official infrastructure meant that trade was carried out primarily by smugglers and pirates. European merchants knew that China was the largest economy in the world and therefore represented a huge economic opportunity.[12] Once they figured out how to get there, Europeans became part of the environment. Certain individuals and groups in China adapted accordingly, integrating the opportunities the Europeans offered into the trade ecosystem.

The disruption caused by the arrival of the Europeans with

their goods created opportunities for smaller players to compete with those traditionally at the top of society. The result was an extensive criminal network that soon threatened the power of the government, and that became a contributing factor to Beijing repealing the trade laws and opening up somewhat for business.

The second lesson about ecosystems comes from looking at what happened in China when trade was opened up. To start, we need a little background. Another motivation for the trade policy change was that Beijing needed money. The traditional currencies, either bronze or paper, had been rendered completely useless by shortsighted policies that put political image ahead of economic sense. By the time those European ships sailed up, everyone in China was paying for goods with little silver bits and shaved-off lumps carried around in their pockets. The problem was that China's silver mines were depleted. There was no way to infuse new currency into the system when it was needed, and an economic system without the raw materials to produce new currency is like a forest that stops getting light. The Chinese government needed the Spanish ships with their tons of silver mined in the Americas.

Trade policy changes can be likened to an environmental change that impacts an ecosystem—a new, invasive species, a persistent change in the amount of rainfall. Changes that affect the environment in a widespread fashion will inevitably produce successes and failures. Some species will adapt and take on new territory or create a new niche, and others will die off, unable to respond to the challenges. In China, there were many individuals and groups who adapted, capitalizing on the instability brought about by the changing trade laws. These adaptations in turn forced others one or two steps removed from direct trade to adapt to the resulting new businesses with their labor and land requirements.

Thousands of acres were planted with the trees that hosted the worms that produced silk. Raw silk was produced by the ton. And now that the Chinese had a market, other adaptations to the changing ecosystem followed.

> As they got to know their customers (according to Quan Hansheng, the Taiwanese historian) they acquired samples of Spanish clothing and upholstery and in China made perfect knockoffs of the latest European styles. Into the galleons went stockings, skirts, and sheets; vestments for cardinals and bodices for coquettes; carpets, tapestries, and kimonos; veils, headdresses, and passementeries; silk gauze, silk taffeta, silk crepe, and silk damask.[13]

According to Charles C. Mann, who charts the changes to China that were a result of the silver trade in his book *1493*, the Chinese began making an exceptional variety of goods to sell to the European market. Whatever the Chinese charged, it was still cheaper than the goods the Europeans could make themselves, and China paid more for silver than anyone else in the world.

The leadership in Beijing didn't adapt so well to the changing economic ecosystem. They could not direct the resulting business boom to stave off inflation, and the silver itself was a double-edged sword. It financed state projects, but the silver "was ever a political threat to the dynasty, because it controlled neither the trade nor the source."[14] And "so much silver flooded into China that the price eventually dropped," resulting in significant loss of revenue for the government.[15]

When ecosystems change, new species can become dominant and keystones as the interaction between species alters. Silver changed the economic ecosystem so significantly that the power relationships between various groups in China changed and evolved.

The third interesting lesson regarding ecosystems comes from the mini-ecosystem that grew within the larger changes to China's trade policy: a very resilient Chinese community in Manila, Philippines. This community originally started when trade with the mainland was outlawed, presumably to have a place to actually conduct trade. The community grew, and when the trade policy was changed it grew some more. As Mann describes, Manila's Chinese inhabitants far outnumbered their Spanish counterparts in the European enclave in the city. The Spaniards were constantly uneasy about this Chinese community. They didn't understand it and looked down on it, but they were also quite dependent on it. The Chinese could produce better goods at lower prices than the Europeans could produce or import themselves, but their foreignness and their numbers meant that the Spanish were always psychologically on the defensive.[16] It was like the Spanish were rare components in the ecosystem of Manila, who did not appreciate the value the far more common components, the Chinese, provided.

There is no evidence for any Chinese plot to oust the Spaniards— which would have made zero economic sense—but perhaps the legacy of a century of conquering caused the Spanish to view all Chinese actions through the lens of potential aggression. Whatever the reason, the Spanish introduced restrictions that caused rebellion by the Chinese, which the Spanish took as reason to massacre the population.[17]

However, the ecosystem of Manila was very resilient. The abundance of both Chinese goods and people that could keep filling a necessary role in this ecosystem was the source of resiliency. Despite the Spanish committing seven separate massacres of the Chinese population in Manila, the trade and the town always came back.

New residents came; more goods were exchanged. The value of the trade, to both the Spanish and Chinese, from the level of individuals to government, created a system that could bounce back after each significant event, and there was no shortage of the raw materials and humans that the community required. The economic infrastructure was valuable, attractive, and efficient. It got goods moving, made a lot of people some money, and made a few people wealthy. The trade also facilitated a projection of power for both the Chinese government (via the infrastructure developments they made with the silver) and the Spanish (via perceived control over lucrative overseas trade). So, despite the periodic catastrophes of widespread murder, the system had evolved to have high resiliency.

> The diversity of species present seems to impart long-term survival to an ecosystem.
>
> —RAFE SAGARIN[18]

A New Approach to Building the Perfect Football Team

The lessons we can learn from ecosystems are ones that we can apply in our organizations. After all, any business is dependent on a web of interactions and influences that includes employees working in different areas, customers, competitors, regulation and governments, and trends and changes in the global environment. So how can we integrate the value of considering the system in how we develop our businesses? We can look at an example from the world of American football.

In 1979, Bill Walsh became the general manager and head coach of the worst team in the National Football League. By 1989, he had developed a dynasty of championship winners. His accomplishment is credited to one meta-factor: he created a culture in the San Francisco 49ers' organization that recognized the exceptional value a well-functioning ecosystem can provide. As Michael Lombardi explains in *Gridiron Genius*, "Walsh took over a team with no high draft picks, no quarterback, and no hope. Three years later, that team won the Super Bowl. It got there by following Walsh's formula, what he called his Standard of Performance: an exacting plan for constructing and maintaining the culture and organizational DNA behind the perfect football franchise."[19]

Walsh recognized that a football organization's culture is ultimately the system that will determine if a team can sustain the effort needed to win a championship. When he took over the 49ers and began rebuilding the organization, he was "relying on one premise . . . that all the components of the Forty Niners' structure had to be a single unitary construction, all pointed toward the same direction, all generating the same energy, interdependent in the goal of creating a great football team, from the janitors on up."[20]

In an ecosystem, all species have a role to play. On the African savannah, the elephants and lions may receive a lot of the attention from tourists, but their survival depends on the less glamorous beetles and baobabs making their contributions. Walsh believed that "everyone has a role and every role is essential."[21] By making this philosophy a cornerstone of the 49ers' culture, Walsh sought to demonstrate that winning football is the product of a well-functioning system; each individual knowing what was required of them and what their contribution was supposed to be was vital for success. It was the organization that was going to win. Not the coach. Not the individual players. "The critical factor whenever people work together," according to Walsh, "is that they expect something of each other. It's not just that the coach expects a lot of the players—it's the fact that the players expect a lot of each other."[22]

Species migrate. Players get traded. Walsh was determined to build a culture that could survive and positively respond to inevitable change. In his book *Finding the Winning Edge*, he wrote, "The structure of an organization must have the flexibility and adaptability to meet unexpected obstacles, crises, or developments."[23] The stronger and more resilient a system, the more easily it can adapt and bounce back. This is why, for Walsh, a successful organization wasn't about superstar players or running a particular offensive formation. It was about building a culture that could be flexible in effectively responding to ever-changing environmental pressures.

Walsh also understood that his cultural ecosystem wasn't closed. What happened off the field in the personal lives of his team could have an impact on their ability to maintain the 49ers' culture. He thus expanded the culture to include initiatives that could help prevent disturbances from which his ecosystem might not be able to recover. One of these was a "Life Skills Program" for the players, which had "four major thrusts, all aimed at equipping otherwise unprepared players for adult life."[24] There was a continuing-education program, a confidential personal and family counseling program, a confidential drug counseling program, and a financial advisory program. As David Harris observes in *The Genius*, "Most coaches just use a kind of one-size-fits-all approach, but Bill understood that different guys have different buttons. Fifty guys weren't all motivated the same way. Bill put in the extra work to figure out each of their personalities and what drove each."[25]

In scouting for talent, Walsh said, "Don't just say he can't do this and can't do that. Find every player's possible contribution and identify the reason to take him rather than just the reasons not to."[26] Maybe the way a player could contribute wasn't needed by the 49ers at that time, but Walsh seemed to recognize that it takes a wide array of skills and specialties to help a team reach optimum performance, and thus it was important to keep an open mind when looking for talent.

One other fascinating property of ecosystems is that different organisms produce different systems, even if the environments are extremely similar. The look and operations of a desert in the Sudan are not identical to those of a desert in Australia. This concept might explain why teams following the same system do not necessarily produce the same results. As Michael Lombardi explains, "Many have tried to copycat Walsh's offense by hiring his former assistants and associates or anyone else who could lay claim to the West Coast lineage, believing that simply employing someone to run the scheme is enough to create the kind of success Walsh had with it."[27] Most of them failed. Why? Essentially, ingredients matter.

Finally, with all complex systems, which ecosystems are, the results of the interactions are not always predictable. Accordingly, the culture of the organization did not always translate into an output of wins. The 49ers didn't win the Super Bowl all the time. The dynamics involved in winning a football championship are too complex to be able to identify and adjust for every factor. Walsh's system, though, did better than anyone else's. He won three Super Bowls in his ten years with San Francisco, which is an exceptional achievement in that league.

The Reality of Living in a Web

Too much of any one external factor can effectively kill a system. If you think about the narrow range of temperatures that humans can exist in, compared with all the possible temperatures that exist in our solar system, you can appreciate the fact that significant change in external factors like light, air quality, and so on can devastate the stability of an ecosystem. So too with any business. External stability is important for overall success. Even if you can't control the external factors, you must pay attention to them. In order to have customers, you need a large pool of people with enough money to buy your product. In order to run an office, you need a stable economic environment and tax system. In order to have employees, you need a strong education system that teaches the skills you require, and an urban structure that allows people to live a satisfying life on the income you provide. If we love our system, we must also do what we can to influence the external factors that are required to keep our system going.

Conclusion

Nothing exists in isolation. Everything is connected. The ecosystem lens reveals that each species plays its part in a delicate balance of competition and cooperation. The actions of any one species can have consequences for many others in the same environment.

In biology, an ecosystem is a community of living organisms interacting with each other and their physical environment. In an ecosystem, nothing exists in isolation—every creature is both predator and prey, both producer and consumer, locked in an intricate dance of energy and nutrients.

Yet the concept of an ecosystem extends far beyond biology. You can see it nearly everywhere you look. Businesses operate within a complex network of companies, customers, competitors, suppliers, and regulators. Each entity relies on and influences the others, creating a dynamic interplay that determines which businesses thrive and which do not. Economies are also vast ecosystems consisting of various sectors (like agriculture, manufacturing, services) and actors (like workers, consumers, governments). These components interact under the rules set by economic policies and market forces. Economic theories often explore how changes in one part of the ecosystem can lead to significant outcomes in another, much like the ripple effects seen in biological ecosystems.

What all ecosystems have in common is their inherent complexity, their reductionist analysis. In an ecosystem, the whole is always more than the sum of its parts. The behavior of the system emerges from the countless interactions of its components, often in surprising and unpredictable ways. This suggests that to truly comprehend a complex system, we must look beyond the individual elements and consider the patterns of relationship and feedback that bind them together.

Left to their own devices, many systems can take care of themselves, possessing abilities to correct and compensate for changes and external pressures. No matter how well intentioned our interventions, they often lead to unintended consequences as the solution to one problem quickly causes another, bigger problem. Be slow to intervene and if you do, take the time to understand how actions in one part cascade into others. It pays to remember the motto of physicians, "First, do no harm."

Niches

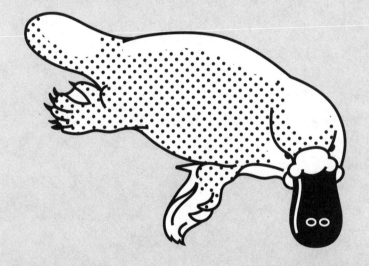

Find a good fit.

There are riches
in niches.

—ATTRIBUTED TO
SUSAN FRIEDMANN

In the biological world, some species are categorized as generalists, which cover a large territory and face more competition but are flexible in meeting their needs. Others are specialists that occupy a smaller territory and face less competition but are more rigid in their requirements. Both are vulnerable in their own ways. It is not always better to be one or the other, but knowing which you are can help you strategize your continued survival.

The ecological niche of a species refers to the role it plays in the ecosystem in which it is found. Every species in an ecosystem has a niche. A species' niche includes everything that affects its ability to reproduce and survive. For example, the amount of water and sunlight it needs, the temperatures it can tolerate, and how much space it requires to live are all part of its niche and are called "abiotic factors," meaning the nonliving aspects of an ecosystem.

Generalist organisms have a broad niche. Those with a broad niche can survive in a variety of places, as they are usually capable of eating different foods and are able to tolerate different environmental conditions. This usually means that they can protect themselves from different predators, tolerate hot and cold or wet and dry conditions, and eat a wide variety of meats and plants and other foods. For this reason, generalists are not greatly affected by rapidly changing environmental conditions and so they can maintain large populations. Such organisms include cockroaches, rats, raccoons, and humans.

> Generalists can survive and flourish in just about any setting. But specialists tend to be much less comfortable with habitat change.
>
> —PETER UNGAR[1]

Specialist organisms, on the other hand, have a very distinct set of roles in the ecosystem. For example, some specialists can survive only in specific locations or eat particular foods. They are more prone to extinction. Specialists, therefore, have a harder time maintaining large population sizes because it is common for land conditions to change and for resources such as food to diminish over time. However, in places like tropical rainforests with stable environmental conditions, it is advantageous to be a specialist because they tend to have fewer competitors, whereas most of the generalists must compete against each other.

Another reason why specialists do well under stable environmental conditions is that they possess mechanisms that allow them to not only survive but to thrive in those particular locations. For example, some animals can eat foods that are toxic to other animals, and tiger salamanders have developed the unique ability to seek out and breed only in ponds without fish, so their larvae will not be eaten.

Specialists thrive in environments full of their particular requirements but do poorly when they are placed in environments that are lacking these. Think of koalas and their particular diet of eucalyptus, or the giant panda struggling to avoid extinction in part because its specialized diet consisting mostly of bamboo makes it unable to adapt to changing environmental conditions.

Success is often a product of environment. Understanding how environments impact performance changes how you hire. Someone who thrives in one environment easily fails in another if part of their performance was the operating environment. This is why hiring a superstar away from a competitor, without understanding the role of environment on performance, often disappoints.

> The generalist method is adequate if stakes are low, but increasing specialization is often mandated when the stakes—the standards of performance in competition—are high.
>
> —GEERAT VERMEIJ[2]

Social animals allow for divisions of labor within their groups, such as having defense specialists. For humans, the species may be a generalist, but as individuals we strongly specialize.

Competitive Exclusion Principle

The competitive exclusion principle, also known as Gause's law, states that perfect competition between two species requiring the same resources to survive in the same niche is impossible. Georgii Frantsevich Gause first identified the principle in 1934 when he found that two species of bacteria requiring the same resources could not coexist in a petri dish. One species will find its own niche by becoming increasingly specialized to require different resources than the other. This is known as resource partitioning. If it doesn't, the second species' slight advantages will become significant enough to wipe out the first. For instance, if there are two carnivores in the same area that hunt the same prey animals, one species will always have some meaningful advantage, like greater speed or camouflage. This will enable it to outpace its competitor, which will have to find another food source or face extinction.

The competitive exclusion principle explains why we see such a diverse range of organisms within ecosystems. Even though they inhabit in the same area, each occupies its own niche and has traits that distinguish it from its neighbors. Natural selection allows only the fittest organisms to survive. Fitness refers to not only how well suited a population of organisms is to its environment but also how well adapted it is in comparison to its competitors.

For instance, red squirrels were once the UK's sole squirrel species. They thrived in coniferous forests and deciduous woods for around ten thousand years. In the 1870s, gray squirrels were introduced to the UK. Since gray and red squirrels inhabit the same biological niche, living in the same areas and eating the same foods, they couldn't coexist. Red squirrels have now been eliminated from many areas of the UK. They survive mainly in areas where the two species are kept apart, such as on islands. Population figures are estimated at around 140,000 red squirrels and 2.5 million gray squirrels.[3] The larger numbers of gray squirrels mean they consume the available supply of acorns first and take over suitable shelter. They also carry a virus that can be deadly to red squirrels.[4] Gray squirrels have stronger digestive systems, so they can derive more energy from their food. Despite extensive conservation efforts, it is possible red squirrels will be extinct within years.

> Species that can't handle an environmental makeover have three options: move, die, or change.
>
> —PETER UNGAR[5]

Surviving and Thriving

Invention is an area where this model fits well. If the invention is useful for everyone, like the light bulb or telephone, it's essentially a generalist forging into new territory. Specialists from your previous environment can't follow quickly because they don't have the capacity to adapt easily to the new environment. But once that new environment is open for competition, the other generalists will be right on your heels. You need to lock down as large a territory as you can defend before the other generalists arrive. This territory must have everything you need to reproduce and survive. If it does, it becomes your base, the place from which you can continue to grow and take on the other generalists.

Specialized invention, in contrast, focuses on catering to a smaller niche. The advantages of this are that once you own the niche, you are incredibly hard to dislodge. Your invention fills the niche so completely, there is very little incentive for anyone to invest in developing a competing product. Your growth is capped, but as long as the environment remains stable, as long as there is a continued need for your invention, you have significantly less competition to deal with than the generalists. An example of specialization is Zildjian cymbals. The company has been around since 1623 and has become so synonymous with great music and the artistry of drumming that they have no real competition among professional drummers. The group of professionals is small enough that there is no incentive to try to compete with Zildjian cymbals.

A generalist faces more competition every day. Surviving and reproducing are a constant struggle. Stress is part of existence. To exist means to compete—for territory, for food, for a mate. This is reflected in how we talk about the large, generalist companies: the constant fight for market share to stay ahead of the changing conditions by offering new and better products and merging with or taking over other companies to grow even bigger.

Specialists, on the other hand, have less of a daily struggle. No one else wants their territory, like the fishless ponds where tiger salamanders breed, or their food, like the panda's staple of crunchy, nonnutritious bamboo. Their day-to-day stress is lower. But as soon as the environment starts to change, the stress explodes. Being unable to adapt means death. At the species level, it means extinction. When no one needs what you are selling anymore, like encyclopedias to put on your bookshelf, there is nowhere else to go. Your niche disappears.

Most people don't realize that the fax machine, something that sends images over wires, was invented in the 1840s. We tend to think of it as this failed technology that started with a short-lived boom in the early 1980s. But no, as soon as we could send information over wires, we experimented to discover what the full scope of that information could be. Images were an early example of what could be sent. The fax survived for more than 150 years in part because it lurched from niche to niche, staking out the few small but often powerful areas where the ability to transmit images was game-changing. How did it do this?

To start, fax users didn't exist. If you never had the ability to send images, if you didn't even know it was possible, then it isn't something you were likely pining for. Therefore, developers of fax technology identified and sought out small groups of potential users to create a market. Appealing to small, unrelated groups was one of the main challenges for the technology for almost a hundred years. It was never very obvious whom the technology would be extremely useful for. As Jonathan Coopersmith explains in *Faxed*, "Despite numerous efforts by inventors and some state support, pushes to develop facsimile technology never created corresponding significant pulls by market demand."[6]

In addition, the fax niche was a protected environment. "For facsimile, that protected niche was both institutional and technological.... These protected environments allowed a fragile and expensive technology to survive." Fax developers deliberately sought out markets with less competition, "where faxing received greater resources (including users willing to pay the high costs) and support, giving it an opportunity to mature and develop."[7]

Faxing needed a specialist niche because it couldn't compete with the early generalist of the telegraph. The telegraph "had enormous advantages of easier use, much lower cost, less interference in transmission, and an already-developed infrastructure as well as users who had by now incorporated the standard telegram into their business routines."[8]

Fax's first niche was with the newspapers—a niche that it helped solidify by creating an expectation that only faxed photographs could fill. "Judged strictly by numbers, facsimile was a minor technology. Less than a thousand transmitters and receivers existed in 1940. Their impact was greatly out of proportion to their numbers, however, because they enabled newspapers to print the latest photographs with the latest stories, visually transforming the news and strengthening the role of photographs in newspapers."[9] Once the public had photographs with their news, there was no going back. It might have been a small niche, but it was one that, at the time, only faxing could fill.

Faxes stayed around and progressed because there were some niches that it fit perfectly. The military was another early consumer, and its requirements were filtered back into the development of the technology. Anyone who needed images was interested in fax, as well as anyone who needed messages with as little room for error as possible. Both of these were requirements for the military. From weather diagrams to direct orders, by exactly copying images, faxing ensured that as long as the technology and necessary infrastructure worked well, nothing was lost in translation.

There was a downside to focusing on niche markets. It allowed the technology to develop with complete incompatibility across the different manufacturers as they competed for the same small pool of clients. "In reality, deliberate incompatibility fragmented the market and scared away potential users fearful of choosing the wrong system."[10] In the world of business, fax was originally adopted as an intra-office tool, and machines compatible with those of another organization were not needed. This lack of compatibility and standards had to be addressed before fax could become the generalist of the 1980s and '90s. "Starting in the early 1980s, the combination of increasing deregulation, true compatibility, quickly dropping costs, and rapid technological change created a blossoming of new machines, applications, and services."[11] Fax was finally able to survive out of the niche.

In terms of information over wires, telegraphy, then telephony, became the generalists in the environment. Faxing could not compete with their lower cost and ease of use. It was through identifying and marketing to niches that fax managed to survive until the conditions changed and the technological advancement and social interest allowed it to flourish as a generalist for a time.

> Natural selection has a limited repertoire of potential forms from which to choose, and convergent evolution is the result.
>
> —GEORGE R. McGHEE[12]

Convergence

In biology, "convergence" refers to the process wherein organisms evolve analogous traits that were not present in their last common ancestor. In other words, species that are not closely related to each other will find the same solutions to the same problems in their quest to survive. This occurs when various unrelated species occupy niches with the same qualities and constraints; for instance, if two species live in areas at a high altitude with little water, or in densely wooded, humid areas—but on different continents.

We call traits that emerge through convergence "analogous structures" or "homoplasies" (convergence is also known as homoplasy). Homoplasies can include body shapes, the presence of organs, behaviors, markings, types of intelligence, social structures, vocalizations, breeding habits, and so on. While they are unlikely to be entirely identical, they have the same form or purpose. Convergence is fascinating because it shows us that biology does involve a degree of predetermination. Evolution is not an entirely random process. Certain features and behaviors recur again and again for the simple reason that they are the best way of surviving within an environment with certain characteristics.[13]

Take the example of flight, an ability that has evolved in birds, bats, some types of dinosaurs, and insects. Each species is unrelated, and each evolved wings as a means of getting around, tens of millions of years apart. The wings of both birds and bats started off as regular limbs for land-based locomotion and still contain traces of finger bones. Take a look at the bones in a bat's wing and you'll see something with a structure not unlike that of your own hands, elongated into the spidery structure of a wing. There are obvious differences. A bat's wing consists of thin skin stretched over bones, whereas birds' wings are covered in feathers. The reason why bats and birds converged is simple. Both lineages evolved in niches where flight became essential for their survival.[14] The number of potential ways to fulfill a function is finite.[15]

A more widespread example is the evolution of eyes. It might seem natural to us that most animals, except those living underground or in the depths of the sea, have eyes. But the fact that so many unrelated lineages evolved organs that look the same and function in the same way is extraordinary. The eye of a squid has much the same structure as that of a spider. Human and octopus eyes are similar, despite the closest common ancestor having lived 550 million years ago and only possessing a basic eyespot.[16] Echolocation, another way of "seeing," evolved in unconnected lineages: cetaceans, bats, shrews, tenrecs, some birds, and possibly hedgehogs. Clearly these are the best possible traits for certain types of biological niches.

Due to convergence, we can tell by looking at a niche what kind of organisms would occupy it even without seeing them. For instance, if scientists discover a new nectar-producing plant, they can also predict the existence of an insect specially evolved to feed from it, even if said insect hasn't been discovered yet. If there's a keyhole, there's also a key somewhere that fits it. In popular culture, organisms from other planets are generally depicted as wildly different from anything on earth. But convergent evolution suggests that might not be the case and that other life forms could have evolved to be recognizably similar to ones on earth.

As humans, we are in part the product of the pressures of our environment. Each of us occupies various niches throughout our lives, which we must adapt ourselves to fit. By and large, the same pressures acting on people and the same incentives seem to produce the same outcomes. If you took a baby from an Amazonian tribe and switched it with a baby from a wealthy family in Canada, would it grow up any different from other Canadian babies? Probably not. While some traits may be inbuilt, it would have to adapt to its ecosystem.

Convergence explains why people in disconnected cultures throughout history have made similar tools, told similar stories, organized themselves in similar social structures, cooked similar food, and generally found analogous solutions to the problems they faced. John Thomas Osmond Kirk, writing in *Science and Certainty*, compares biological traits to mathematical concepts in the way that they seem to exist beyond our definition of them, reappearing again and again everywhere we turn, as if they are laws of the universe.

It's important to understand that it is the environment that makes the organism. When we look at the behavior of others, it's easy to imagine we would never do the same if we find them abhorrent. For instance, a corrupt politician stealing aid money or a neighbor turning on a neighbor during a genocide. But it's possible that if we were in the same circumstances, we would act in much the same way. It's a lot easier to be empathetic if we look at the environment that shaped someone instead of merely considering the result. To a certain extent, we are all more predictable than we would like to admit.

We misunderstand that equivalent problems tend to have equivalent solutions, as convergence shows us. Our own problems often feel unique, which leads us to ignore the solutions that worked for others in equivalent situations. Yet just as bats and birds found analogous ways to solve the problem of flight, often what works for others would work for us too.

Defining a Generalist

Generalists face more daily competition, but they are more adaptable. They maintain a large population that occupies a broad niche. In the world of consumer products, Coca-Cola used advertising to become one of the world's most successful generalists. Coke's spread and ability to compete in most geographical and socioeconomic markets was all down to its advertising campaigns.

Coke's first advertising efforts were a turn away from its roots as a medicinal tonic, marketing its product as a beverage for "relaxation and enjoyment."[17] As the nineteenth century turned into the twentieth, the brand created an image associated with refinement and the upper class. But instead of isolating its product as out of reach, Coke set one of the first examples of selling an idea before a product. Anyone could join that upper echelon by buying the right brand, in this case a five-cent Coke.

Using pretty women, celebrity endorsements, and vast sums of money—$750,000 in 1909 alone, which is more than $18 million in today's dollars—Coke convinced consumers that they weren't just buying a drink. They were buying a lifestyle. "By the 1920s, Coke had established itself as *the* national brand of soft drink."[18] Its advertising created an image in which everyone could participate. To drink Coke was to live a better life.

In *The Coke Machine*, Michael Blanding writes, "As it became more and more a part of the landscape, lifestyle started imitating advertising: Films began incorporating the drink into scenes, music started spontaneously referring to it in lyrics." Thus, Coke became a ubiquitous part of life. It was just there. Everywhere.

From these roots, Coke attained success as a generalist. It survived in different environments because it appealed to a diversity of consumers. There were no class or ethnic barriers to Coke. The lifestyle associated with it was available to everyone. Whereas other brands had previously tended to market by class or gender or location or other identifiers, Coke just sold itself to people. That was arguably the company's greatest innovation.

The 1920s saw the company come up with the first of many memorable slogans. By far the most popular at the time was "The pause that refreshes." This slogan positioned Coke as "a momentary time-out."[19] Again, this is a generalist approach, because a break from the frantic pace of each day is something everyone wants and needs. Who doesn't want a pause that refreshes? Coke's slogans became particularly captivating during the Depression, a period in which its sales did well. Drinking the beverage became a momentary escape. "A better life was only the pop of a bottle cap away."[20]

World War II made Coke international as bottling facilities started operating all over the world so that American troops could have easy access to the drink that reminded them of home. When times change, generalists can adapt more easily, and this was what happened with Coke during the war. The company used the sentiments of soldiers and its new international presence to inform new advertising campaigns that associated Coke with US prosperity. Directed at soldiers, the campaigns reminded them what they were fighting for, and in the war-torn international markets, it offered foreigners a piece of American luxury.

When Coke had to position itself against Pepsi, its most significant competitor, Coke "marketed itself as the product for everyone—workmen and businessmen, soldiers and socialites—[while] Pepsi focused solely on young middle-class families."[21] Pepsi tried to carve itself a small niche in Coke's vast territory.

Over time, everyone from Santa Claus to polar bears has been seen drinking Coke. In 1963 Coke had the number-one ad budget in the United States, spending $53 million a year on ads and targeted consumer research. "After the challenge from Pepsi, Coke redoubled its efforts to associate Coke subliminally with almost *everything*."

Around this time, the company created its first successful slogan in years: "Things go better with Coke." According to Blanding, "*What* went better didn't matter so much—Coke could just as well spark romance as childhood friendship. It was left to the consumer to fill in the blank."[22] Advertisements no longer talked about what Coke tasted like or contained. It didn't matter. In such vast territory, Coke had to be adaptable to different environmental pressures. It was this flexibility that was the key to its success. The general image could be adapted to suit any particular.

Being a generalist in the world of beverages wasn't about taste. People were attached to Coke not as a drink but as a representative of the nostalgia of good moments. Coke's malleability was how it conquered such a large spectrum of the population.

Conclusion

A niche is a special place where a particular species or idea can thrive. It's the ecological equivalent of a custom-fitted suit, tailored to the unique needs and abilities of its occupant. In a niche, you don't have to be all things to all people—you just have to be the best at what you do.

In biology, a niche is the specific role and position a species occupies within its ecosystem. It's the unique combination of resources it consumes, the habitat it lives in, the interactions it has with other species. A place where a species' adaptations flourish.

But the concept of a niche extends far beyond the realm of ecology. In business, we talk about "market niches"—the specific segments of customers with particular needs or preferences. A company that focuses on a niche can often outcompete larger, more general rivals by specializing, by becoming the best at serving that particular slice of the market or moving with velocity.

The same principle applies to careers. By specializing in something unique and valuable, you can create a space where you can excel, where your combination of skills can thrive. The key is to find the niche that fits you, that rewards your strengths and neutralizes your weaknesses.

This isn't to say that occupying a niche is without risks. In fact, you become very fragile. If the environment changes, if consumer preferences shift, a once-cozy niche can quickly become a tight squeeze. That's why successful niche occupants are often those that can adapt, that can evolve their niche as the world around them changes.

Specialists have less competition and stress, but only in times of stability. Generalists face greater day-to-day challenges for resources and survival but have more flexibility to respond when times change.

Self-Preservation

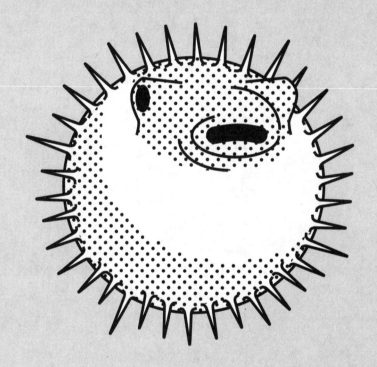

Survive to thrive.

Self-preservation is
the first law of nature.

—SAMUEL BUTLER[1]

Self-preservation and survival instincts are innate behaviors that all organisms possess for the sake of protection from harm. They are considered both fundamental and useful, and they govern a lot of our behavior.

Surviving and thriving are very reliable human biological motivators. We all want to live the best life possible. However, how each person responds to these driving forces is different. There is no universal human definition of a great life. Sometimes these instincts push us to reject the status quo, leading to new opportunities. And sometimes they hold us back, preventing us from realizing our potential. Knowing how to manage your self-preservation instincts can help you truly understand how to motivate yourself and others.

Think of reflexes. These are involuntary, automatic actions that our bodies perform in response to a stimulus. For example, if you put your hand on a hot stove, a reflex will cause you to remove your hand right away, even before a "Hot!" message is sent to the brain. This reaction protects the body from serious burns. Blinking is another example. When dust or bugs approach the eye, the eyelid automatically closes, without you having to voluntarily contract any muscle to close it. These simple examples demonstrate that self-preservation is hardwired. The better your survival reflexes, the greater your chances of survival, and so these systems are easily selected for in the evolutionary process.

A more complex self-preservation instinct is the fight, flight, or freeze response in humans and other mammals. When human beings are faced with imminent danger, this mechanism kicks in with the mobilization of the sympathetic nervous system. The results in the body are a sharp increase in blood sugar levels, constriction of blood vessels, increase in heart rate, and the diversion of blood from nonessential organs to heart and skeletal muscles. These are responses that help the mammal deal most effectively with the situation they are in.

Sometimes the survival of a group can require the sacrifice of certain members. The survival of some species is contingent on sacrifices within the breeding process. This is known as "kin selection" and is a form of natural selection concerning populations, not individuals or individual lineages. Many species of animals stick around only because individuals have evolved to display completely selfless behaviors. If a behavior is beneficial for a population overall, despite its impact on the individual, it is likely to be selected for.

Just like human mothers, many animals are willing to go to great lengths to ensure the survival of their offspring and therefore their species. Some will literally sacrifice their own lives, like the black lace-weaver spider, which will allow its babies to eat it. Some animals, like African elephants, zebras, and sea lions, will work together in large groups to protect the offspring of others. Orcas and dolphins remain awake for a full month after the birth of their young to care for and protect them. Other animals, including polar bears and penguins, may go months without eating for the sake of their offspring. Marmots will delay their own reproduction if others in their group need help with childcare.

Worker honeybees even completely neglect to reproduce so they can look after their queen's babies—and if they don't, the other bees destroy their eggs.[2] Once the workers become too old to be useful for foraging, the other bees will either kill them or refuse to let them into the hive, leaving them to starve to death. Drones, which are male bees, die during the mating process, having successfully passed on their genes. Any drones that don't manage to mate are likewise killed by other bees so the hive does not need to waste resources feeding them. Bad for the individuals, excellent for the hive.[3]

From a natural selection standpoint, this makes sense because it ensures the survival of their own genes. Even in a herd, protecting the offspring of others makes sense because the animals in that population are likely to be at least distantly related or even immediate family. This has the long-term effect of selecting for altruistic genes and not selecting for selfish ones.

Other animals will end their own lives to protect their buddies. One species of ant, *Colobopsis explodens*, will explode when threatened by a predator, killing the individual but helping the group survive by releasing a poisonous substance. Bees and some types of termites behave similarly, attacking predators by destroying themselves.[4] Belding's ground squirrels announce the presence of a predator through alarm calls that make themselves more conspicuous and therefore vulnerable.

Why are automatic reactions programmed in? The desire for survival seems a given, but it exists in organisms that don't have anywhere near the size of cortex that we do. These widespread instincts exist without the ability to philosophize about them because the longer an organism survives, the greater its chances of passing along its genetics, and that is the ultimate point of evolution.

Humans are also, however, capable of overriding our own biological survival instincts. Sometimes it is innocuous, like when we go on a roller coaster. We tell ourselves it's perfectly safe, so the biological reaction of terror gets processed as a thrill. Sometimes, though, we override them because our circumstances seem to demand it, and we put ourselves in situations of chronic stress and pressure. So self-preservation instincts are complex. The biological motivation is to ensure one's own survival, but not if it comes at the cost of the survival of one's own genes.

Territorial Behavior

A core component of self-preservation for all organisms is ensuring access to the resources necessary to survive. This manifests as territorial behavior. An organism or population's territory is loosely defined as the geographical region containing both the resources it needs to survive and the mating opportunities needed to ensure the survival of its species.[5] Only the areas that an organism makes an active effort to defend count as its territory, as there may be additional areas where it also lives.

For an organism to maintain its territory, it must compete with other species, or with other members of its own species. Some animals use scents to mark out their territory, as a warning to others to stay out. Others release unpleasant chemicals or make visible markings. Some actively guard their area, attacking any intruders. Others, birds in particular, use threatening calls.

Maintaining a territory often requires a great deal of time and

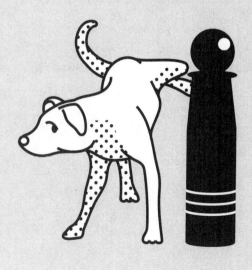

energy, which is always a signal that a trait confers some serious survival advantage. Territorial behavior is not necessary if resources are abundant, and organisms will generally cease to engage in it over time if this is the case. The scarcer resources prove to be, the more aggressive the territorial behavior is likely to be.

Self-Preservation Means More Than Survival

At first glance, self-preservation seems straightforward. You run from a suspicious-looking person on the street. You fight back against a bully. You freeze when your boss yells at you for the fourteenth time in one day and you are too vulnerable to do anything else.

We choose fight or flight when we think we have a chance to succeed. Freeze mode usually takes over when the accumulation of stressors is so great that we can no longer really function. By freezing we hope to preserve the little life we have left. The drive for survival is deeply ingrained in our behavioral responses.

How, then, do we understand people who risk their lives for a cause? What propels someone to put their immediate survival in jeopardy in support of a possible future?

Gioconda Belli was not an obvious choice to join the Sandinista revolution in Nicaragua in the 1970s. She was married with two young daughters. She came from an upper-middle-class family and had a decent life under the Somoza dictatorship that had been in power in Nicaragua for forty years. However, she didn't like the oppression, corruption, and poverty she saw in her country. She sought political and social change and concluded that joining the revolutionary Sandinista organization was the best way to achieve it. In her memoir, *The Country Under My Skin*, she writes that she knew "joining the Sandinistas was a risky proposition. It meant putting my life in the line of fire."[6] From the beginning of the Sandinista movement, suspected revolutionaries were arrested and tortured by the Somoza dictatorship. As the revolution progressed, there were horrific accounts of the measures the regime took to suppress the revolutionaries, including throwing people to their deaths from helicopters.

Deciding to face potential torture and death seems to be the opposite of self-preservation. Belli deliberately and knowingly put her life at risk to try to achieve political and social change that was far from guaranteed. Self-preservation is such a useful model because it helps us understand seemingly counterintuitive actions: sacrificing short-term guarantees for long-term possibilities, like the animals we looked at who sacrifice themselves for their offspring or their group.

Belli was not fully committed to the revolution right away. She had moments of doubt, both about the Sandinista organization and about the wisdom of putting her daughters in a position in which they might have to grow up without a mother. She quotes a friend of hers trying to help her reconcile being a revolutionary with being a mother: "Your daughter is precisely the reason you should do it," he said. "You should do it for her, so that she won't have to do the job you are not willing to do."[7] Belli was motivated by trying to create a world for her daughters where they would not have to make a similar sacrifice. We can understand it as deferred preservation: a more equitable and stable world would give her genes the best possible chance of carrying on.

It's important, however, not to frame her choice simply in terms of calculated biological preservation. Belli explains that when she was contemplating committing to the Sandinistas, she saw participating in the revolution as her "only way into a more meaningful existence."[8] There is a nuance here: that for humans, survival is not merely a binary, like dead/alive. We don't want to just continue breathing, but to have a life that we perceive as having meaning, value, or at least a point.

Working with the Sandinistas was perilous. Belli writes of being followed, interrogated, and exiled to neighboring Costa Rica after having been convicted by the Somoza government of being a traitor. She spent a lot of time separated from her children and went through personal turmoil as she tried to navigate two marriages that failed under the pressure of her activities. Watching many comrades jailed or killed, she writes, she was afraid that "so many dreams and efforts might be wasted."[9] Belli was, however, driven by the desire to stop the actions of the Somoza regime that kept so many Nicaraguans poor and desperate while the leaders lined their pockets with international aid money. She explains: "At twenty-four, I was a citizen of a terrible, destitute country, but no misfortune seemed eternal to me. I was sure we could change everything and build a bright future."[10]

Working with the Sandinistas meant joining a tribe of sorts. Belli explains, "I understood how strong the bond between those of us who were in the struggle was."[11] Therefore, individuals were prepared to take actions that put their own lives at risk to increase the chances of survival of the group. Belli writes of the many times she smuggled guns, money, and fake identification across borders, bringing them to others in the revolution, jeopardizing her own freedom to help the Sandinista movement.

She admits to questioning the desire of people to put the group first. "Were we all mad?" she writes. "What mystery in human genes accounted for the fact that men and women could override their personal survival instincts when the fate of the tribe or collective was at stake?"[12] What makes us take a risk on an uncertain future instead of sticking with guaranteed immediate survival? Belli herself offers an interesting perspective when she explains how she pushed through the setbacks and stress of exile: "If I gave in to fear, I would end up killing my soul to save my body."[13] She also writes of explaining to her children "the obligation to be responsible to other people,"[14] to be responsible to the group.

The Sandinista revolution was successful in that it removed

Somoza from power in Nicaragua. With the dictatorship gone, the Sandinistas tried to rebuild the country's political and social infrastructure based on the ideals they had developed and refined as a revolutionary organization. Belli's main contributions to the ultimately successful revolution were in communications and public relations. She wrote press releases and recruiting letters, trying to explain the goals of the Sandinistas and recruit people to the cause. She traveled abroad many times to represent the movement and gain international support. But, she explains, "Sandinismo was a fundamental element of my identity,"[15] which propelled her to take whatever action necessary to support the group. As the revolution approached, she continued her efforts from her exile in Costa Rica, "but I was anxious for the moment when I could join in the one, most basic contribution to the struggle: combat in Nicaragua."[16] Very often, her course of action had her saying goodbye to her children as if it could be the last time she saw them. But she did it anyway. Her self-preservation instincts were focused on doing everything she could to see her children grow up in the world "safely and happily."[17]

Permanent Record

We humans preserve ourselves not just through the genetics that we download into our offspring but by maintaining a record of who we are. Around the time that humans first started writing, we began to keep the most permanent records we could in libraries. Almost immediately we decided that it wasn't enough to record but far more important to preserve our records. The knowledge that we have captured over millennia allows us to leave a legacy of remembering who we are.

In 1849, Austen Henry Layard found Nineveh, an ancient Assyrian city that had once been the center of a civilization. It had been completely destroyed by fire in 612 BCE, and in the intervening millennia had been reduced to fiction. The destruction by fire, however, had an extremely valuable side effect: it had preserved the clay tablets that were contained in the city's remarkable library. The city's last king, Ashurbanipal, had collected texts from all over Mesopotamia, so the library was full of tablets chronicling not only Assyrian life but Sumerian and Babylonian as well. Finding the library brought to life people, cities, and customs that had disappeared from history.[18] The "library contained dictionaries and grammars, treatises on botany, astronomy, metallurgy, geology, geography, chronology, tracts on religion and history, and a collection of royal edicts, proclamations, laws, and decrees."[19]

The find gave us more context to understand human history. A tablet was discovered that chronicled a flood story similar to the one found in the Bible, but from centuries earlier. Another find, the Law Code of Hammurabi, provides insight into cultural norms that influenced later civilizations. Knowledge like this helps to trace, with more and more comprehension, the story of humanity. Without what is contained in libraries, we would have had to reinvent and reimagine everything all the time. Preserving knowledge allows us to transfer it more easily, supporting the preservation of the species.

Derinkuyu: Turkey's Ancient Underground City

It may be a myth that ostriches bury their heads in the sand, but during times of danger, humans have often looked beneath their feet for safety. During the Great Fire of London in 1666, people buried valuables in their gardens. The Dead Sea Scrolls were found underground in a cave. And in the Central Anatolia region of Turkey, a number of persecuted groups over the course of thousands of years transferred their lives beneath the ground in a move that illustrates the incredible lengths we will go to for self-preservation.

Derinkuyu is the deepest of the cities yet discovered beneath Cappadocia. In 1963, a Turkish man renovating his basement found something astounding: an entire room behind its wall. From there, archaeologists discovered a whole city snaking beneath the ground, carved into the soft yet sturdy rock.

Descending 200 to 280 feet underground, it has 18 different levels capable of housing as many as 20,000 to 30,000 people at a time. Future excavations may find it to have been even bigger than that.[20] Derinkuyu is far from being just a maze of tunnels to huddle in and wait for danger to pass. It is a complete city, containing everything its residents needed to comfortably thrive for a while, not just survive. Archaeologists have uncovered schools, areas for worship, bedrooms, bathrooms, areas for storing food and equipment for making olive oil and wine, tombs, stables for horses and other animals, and community meeting spaces. In addition to fresh food and water, the residents had fresh air from above through at least fifty-two shafts that kept the city well ventilated.[21]

Some experts attribute the construction of Derinkuyu to the Phrygians, an ancient race of Indo-Europeans from the southern Balkans who migrated to the area in the twelfth century BCE, according to accounts by the Greek historian Herodotus. The Phrygians may have built it to hide from the Assyrians. Derinkuyu could also be the work of the Persians or the Hittites. Historians have suggested that the Hittites may have dug tunnels for storage before other groups turned them into cities.[22] Alternatively, the Hittites may have sheltered in Derinkuyu during their twelfth-century BCE war with the Thracians. Romans, early Christians, and Turks all used the tunnels at various points. Some archaeologists go as far as to claim they are prehistoric, first dug as protection from the heat, due to the discovery of ten-thousand-year-old stonecutting tools in the area. The variation in the quality of the tunnels lends support to this theory.

Regardless of who dug the first tunnel, subsequent groups expanded upon and advanced Derinkuyu to the extent that it is hard to view it as the property of any single group. Derinkuyu belongs to the region.

The region of Anatolia has spent much of its history in a stew of conflict and uncertainty. Its position between Asia and Europe made it an appealing target for major world powers who, again and again, sought to control the region. For the residents to survive the endless wars and confusion, they needed to take drastic action. Derinkuyu and the other underground cities in Cappadocia repeatedly saved the area's residents from extinction. During the seventh century, the Persian Wars took place in Cappadocia, tearing the region apart. That conflict was scarcely over when Muslim Arab armies arrived and caused a complete civil breakdown.[23]

Based on its design, Derinkuyu was intended to provide protection during conflict, like a turtle retreating into its shell. The tunnels were narrow enough to require walking along them in single file, hunched over. This would have prevented attackers from moving into Derinkuyu, as the residents could easily pick off soldiers emerging one by one from tunnels. Huge carved stone disks weighing eleven hundred pounds were rolled in front of entrances when the residents wanted to prevent anyone else from entering, with small holes in the middle through which arrows may have been fired.[24] Derinkuyu even had a tunnel, based on preliminary excavations, stretching several kilometers to another underground city. If its defenses were somehow breached, the inhabitants could hastily take refuge elsewhere.

When we feel threatened, flight is often the first response. We want to get away from the danger and hide. The people who sheltered in Derinkuyu and other underground cities in the region did so because it put them in a situation in which they had maximum leverage. They had everything they needed to survive in relative comfort for long periods of time. Even if any attackers did manage to get into Derinkuyu, they could only do so one at a time and were easy to defeat.

The strategy of fleeing and hoarding worked well for the residents of Cappadocia, but this self-preservation response can backfire. Hoarding supplies beneath the ground may have made sense for them in the short term. While there is much left for researchers to learn about Derinkuyu, it seems unlikely that people could have remained entirely underground in the long term. They could store only so much food, and over extended periods of time would have suffered serious vitamin deficiencies from the lack of sunlight and fresh food. If their enemies had decided to start a siege, it wouldn't have worked so well.

An underground city is a vivid image, but the ways the same impulse can influence our behavior can be less obvious. Acting in survival mode is not sustainable long-term. Hoarding and hiding are not lifelong strategies. As humans, we're always on hair trigger to hoard at the slightest sign of scarcity, even if doing so ends up worsening that scarcity. If people at a company fear impending lay-offs, they may make like the residents of Derinkuyu and metaphor-ically hide away from everyone else, hoarding information, because they feel that keeping all the information to themselves will make them more valuable to the company. They might hoard work, re-fusing to delegate and taking on irrelevant responsibilities. It might make them indispensable in the short term, but in the long term trust breaks down and less work gets done, putting the company, and thus their job, at risk. In reality, this self-preservation instinct has the opposite effect. Not helping others or sharing the leverage is worse for everyone.

Anytime we're fighting to preserve ourselves in an emergency situation, we need more of a concrete plan than hiding and hoard-ing. In addition to our natural instincts, we need to move beyond our evolutionary programming and consider how we can survive long-term. Sometimes our immediate self-preservation instincts can backfire, putting us in situations of little long-term benefit.

Conclusion

Self-preservation is a core instinct that drives all living things to protect and sustain their own existence. It's the biological impera-tive that makes a gazelle run from the lion, the roots of a tree seek water, and bacteria evolve resistance to antibiotics. In the game of life, self-preservation is the only rule: stay alive.

For humans, self-preservation goes beyond physical survival. It encompasses the protection of our psychological well-being, our social status, our sense of identity. Anything that threatens how we see ourselves becomes a threat.

While self-preservation is a necessary instinct, it can also be a limiting one. When we're too focused on avoiding threats, we can easily miss opportunities right in front of us. Left unchecked, self-preservation can lead to stagnation. The key, then, is to find balance: to protect what's essential but also be willing to let go of what no longer serves us.

Listen to the voice that tells you when to be cautious but don't let it be the only voice you hear. Often the greatest risk is to not take risk at all.

Replication

Copy copy copy.

There must be a certain amount of imitation, copying, in outward technique, but when there is inward, psychological imitation surely we cease to be creative.

—JIDDU KRISHNAMURTI[1]

Replication in biology is ultimately about the ability of DNA to make a copy of itself during cell division. This is how we start life, and it is a process that continues in some of our cells until our death.

Let's think about this process at the small level: cell replication. Our skin cells flake off by the millions every day, yet throughout our lives we never run out. That's because there are skin cells making copies of themselves all the time. This ability to make perfect copies is built into their structure, and without it we wouldn't last very long.

This type of replication is called "mitosis." It refers to the entire process of replication of nonsexual cells, the result being two genetically identical daughter cells. Mitosis is the process that gives us more skin, more hair, more nails. This replication is far from mysterious and can be conceptualized as having certain basic requirements.

In an adapted unit, most variation introduced by errors (mutations) in copying are harmful. For an adapted entity, therefore, increasing fidelity in copying, or mechanisms

You need three things for replication to occur:

1. A code that represents what you wish to replicate

2. A means of copying this code

3. A place to process the code and construct the replication

This is how our skin cells are constructed. They possess a code of themselves, a mechanism to copy the code, and a place to execute the code—all to produce more skin cells. Furthermore, this replication machine is phenomenal. We never run out of skin.

Replication is useful beyond skin cells. It has another amazing property: combination. Replicas don't have to be exact copies. The components of cells can be combined in new ways to give us unique instances of existing things. This is sexual reproduction, or "meiosis," and it creates new opportunities. A sex cell contains a copy of half a female's chromosomes and is combined with half a male's chromosomes to produce a new whole. The offspring of these parents are genetically unique due both to having two sources for their genes and to variation that occurs in the copying.

Sexual reproduction is prevalent all over the biological world. Mammals, fish, and plants all partake. Why? Because over several generations, a lack of sexual reproduction means less genetic variation, which leads to fewer options when the environment changes. And if you can't adapt to a new environment, you die.

Replication, then, is what allows for diversity in traits that can improve fitness and increase the chances of survival. Exact copies perpetuate bad mutations. The power of replication combination prevents the accumulation of traits that impair fitness and lets us, as a species, try out new behaviors that can be super beneficial. Of course, there is a significant cost. We have to work hard to find another half with which to combine and not be intimidated by the diversity that might offer the best chance of producing successful adaptations.

Keeping It All in the Family

When we have replication without diversity, the outcomes are disastrous. Replication can be thought of as sharing information, and "thus, like all forms of transmitting information, replication is inevitably accompanied by some degradation, or at least change, in content."[3] It's not enough just to copy; there also need to be innovations and improvements to compensate for the errors that are inevitably introduced.

Beginning in the eleventh century and ending in the eighteenth, the Habsburg family dynasty ruled over a significant portion of Europe. Members of the family at various times ruled over Germany, England, Hungary, Ireland, Portugal, Spain, and other countries. As Benjamin Curtis writes in *The Habsburgs: The History of a Dynasty*, "The family's members were sure that they were born to rule. . . . Their preeminence was longer lasting and their ambitions more grandiose than almost any other royal family." The Habsburgs guarded their power so jealously that they loathed marriages that required them to share it with other families. Whenever possible, they chose to marry close blood relatives—first cousins or nieces and nephews—to keep their veritable empire intact. One of their mottoes was "Let others wage war; you, happy Austria, marry."[4]

Unsurprisingly, the lack of genetic variation caused by these consanguineous marriages carried serious consequences. The best-known result of the Habsburgs' lack of diversity was their unusual jawline, with an enlarged chin, underbite, and thick lips. Even in their most flattering portraits, this feature is unmistakable.

As the generations progressed, the results of their inbreeding led to extreme difficulties with basic things like speaking and eating. The Habsburgs' infant mortality rate was far higher than that of even the poorest members of society at the time. Between 1527 and 1661, the Spanish branch produced thirty-four children. Of these, half died in their first decade, and another ten before their first birthday.[5]

Closed systems, those without any new inputs, die in changing environments. Ultimately, after sixteen generations of intermarriage, the Habsburgs ended up with such serious disabilities that they wiped the family out. Their success in controlling Europe proved to be a Pyrrhic victory. The final member, Charles II, was infertile and thus unable to produce an heir.[6] He also experienced dire health from birth. He did not learn to speak until the age of four due to his distended jaw, could not walk until he was eight, frequently drooled, was of low intellectual ability, and was barely able to speak comprehensibly. His infertility may have been the result of a pituitary hormone deficiency, and he also suffered from kidney problems.[7] Charles II died in his late thirties, young for someone of his wealth even at the time. He reportedly had the intellectual capabilities of a small child.

Replication is necessary but not sufficient for survival. The more you copy something, the more it weakens. Thus, replication alone is not always beneficial. Imagine a teacher photocopying a worksheet for a class and then throwing away the original. The next year they make photocopies of the photocopies and again throw away the originals. As the years go by, the quality of the sheet progressively gets worse because each copy will pass on errors and introduce new ones. Minor problems compound with each copy. The same happened to the Habsburgs. Without genetic diversity, recessive mutations that would have otherwise failed to show up in children were reinforced and compounded over generations.[8] Only with the relatively recent discovery of genetics did it become clear why this happens. Without diversity, replication only works if the original is perfect. Otherwise errors build upon themselves.

The German Secret to Hitting the Replication "Sweet Spot"

There is a sweet spot to replication. The components have to be rigid enough to be easily copied but flexible enough to adapt to inevitable changes. As with genetic mutations piling up, replication of errors compounds errors in all fields of human endeavor. We often think of new things as polluting or diluting and try to stick with the old, but this doesn't work. We need to inject newness, or the lack of variation proves destructive. Relevant to everything from military campaigns to venture capital, figuring out how to replicate strategy or success is critical. How do you allow for adaptability and innovation without sacrificing your goals, values, or vision?

After the Germans kept getting humiliated by Napoleon on the battlefield, they realized that his methods in war were different than any they had previously come across. If they wanted to win, they needed to change and try new tactics. Early in his career,

Napoleon employed the strategy of inserting his army between two opposing forces and then striking at both before they could coordinate and combine. He wrote, "It is contrary to all principle to make corps which have no communication act separately against a central force whose communications are open."[9] The traditional German armies, with "their linear tactics, iron discipline, blind obedience and intolerance of independent action,"[10] were initially unequipped to deal with Napoleon's approach. Recognizing the need for a new strategy, the Germans developed *Auftragstaktik*, or what we now call commander's intent, which is the idea of sharing the information necessary "to empower subordinate commanders on the scene."[11] The theory underpinning commander's intent is all about trying to construct the right circumstances for replication.

Any given side in a confrontation wants to replicate their strategy to the point of execution. What is the best structure for this? Too rigid and the guy on the ground can't adapt and innovate to execute the strategy when the circumstances change—which they will. There is a direct connection to the challenges of replication in biology: "Rigid specialization—by a genetic code, for example—is not feasible, simply because the code would be excessively large, prone to breakdown, and inadequate for anticipating the many challenges and opportunities an economic entity is likely to encounter during its lifetime."[12]

When the Germans faced Napoleon, they were experiencing problems related to their rigidity of organization. The guys on the front lines couldn't adapt. Discouraged from ever considering the why or the rationale behind an order, the German troops had nothing to draw on when Napoleon changed his tactics mid-battle.[13] The environment always changes, which is why successful replication has a bit of flexibility built in.

If there is not enough fidelity in the copying, however, the strategy gets polluted with too many errors and cannot be executed. Empowered subordinates can adapt to changing battlefield conditions, but giving flexibility cannot cost the commander the ability to synchronize events to execute the strategy.

As Clausewitz explained in *On War*:

> Strategy is the employment of the battle to gain the end of the war; it must therefore give an aim to the whole military action, which must be in accordance with the object of the war; in other words, strategy forms the plan of the war, and to the said aim it links the series of acts which are to lead to the same, that is to say, it makes the plans for the separate campaigns, and regulates the combats to be fought in each. As these are all things which to a great extent can only be determined on conjectures, some of which turn out incorrect, while a number of other arrangements pertaining to details cannot be made at all beforehand, it follows, as a matter of course, that strategy must go with the army to the field in order to arrange particulars on the spot, and to make the modifications in the general plan which incessantly become necessary in war. Strategy can therefore never take its hand from the work for a moment.[14]

How do you hit the sweet spot between execution of strategy and flexibility to adapt to changing conditions? There are four elements of commander's intent: formulate, communicate, interpret, and implement. The first two are the responsibility of the senior commander, the latter two the job of the subordinate commander. In order to develop these skills, commanders must consider four criteria:

1. Explain the rationale (not just the what and why, but how they arrived at a decision)

2. Establish operational limits (identify what is completely off the table)

3. Get feedback often (a continuous loop between levels)

4. Recognize individual differences (the unique psychological makeup of each subordinate)[15]

In combination, these criteria, when executed properly, hit the sweet spot of replication. They allow for the continuous application of strategy, while having room to adapt and innovate in the face of changing conditions.

Replicating a Culture

The model of replication can also be used to help us understand why some products or customs propagate around the globe. Often, when exposed to other cultures, we notice the differences: the things those others do or say that we find foreign and almost nonsensical; ideas that seem to be barriers to communication and understanding. It is possible, however, to see these customs as being too rigid to allow for the necessary development that comes when new ways of doing things have to fit into existing cultures. There are spectacular examples of customs that are near global, something that otherwise disparate cultures partake in, albeit in slightly different ways. One of the products that have had the flexibility to take root all over the world is tea. How it was able to replicate not just biologically, but culturally, speaks to the value of being able to adapt.

Tea-drinking cultures are all over the world. From China, Japan, and Russia, to Iran, the United Kingdom, and Kenya, tea has spread everywhere.[16] In most places, the development of a tea culture—simply understood as a place where a lot of people like drinking tea—followed a typical pattern. First, a place was exposed to tea, from explorers, voyagers, or invaders. Once people got a taste for it, the country began trading for it. Then, after its uptake into the culture, countries would try to grow it themselves, climate permitting. This was a pattern that played out in many areas around the globe.

Tea first started in China, as the tea plant is native only to a small region encompassing southwestern China and parts of India and Myanmar. Cultivation of the tea plant started there at least three thousand years ago and as early as 400 CE was being described as a drink that "lightens the body and changes the bones."[17] Tea can taste wonderful, but now we also know that it has caffeine, which is no doubt a huge part of the reason for its initial and ongoing popularity.

Tea has played a lot of roles in China. For many centuries it was one of the country's greatest exports, and it has played a significant part in the country's international relations with everyone from the Mongols to the British. Tastes changed and evolved over time in China regarding the right way to brew a cup or the right tools required for serving. However, when it comes to tea, China is the original consumer of the plant, and it was ultimately from there that everyone else replicated the tea culture.

Traveling Buddhist monks brought tea to Japan, where it and its associated ceremonies became related to both political power and cultural expression. Tea came over from China a few times, but as Victor Mair and Erling Hoh explain in *The True History of Tea*, "It was not until 1191, when the Buddhist monk Myōan Eisai, having returned from studies in China, began to propagate Zen as a teaching that could save Japan, and tea as a medicine that could restore the Japanese people to health, that Japanese tea culture began to develop in earnest."[18] Once the culture had started, the Japanese began to cultivate the tea plant themselves. Tea consumption became part of a much more elaborate cultural expression. The tea ceremony, or chanoyu, was long and complicated, and each participant was required to know their role going in. But far from being a turn-off, this complicated way of consuming tea "was perfected as an art form that fuses nature, the crafts, philosophy, and religion, lending poignant expression to the Japanese spirit."[19] Tea had undergone its first total replication, leading to new cultural expression in Japan.

In the seventeenth century, trade routes developed linking China and Russia. Tea was one of the most important commodities, making its way from China to Moscow, more than four thousand miles away. The Russians took to tea almost immediately. "From the gilded halls of the Kremlin, to the tarred cabins of the country's peasants, tea became Russia's national temperate drink, and the samovar, a metal urn used to boil water, the embodiment of the warm, hospitable Russian hearth."[20] The Russian temperance movement actively promoted tea as a means of reducing vodka consumption. Initially, Russia sustained its tea habit through trade with China. However, as time passed, Russia wanted to change its dependence on Chinese tea. So, "in 1893, the Popoff tea firm established the empire's first tea garden in the Caucasus near the Georgian town of Batumi."[21] Thus, Russia began to cultivate its own tea, creating another cultural and industrial replication.

The last place we will look at for the development of tea culture is Persia, the region now known as Iran. Tea came to this area not directly from China, but via the groups in central Asia who had already become addicted to it, and who carted it into Persia for trading purposes. There, "by the first half of the 17th century it had become part of daily life."[22] Tea was well suited to Islamic culture given its prohibition of alcohol. It provided a religiously acceptable little boost. Tea taverns developed "where persons of good repute went to drink tea, smoke tobacco, and play chess."[23] Persian pilgrims took tea to the countries of the Arabian Peninsula, much like the Buddhist monks had taken tea all over China and to Japan. As tea culture firmly took hold, Persians too desired to reduce their dependency on outside sources for the plant. So "tea production was initiated at the beginning of the 20th century, when the Persian consul to India succeeded in smuggling some 3,000 Assam tea seedlings back to his country and had them planted in the Lāhījan region on the southwestern side of the Caspian Sea."[24] And thus did the replication of tea as both industry and culture continue.

What is it about tea that allowed it to be replicated all over the globe? For starters, it has an inherent flexibility. There are multiple ways to make and consume tea, which can be modified based on cultural norms and social desires. Different degrees of oxidization of tea leaves will produce green, oolong, or black tea. Each of these can be flavored with different spices or milk, or whatever else is locally available. It lends itself to different brewing techniques based on equipment and resources. But all outputs of steeping tea leaves in boiling water are uniformly called "tea." So there is also a core structure that cannot be changed. Tea comes only from the tea plant.

This combination of a firm concept within a flexible package is one clear explanation of how tea managed to spread from a tiny geographical location to have acolytes in almost every country on the planet.

Conclusion

Replication is the molecular magic trick that allows organisms to make copies of themselves, to pass their genetic blueprints from one generation to the next. In the grand ballet of evolution, replication is the music that keeps the dance going.

At its core, replication is about information transfer. It's the process by which the instructions encoded in DNA are faithfully copied and transmitted. Every time a cell divides, every time an organism reproduces, the replication machinery swings into action, ensuring that the genetic message is preserved and propagated. But replication is not a perfect process. Errors creep in, mutations occur. And it's these imperfections that fuel the engine of evolution. Without the variation introduced by replication errors, life would stagnate, unable to adapt to changing environments.

Replication is useful outside of biology too. As a mental model, it teaches us that we don't always need to reinvent the wheel. When you're just getting started, the quickest way to make great leaps is to imitate what others are already doing. This establishes an average baseline of performance. Once you get a sense and a feel for the environment, you can innovate and adapt to set a new baseline.

The power of replication lies in its exponential nature. A single replicated entity can give rise to countless copies, each of which can replicate further. This is the power that viruses and viral ideas harness—the ability to spread explosively by exploiting the machinery of replication. Memes, beliefs, and practices also replicate, spreading from mind to mind, shaping the contours of our shared reality.

But replication also comes with risks. Unchecked replication can be cancerous, leading to uncontrolled growth that threatens the health of the larger system.

Effective replication requires enough structure and space to produce a copy and enough flexibility to adapt that copy to changes in the environment. Just because something has worked for a while doesn't mean it will be effective in perpetuity. Maintaining a successful approach requires an ability to grow and modify that approach as required.

As we contemplate the role of replication in life and in thought, we must recognize both its creative and destructive potential. We must strive to create conditions that favor the replication of what is true, good, and beneficial, while resisting the spread of what is false, harmful, or malignant.

Cooperation

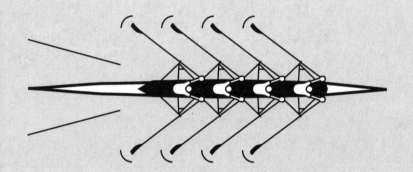

Work together.

If you want to go quickly, go alone. If you want to go far, go together.

C ooperation, or symbiosis, in biology rests on the idea that an organism that cannot perform an important function alone fills this particular gap by using the physical body of another organism, who also benefits from the interaction. It's often a way to increase species' competitive prowess by giving them an advantage over their competitors. "All organisms are constrained in their adaptability at some point, and symbiotic relationships allow them to extend their inherent adaptive capacity to exploit new resources and environments or adapt to their own environment as it changes."[1]

We commonly think of biological cooperation as a win-win arrangement for the parties involved. You have a need. Someone fills it in. In exchange, you fill one of their needs. You don't require cooperation to survive, but with it the quality of your life improves. A shark doesn't need little fish to clean its teeth in order to live that day, but overall the quality of the shark's life is enhanced because clean teeth mean healthy teeth, which will give it more years to feed on prey. Cooperation significantly expands what's possible, by creating emergent properties that have more power than the individual components.

The origin of mitochondria is an excellent example of cooperation in biology. Mitochondria are the energy-producing organelles of cells. They are now an indispensable component of cells, but they do not exist as a product of natural selection. We are here because at some point a mitochondrion and another cell cooperated.

According to one theory, mitochondria originally existed in nature as free prokaryotic (simple) cells and that one such mitochondrion was then acquired by an anaerobic, already eukaryotic (complex) cell for the purposes of converting toxic oxygen radicals into harmless water for the host. Another theory states that both the mitochondria and the host cell were prokaryotes and that the eukaryotic cell that now powers the vast majority of living organisms was created as a result of the cooperation.[2]

Either way, the ancestor of mitochondria was a bacterium that got incorporated into a cell, from which a mutually beneficial relationship developed. Mitochondria produce adenosine triphosphate, or ATP, which can be thought of as the energy currency of the cell. Most chemical reactions in the cell need a lot of energy. These reactions are possible because the mitochondria are on board to create a rich energy source.[3]

Because of the success of this new cell, the mitochondria began "living" in the host cell, and over time became a part of the cell and reproduced. These events took place more than a billion years ago. Without this cooperation between two types of cells, complex organisms would not have been able to evolve.

The symbiosis between cows and the bacteria that live in their digestive systems is also interesting. These bacteria digest the cellulose found in hay and grass for the cow, while the cow offers a nutrient-rich environment for the bacteria. It's a win for both organisms. Combined with their multilayered stomach and short appendix, this relationship means cows can eat tough plant foods. Humans cannot digest cellulose in part because they do not have cellulose-digesting bacteria in their digestive systems!

A final, fascinating example is the interaction of the Hawaiian squid and a bacterium, *Vibrio fischeri*. The bacteria emit light and live in the light-producing organ of the squid. This is a relatively safe environment for the bacteria, as anything that wants to consume them has to get through the squid. The squid, in turn, uses the light produced by these bacteria to camouflage itself from predators in oceans.

> Cooperation . . . is its own evolutionary force that contributes to an organism's immediate survival but also creates the possibility for adaptive responses to future challenges.
>
> —RAFE SAGARIN[4]

Progress Takes the Fast Track

In some cases, cooperation can be so valuable to the organisms involved that they evolve to become part of each other permanently. As in the mitochondria example, the benefits realized by those organisms' cooperation provide a foundation for further development. When you can depend on the cooperation and the needs it addresses, you can leverage the freed energy to support growth and innovation.

A human example of this is the development of the railroad and the telegraph. As inventions they were completely separate, but the cooperative relationship that developed between the two allowed them to take over the world. As Alfred D. Chandler Jr. writes, "The railroad and the telegraph marched across the continent in unison."[5] The telegraph provided train companies with a mechanism for communicating the progress of trains on the line—if they were late or early—so people could be ready to unload perishable goods and otherwise adjust their schedules. This extreme efficiency was key to the railroad being profitable. In return, the rail lines provided telegraph companies with an infrastructure on which to construct their system—from the poles and wires linking cities to the stations that often housed telegraph offices.

The cooperation was so successful that very quickly neither industry could conceive of doing business without the other. Their businesses became linked because of the mutual benefit each provided, as well as the benefits that further accrued from their symbiotic relationship. The interactions between the two technologies "intensified the speed and volume of the flow of goods, passengers, and messages."[6] They helped each other to be better, and similar to cooperation among biological organisms, "what matters is that partnerships develop according to how effectively tasks are accomplished."[7] The attachment between the railroad and telegraph was so strong that it could be depended on completely, allowing each industry to free up resources that would otherwise be spent on duplicating the other's technology and infrastructure.

The lesson here is to consider how often you look for opportunities for collaboration. We frequently talk of the competition—what they are doing, what direction they are headed—so we can keep up where we need to and not get blindsided or lose too much market share. But how many of us devote resources to looking for "the cooperation"—companies or industries with whom we can partner for mutual benefit?

Exceptional Harmony

Writing about lichens, which are essentially a new organism produced through the symbiotic relationship between algae and fungi,

Rafe Sagarin says of symbiosis that it "creates emergent properties that you wouldn't predict from just looking at the two organisms on their own."[8]

There is possibly no better example of the power of cooperation to transform existing structures and create new capabilities than the relationships required to achieve success as a symphony orchestra. The interaction between the musicians, and theirs with the conductor, involves a huge amount of trust and commitment to produce something that is greater than the sum of its parts.

Alexander Shelley, conductor of the National Arts Centre Orchestra in Ottawa, Canada, describes the interaction of its members as such: "In the best-case scenario, they start to behave like a flock of birds. When you see a flock of birds moving around, you're not quite sure who's leading it or what's happening."[9] This speaks to the unusual collaboration that happens in symphony orchestras. It's not a leader with a bunch of followers. It is not a rigid hierarchy of responsibility. Shelley says, "When it's functioning correctly, it's a symbiosis between me and the eighty musicians on stage."[10]

Why does an orchestra pursue its goals in this way? Because this is what all the participants believe is required to truly make the music. Perfect cooperation is the difference between good and inspirational. Shelley describes an orchestra by saying, "When things are working well, a conductor and orchestra are in this state of absolute coordination where the music is speaking the way it needs to speak."

Other conductors have made similar points. Conductor Valery Gergiev says, "I just go straight to the most important thing—what is the color, what is the character of this music, what is the principal voice? And that means we are working immediately on . . . the relationship between all the parts, which is a huge coordination between all of us."[11]

Conductor Mariss Jansons defines that moment of success for an orchestra as "when a good performance becomes a great one, a coming together of the piece, the performers, and the audience that creates a positive feedback loop of continuous enrichment and enchantment."[12]

Therefore, trust is an essential component of successful symphony orchestras. Each musician hears the instruments closest to them best, and in some halls they cannot rely on their ears at all if they have to collaborate with an instrument in a different section. To cooperate fully as a group, they have to trust each other, and they have to understand how their individual part contributes to what the rest of the orchestra is doing. In *Music as Alchemy*, Tom Service describes the musicians in the Berlin Philharmonic orchestra as "a group of players who value themselves enormously as individual musicians, but who together create an instantly identifiable single sonic body in their performances."[13] It's the complete cooperation that allows the emergence of the musical experience.

An orchestra has to come together on many levels in order to make music. To achieve the trust required to anticipate the needs of the performance, the cooperation must be absolute. Each member has to be all in.

An orchestra is an all-or-nothing situation. If one member is messing up and playing terribly, they can ruin the whole performance. Their playing jars with everyone else and throws them off. It requires total cooperation.

A remarkable example of this cooperation and trust is the Montreal Women's Symphony Orchestra. Started in 1940, they were "the only complete all women's symphony orchestra in North America at that time—conducted by a woman, managed by women, and composed of women."[14] This orchestra was born at a time when it was rare for women to play in orchestras, and if they did, they were confined to certain instruments that were considered "ladylike," such as the harp. Anything happening in the public sphere, even music, was still very much considered the purview of men. Of course, not everyone agreed, and two women, Madge Bowen and Ethel Stark, decided that there was enough untapped female talent in the city of Montreal to put together an all-female symphony orchestra.

The only requirement to join the orchestra at the beginning was commitment and passion. Thus, the orchestra comprised women from many walks of life—professional musicians and amateurs, housewives, socialites, working class, and upper class. There were Jewish women, Christians, French, English, and white and black women, including Violet Grant, the first black Canadian to be a permanent member of a symphony. Their emphasis, under the guidance of their conductor, Ethel Stark, was on teamwork and inclusiveness, so that "despite their differences, they came together for one purpose: to make music."[15]

The diversity of the group required a staggering amount of cooperation in order to make the orchestra succeed. They had to deal with social tensions that are still unresolved in contemporary society. Before the instruments could cooperate to make music, the cooperation of the members was required to create the orchestra. Class divisions had to be set aside during rehearsal time in order for their dedication to the music to achieve fruition.

Cooperation often comes about in a biological context because of the latent understanding that no one can do everything. No species or individual is perfectly adapted to deal with the entire spectrum of possible environmental conditions. This applies equally well to an orchestra. There is no music without all the instruments, and these instruments cannot work together without people who are willing to trust each other to respond correctly to the demands of performance.

The Montreal Women's Symphony Orchestra devoted themselves to their music, demonstrating, as Maria Noriega Rachwal describes in her biography of the group, "the power of music to transcend boundaries."[16] Their dedication and talent were recognized after years of practice in basements and drafty industrial buildings, squeezing the music in between factory work and child-rearing, when the group became the first Canadian orchestra to be invited to play at Carnegie Hall in New York. The performance was exceptional; the music flowed out to rave reviews. Building on this success, the orchestra toured all over the world, as well as performing on television and radio. Never well paid, the Montreal Women's Symphony Orchestra eventually had to shut down after being denied funding that was made available to other Canadian symphony orchestras.[17] So it is truly their commitment to music and each other that led them to the successes they had. In terms of cooperation, theirs was absolute. The women in the orchestra were all in.

Shared Belief

In the book *Sapiens*, Yuval Noah Harari explains and examines how humans cooperate in extensive systems of shared belief.[18] He points out that, uniquely among species on the planet, humans are able to imagine things that have no physical counterpart, and furthermore that this imagining allows us to function in the large, complex societies that we have. These shared beliefs are requirements for our lifestyles—"large numbers of strangers can cooperate successfully by believing in common myths."[19]

These shared beliefs frame every aspect of our lives. Our belief in the value of currency, laws, corporations, and nations is what allows us to work together and to live together. Without these shared beliefs, we wouldn't own anything or have homes, jobs, or any social infrastructure. According to Harari, it is this ability to trust in shared beliefs that allowed humans to move from small groups focused on daily needs to the large, interconnected population that studies the past and worries about the future.

Whether or not this gets a value judgment of "good" can be debated. As Harari argues, "most human cooperation networks have been geared toward oppression and exploitation."[20] After all, it is only shared belief that explains why some people's lives are easier than others—if we didn't all buy into the myth of money, it wouldn't exist, let alone be useful to accumulate. And there is an element of inertia here. The more encompassing a shared belief becomes, the more we forget it is a human construct. Eventually, the mass of belief becomes so large that we consider it an inescapable part of the natural world. There is no doubt that we can no longer operate without cooperating in these shared beliefs.

Conclusion

Cooperation is the surprising secret of success in the ruthless world of survival. If there is any one model that explains humanity, then this is it. Cooperation unleashed the potential of the human species.

At first glance, cooperation seems to defy the logic of natural selection. Why would an organism invest its hard-earned resources in helping another rather than focusing solely on its own survival and reproduction? The answer lies in the magic of reciprocity and shared interest. When organisms can benefit more by cooperating than by competing, cooperative strategies emerge and flourish. Collaboration with others gives us options and opportunities that are unavailable when we insist on going it alone.

But cooperation is not automatic. It requires specific conditions—repeated interactions, shared benefits, mechanisms to prevent cheating.

Cooperation is the foundation of civilization. Our species' success is built on our ability to cooperate flexibly and at scale—to share knowledge, coordinate efforts, and create institutions that incentivize cooperative behavior. From the division of labor in the economy to the norms of reciprocity in society, cooperation underlies our greatest achievements. But, as in nature, human cooperation is not guaranteed. It requires constant cultivation and protection from the forces of selfishness and short-term thinking. It requires norms that reward cooperation and punish defection.

SUPPORTING IDEA:
Dunbar's Number

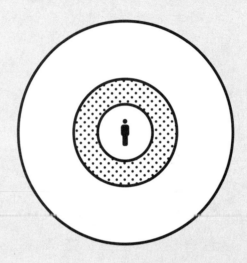

ROBIN DUNBAR, AN EVOLUTIONARY ANTHROPOLOGIST, ARGUES THAT there is a limit to the number of people with whom one can maintain stable social relationships. This limit, of about 150 persons, is set by our neocortex size. He explains that in groups beyond this number, neocortical limitations make it difficult for people to maintain relationships with everyone, as they suffer from information overload. Using studies by field anthropologists working with primates, Dunbar suggests that there is a direct correlation between the number of neocortical neurons and the number of social relationships that can be monitored.[21]

To support this argument, Dunbar refers to historical communities that were about 150 in number. These include hunter-gatherer communities, military units, successful businesses, communities counted in the *Domesday Book*, Neolithic villages, and Christmas-card networks, to name a few.

Dunbar's research suggests that because we are limited by our brain capacity, the fitness advantage of larger social groups was a driver in the evolution of parts of the brain. Other scientists have corroborated this idea that our larger brains are primarily a social versus an ecological adaptation. It wasn't because we happened to have a bigger brain for, say, hunting that we pursued complex social relationships, but rather that these relationships were critical to the evolutionary development of neocortical capacity.

This means that being socially successful is critical for our survival, both as a species and as individuals. There is, however, a limit to how many social relationships we can successfully navigate. Thus, being socially successful is about knowing our limits and investing our time accordingly.

Dunbar identified the following scale of closeness for humans in groups. Note that each group includes the individuals from the smaller groups, and each number is about the maximum that could be maintained at that level.

5 people: This is our inner core of closeness, the people we support and who support us on a daily basis, such as partners, family, and best friends.

15 people: This is our close friend group. These people are integrated into our lives to the extent that we have an excellent understanding of their behavior, even if we may not see them all the time.

50 people: This includes our basic friends and acquaintances. We hang out occasionally, probably more often in groups, and know a bit about what is happening in their lives.

150 people: This is the size at which you feel you are part of a community. "This is the number of people you can have a relationship with involving trust and obligation—there's some personal history, not just names and faces."[22]

500 people: This category includes friends of friends, people you know something about but don't know as well and don't make a sustained effort to know.

1,500 people: This is the upper limit and includes all the faces you can put names to.

Dunbar's number is useful in terms of reminding us about working with our biology. Our brains can process only so much of the information required to maintain social groups. The larger the group, the more brain power required. Eventually we are going to run out. In addition—and we do this all the time—is the cost-benefit analysis. At what point does an increase in our social efforts start to bring diminishing returns?

At around 150 people we max out, according to Dunbar. Too far beyond this and we will have trouble keeping track of who everyone is and how they relate to everyone else. To invest effort beyond this may be more than our brains are capable of doing. Also, less related to scientific research but very relevant to life experience, relationships of any sort require a time investment. How much time we have to devote to social maintenance has a definite cap.

Hierarchical Organization

Know your place.

A civilized society handles hierarchy very politely, but it's still there. It permeates everything.

—PETER D. KAUFMAN[1]

ierarchies can be found across the animal world. They are a form of social structuring characterized by a linear or almost linear dominance ranking between individuals that live close to one another. These types of organizing structures are most common in social mammals such as baboons and wolves, but they are also found in chickens, bears, and elephant seals. All else being equal, hierarchies are relatively stable over time, as the individuals within a lower group are aware and accept their position and thus do not directly challenge those on top. Organizing this way generally means there is less fighting and more order.

Getting to the Top

There is a contract implied in a hierarchy. The dominant member of a group has certain responsibilities to execute in relation to the other members. Specifically, "(a) direction each day for food, (b) protection each day from predators and other dangers, and (c) the maintenance of order every day by orienting members to their places and roles, by resolving conflicts when they break out, and by reinforcing social norms whenever transgressions occur."[2]

It was the Norwegian researcher Thorleif Schjelderup-Ebbe who first studied hens to explore how dominance hierarchies, and consequently peace, were maintained in their flocks. He recognized that peace was found only in already established flocks where a dominance hierarchy had been set—each hen knew whom it could dominate and whom it was subordinate to. Each hen was able to remember the pecking order, and in Schjelderup-Ebbe's experiments, he discovered that one hen had extraordinarily recognized twenty-seven other hens from different flocks. This shows that hierarchical organizations are respected by these birds and form the basis of their way of living.

In chimpanzees, "the alpha male usually wins his position not because he is physically stronger, but because he leads a large and stable coalition. These coalitions play a central part not only during overt struggles for the alpha position, but in almost all day-to-day activities. Members of a coalition spend more time together, share food, and help one another in time of trouble."[3]

One of the drawbacks of hierarchies is the lack of perceived value of those who are at the bottom. "An efficient new gathering strategy devised by a low-ranking chimpanzee, for example, might not get replicated just because of her status in society."[4]

Hierarchies in the human world act as information filters, causing us to potentially miss opportunities and ideas. The way we organize ourselves is often a default to our instincts on leadership and authority. Sometimes this is optimal, sometimes it isn't. If it isn't getting us what we need, either as individuals or as a society, it is within our power to make different choices emphasizing the values and strengths that would be beneficial. Our hierarchical organizations are where we derive our ego, status, and reputation, and they are what conditions us to focus on growing ourselves rather than growing others.

The interesting thing about hierarchies in humans is that their benefits aren't always obvious at first. Few people would say they like them, unless they happen to be at the top of the pile. Most of us hate having to defer to our parents, our bosses, the state. Hierarchies reduce creativity. They put extra stress on those at the bottom, potentially increasing their mortality levels. They put a lot of pressure on those at the top too, forcing them to constantly worry about maintaining their position. Most organizations promote cultures that emphasize rather than de-emphasize an individual's status, power, and place, which is part of the reason they get torn apart. Hierarchies are inherently and inevitably unequal and unfair.

Hierarchies, however, clearly confer a benefit that is large enough to balance out their costs. In the absence of an imposed structure, people have a natural instinct to self-organize. In organizations that claim to have a flat structure with no leaders, people often just end up more frazzled than normal as they attempt to navigate the inevitable unspoken power structures critical to their success. Even anarchist movements end up with leaders. Leadership is important. Getting rid of the title of "captain" or "boss" doesn't change the fact that someone in the locker room or the boardroom is going to set the example for others, so it's best to ask who we want that person to be.

If we can't avoid hierarchies, we need to recognize their presence and focus on structuring them in the most beneficial way for everyone involved, like having prestige associated with belonging to the group rather than being conferred on individuals. The key is to be aware of hierarchies and work with, not against, them. We want to use hierarchies as a tool, not be used by them.

A Place for Everyone and Everyone in Their Place

According to both Plato and Plotinus, another major ancient Greek philosopher, the entire universe is arranged in a hierarchical structure. At the bottom, we have inanimate objects like pebbles or soil. Next, we have plants, then animals, then humans. Then God is at the top of the hierarchy, superior to everything else in the universe. As Charles Van Doren explains in *A History of Knowledge*, it was this idea that informed human society from the very beginning. The assumption that humans can be organized into a hierarchy from the lowest up to the individual with the most power and perceived importance has always been integral to the way we've constructed our world. Look at any ancient civilization and you'll find someone at the top, with only that group's god above them. Following Plato and Plotinus, people used their ideas about hierarchy to justify a stratified society.[5]

Yet people have always, at various times, rebelled against hierarchies. As Van Doren points out, many of the individuals, in particular religious leaders, to whom we've accorded the highest esteem throughout history are those who have questioned and thought against existing, unequal hierarchies. This is especially true when a hierarchy becomes so severely stratified that only a handful of individuals can benefit from it. The French Revolution is one of the most iconic instances of people fighting to overthrow a flawed social hierarchy.

Prior to the revolution, French society was divided into three main groups, known as estates. The First Estate consisted of the Catholic clergy, who oversaw the Catholic Church and had some other duties, like giving the monarch advice. They didn't have to pay taxes, collected tithes, and owned lands. As with each of the estates, it was further divided into hierarchical levels, with higher-ranking individuals in Paris and Versailles having very different lives than rural parish priests. The Second Estate consisted of aristocrats with inherited titles. Like the First Estate, they didn't need to pay taxes, but they could collect them.

Into the Third Estate went everyone else, about 96 to 98 percent of the population. At the highest level of the Third Estate were the bourgeoisie, including those in finance, medicine, law, and trade. They could become wealthy, just without gaining any political power or influence. Next were the sansculottes, artisans, and other city workers. The final layer was the peasants, who labored on farms, paid heavy taxes, and had essentially no rights or influence. They owned land, but few had enough to feed their families. For instance, between 1720 and 1729, and 1780 and 1789, land rents rose by 142 percent, while the prices of agricultural products rose by only 60 percent.[6] About three quarters of peasants had less than five hectares, the minimum amount of land needed to survive. In many areas, at least a quarter of peasants had just one hectare.

At the top of society was the king, who had absolute power and few limitations on his behavior. This system of power, known as absolutism, was popular in Europe at the time. Not only was arguing against it dangerous, but some people did see the system as positive because of its ability to maintain order. It's worth noting that absolutism was not like other monarchy systems, like the ones used during the medieval era, because here the king did not share his power. When King Louis XIV said "L'état, c'est moi" ("I am the state"), he meant it. For everyone but the king and a few nobles, the system was entirely unfair.[7]

During the French Revolution, people fought for a more equal society without the intense divisions of the estates. The vast majority of the French population was trapped in harsh poverty with too little to eat and no rights whatsoever. The wealthy minority merrily spent their tax income and racked up a growing national debt. People began to question the age-old notion of an absolute ruler with a monopoly on force and no restrictions on their behavior. They saw that the social hierarchy was arbitrary and could be overthrown. When the common people seized weapons and means of exercising force in Paris, they upended the hierarchy. What they had more trouble with was finding a system to replace it.

During the interim between the end of the monarchy and the rise of Napoleon, the French people tried out different hierarchical structures and leaders, each of which failed. Here is the summary of those years:

> Between 1789 and 1815 the country went through roughly five phases. From 1789 to 1792 France was a constitutional monarchy. During that time Louis XVI came to be seen as a despot, and in 1792 he was tried and beheaded. That marked the beginning of the most radical period of the Revolution, called the Terror, when France was run by the ... Committee of Public Safety, headed by Maximilien de Robespierre. Robespierre quelled civil war within the country and waged war on the neighboring countries hostile to the Revolution. Some seventeen thousand opponents of his regime were beheaded and another thirty-five thousand jailed, but in 1794 Robespierre himself was led to the guillotine in a counter-coup.[8]

The country was then run for five years by the government of the Directory, staffed mostly by the bourgeois class. What's interesting is that within a few years, the old hierarchy was effectively back in place. When Napoleon came to power in the late 1790s, he reinstated absolutism, although he did not call himself a king. He seized power in 1799, and in 1804 he declared himself emperor. Hardly a revolutionary move. Napoleon had absolute power and was not answerable to anyone. He maintained this by violently quashing any dissent.

France did not emerge from the revolution as a country without a hierarchy. Instead, Napoleon instituted a system that was based more on ability than on class, although it is still debatable whether a meritocracy is even possible or what a true one might look like. In addition, Napoleon saw France as at the top of the hierarchy of European countries and therefore sought to make the others subordinate. This was part of the rise of nationalism, the belief that one's own country is superior to all others and must be willing to fight to expand its borders. Napoleon was then defeated by the British and sent into exile in 1815.

The period from 1789 to 1815 thus saw a constant jostling of the hierarchy in France, as various groups and individuals tried to take and maintain power. One of the lessons of the French Revolution is that upending a hierarchy creates instability, and many people will maneuver to influence what the old hierarchy will be replaced with. A new hierarchy might have different rules and different roles, but it will still be a hierarchy. Surviving the establishment of a new order is by no means easy.

Take the story of Charles-Maurice de Talleyrand-Périgord, "who simply kept reinventing himself in order to ride France's political roller coaster."[9] Talleyrand was bishop of Autun in the Loire Valley when he joined the revolution. When things got extreme, he went into exile. In 1797 he returned, became foreign minister under the Directory (government), and remained there under Napoleon. But in 1807, as Napoleon's ambitions began to become alarming, Talleyrand turned against the emperor. In 1814 he represented France during the peace negotiations of the Congress of Vienna as foreign minister during the brief reign of Louis XVIII. Talleyrand thrived by finding a way to maintain position in the constantly changing hierarchy.

Another important lesson from the French Revolution is that when contemplating the hierarchy we want to live with, it is worth asking what kind of leaders our hierarchical system will produce.

Our hierarchical instincts are not always right in getting us the most efficient organization to deal with the challenges we are facing. Writing about sports teams, Sam Walker argues in *The Captain Class* that the best performers are not the best leaders. We seem to want our leaders to be the alpha performers, the guys and gals who dazzle us with their play.[10] Walker writes, "All too often, the people who propose themselves for positions of power are quick to trumpet their abilities. And those of us who make these decisions [on who should lead] are often swayed by the force of their personality."[11] For example, the leader becomes dominant because of skills displayed in the competitive process of becoming leader— strength, smarts, and so on. This means that the leader is just the most powerful competitor, like Robespierre or Napoleon. Their skills are exemplary for winning the competition of dominance. They are not necessarily the most skilled for actually running the show. Maybe the role would benefit from some of the strengths exhibited by others, but because those traits didn't help in the competitive process, the leader doesn't possess them—to the detriment of the entire hierarchy. We then end up with leaders who don't actually have the skills to lead.

The French Revolution, with its focus on ending absolutism and the subsequent return of absolute power and the rise of nationalism, can show us a lot about our hierarchical instincts. People could not destroy the hierarchy altogether; they just ended up with a new form of it. One of the lessons here, then, is that allowing for the fact of hierarchical instincts is critical in the development and leadership of any organization.

Status Symbol

The history of fashion can be read, in part, as a chronicle of humans trying to establish and negotiate social hierarchies. How we dress communicates information to people about our status. In *Survival of the Prettiest*, Nancy Etcoff says of magazines, "The fashions they feature are as much products of social competition as the finest bird feathers or the sweetest birdsong."[12] Thinking about fashion exposes the ongoing tension in human hierarchies. On the one hand we are comfortable when we can place people quickly in the hierarchy. From their clothing we infer information about their relative power and wealth in the society we inhabit. On the other hand, we continually chafe at the restraints of whatever position of the hierarchy we happen to find ourselves in. I may be limited by my biology, but I certainly don't want to be limited by the messages of the clothes I wear.

Yuval Harari observes, "Hierarchies serve an important function. They enable complete strangers to know how to treat one another without wasting the time and energy needed to become personally acquainted."[13] In different times and places, the hierarchy of fashion has been legally mandated in the form of sumptuary laws. They were often enforced not legally, which was logistically challenging, but socially. If your status meant you weren't allowed to wear purple and yet you showed up at court decked out from head to toe in violet, you were risking a lot. You probably wouldn't be arrested, but you could be snubbed by your peers, laughed at by those higher up, and left off the list for the next social occasion or business opportunity. Fashion laws thus meant that you could easily place people in their social position and act toward them accordingly. Taken to the extreme, some markers of high status were intended solely to convey that status. Black teeth were fashionable in the Elizabethan era to show that one could afford sugar, and very long nails demonstrated the lack of a need to work.

Of course, hierarchies are dynamic, with ongoing challenges for top position. Fashion and accessories were a way to make it harder for those lower in the hierarchy to successfully compete, mostly through cost. Silk, gold, silver, precious stones—these long-recognized components of "luxury adornment" have always put those who could afford them "at the top of the pyramid, setting apart the haves from the have-nots."[14] Cost barriers to various goods are an easy and long-lived way to set up and define social hierarchies.

The upper class also shows status through wearing clothes that are totally impractical for doing any labor, reflecting participation in expensive activities and having more than one actually needs. "Charlemagne owned 800 pairs of fine gloves at a time when gloves were difficult to produce and clean," notes Etcoff.[15] We can admit to ourselves that not a lot has changed; status is still frequently demonstrated through fashion. Labels, fabric, and the cut of a suit or a hoodie communicate a lot. Yes, it is often nuanced. For example, even though luxury goods in some contexts are still markers of status, dressing scruffy when you don't have to is also a form of demonstrating your privileged place in the hierarchy. The academic in a shirt with soup stains, the CEO in battered jeans, the billionaire in a tracksuit—these are all examples of them announcing to the world that their status is so secure, they don't need to indicate it through luxury clothing. In so many cases, what we wear "helps us negotiate our relations with the outside world and provide us with comfort and protection."[16]

"Underground" Hierarchies

Hierarchies are critical in survival situations and in combat. In these scenarios, we primally crave leadership. In chaotic, life-and-death situations, sheepdogs magically appear to herd the sheep. Even in the US Special Operations Forces, which are designed to be as flat as an organization can be within a military division, hierarchical decision-making immediately emerges and takes over in combat or when there are time constraints.

How do hierarchies form and break down? There are, broadly, two components: biological enablers and cultural constraints. These two dynamics influence how our tendency toward hierarchies manifests. To get insight into these dynamics, let's look at the 2010 Copiapó mining accident in northern Chile, when a cave-in at the San Jose copper-gold mine trapped thirty-three miners seven hundred feet underground.

The miners were completely isolated in a physically stressful environment. It was hot, humid, and dark. The ground was unstable, and debris and rocks continued to fall. They retreated to a refuge that had only enough provisions for ten miners for two days.

Luis Urzua was the shift foreman, a position that granted him automatic authority. He "held formal leadership; in the Chilean mining culture the authority of the shift foreman was considered absolute."[17] Urzua, however, had worked at the San Jose mine for less than three months. He hadn't had time to develop a bond with the miners on his team to back up the authority implied by his title. In the small power vacuum created, two other miners, Mario Sepulveda and Mario Gomez, "rallied the miners to explore escape routes and send signals to the rescue workers."[18] Although these two may have had the right characteristics for leadership, they could not take a place at the top of the hierarchy because they lacked the culture-supported authority. Thus, in the first twenty-four hours, "most [miners] felt accountable to no one" and stayed in "subgroups based on kinship and past friendships."[19]

Our desire for hierarchy, for leadership, is most present in survival situations. It will arise. For the miners in Chile, days two to five saw the emergence of spiritual leadership by one of the team who had pastoral experience. A democratic process was instituted to make decisions about allotment of the food supply and bathroom rules. Mario Sepulveda, clearly having natural leadership instincts, used them in a way that exploited the culture he was in; he urged the group to "respect Urzua and suggested that if Urzua were willing to lead, the miners should accept him as their leader. If Urzua were unwilling to lead, Sepulveda would be willing to take charge."[20] Leadership was necessary not only to get tasks done, but for the comfort it would offer to the group.

By day five, "throughout the day, the miners gave more authority and respect to both Urzua and Sepulveda. Gomez was also widely respected for his experience and wisdom. Sepulveda had started to assign specific tasks to people based on their skills, experience, and mental stability."[21] Good leadership is about acting in the interests of the group. In *The Captain Class*, Sam Walker, in one of the most counterintuitive conclusions in his book, explains it this way: "When it comes to competition, most people believe that the leader of a team is the person who does something spectacular when the chips are down."[22] This, however, is actually not true. Walker's conclusions about the real qualities of great captains apply to the dynamics of the miners in Chile. "The great captains lowered themselves in relation to the group whenever possible in order to earn the moral authority to drive them forward in tough moments. The person at the back, feeding the ball to others, may look like a servant—but that person is actually creating dependency. The easiest way to lead, it turns out, is to serve."[23] It's possible that Sepulveda, by supporting the leadership of Urzua, was doing the most valuable thing he could to serve the interests of the group.

The hierarchy developed in the early days held until day seventeen. During this time, there was widespread despair about the success of the rescue efforts, with the miners rationed down to one bite of food every thirty-six hours. Hope was low, but the hierarchy served its purpose of maintaining a structure that supported a maximum chance of survival.

On day eighteen, a "breakthrough shaft" reached the refuge where the miners were located. Not large enough for rescue, it was used to get items to the miners, including food, medical supplies, letters from their families, and a television. At this point the hierarchy of the thirty-three miners began to break down, because there was a new top of the pyramid. Control shifted to people aboveground. The miners were no longer accountable to just each other. "Fights occurred about which channels to watch," and "discipline gradually declined alongside their humility as the miners began to digest the news of their celebrity status."[24]

As the days continued, the hierarchy that had maintained order while they were isolated and scared continued to fade. Miners began developing relationships with doctors and media advisers, fighting for more information from their loved ones. Some miners began receiving drugs in their communications from family, which shifted relationships and allegiances underground. The hierarchy, though, didn't completely disappear. It was as though they were pulled between two different hierarchies, the one belowground that had gotten them this far, and that aboveground, which offered promise of rescue. As they passed sixty days underground, "the miners' behaviors...oscillated between extremes, indulging in petty fights one minute and promising never to break their fraternal bonds the next minute."[25]

The rescue started on day seventy. The miners were lifted out one by one, with Urzua coming up last. They had expressed the desire to leave San Jose as a group, which they did with the world watching.

Boss vs. Leader

There is a nuance here between authority and leadership. Those at the tops of hierarchies have authority that they are expected to use to solve problems and address issues facing the hierarchy. But as Ronald Heifetz points out in his article "Leadership,"[26] we can easily think of examples of people with lots of authority who don't actually lead or who don't have the solutions in times of crisis, and lots of people who exhibit leadership without having any authority.

Conclusion

Hierarchy is the invisible scaffolding that organizes the living world.

Hierarchies in biology aren't just about structure but about function. They allow for specialization and division of labor, for the emergence of complex behaviors from simple rules. In the hierarchy of an ant colony, the queen, workers, and soldiers all play their roles, their interactions giving rise to the sophisticated operation of the colony as a whole.

But hierarchy isn't rigid or fixed. It's fluid and dynamic, with levels constantly interacting and influencing one another. A change at one level can ripple across the entire hierarchy, transforming the system in unexpected ways.

While hierarchy is a way to manage complexity, it can also backfire. Too much hierarchy leads to unrest and instability. Too little leads to chaos.

Most organizations promote cultures that emphasize rather than de-emphasize an individual's status, power, and place, which is part of the reason they get torn apart, as the fight to get to the top of the hierarchy takes precedence over the success of the organization.

In the end, hierarchy is the organizing principle that allows scale from the microscopic to the magnificent.

Incentives

Shape behavior.

Never, ever, think about something else when you should be thinking about the power of incentives.

—CHARLIE MUNGER[1]

Incentives shape behavior. We move in the direction of rewards and take steps to avoid punishment. Humans, when we are thoughtful about incentives, will change our behavior to attain a perceived benefit. We will go through the same behavioral hoops to detour around perceived disadvantages. However, the ability to identify and respond to incentives is an intrinsic part of our biological makeup. Therefore, their influences on our behavior are not always rational. We often evaluate the value of an incentive through an incredibly biased lens made up of our self-esteem, our personal narrative, and our physiological state.

Behavior Modification

Behaviors can be a response to both internal and external factors. Multiple studies have shown, in both rats and humans, that consistent but infrequent rewards can create stronger behavioral changes than those that are given all the time.

A rat learns that a certain lever will sometimes produce food. It's always the same lever, but it doesn't always have food. The rat will continue to press that lever for far longer after food is no longer given than a lever that always gave food then one day just stopped.

Our behavior changes based on both actual reward and punishment and our perceptions of it. If something we did resulted in something good, just the anticipation of having that good thing again is an incentive to repeat the behavior. Same goes with a negative experience. Just the possibility of a repeat of punishment makes us want to avoid similar situations in the future.

The ability to store things such as fat and food gives us flexibility in responding to incentives. Money can be thought of as a form of storage—all the potential purchasing power is stored until it's used to buy things. "Perhaps the greatest economic innovation in human society was the invention of money, an exchangeable commodity that in effect stores the power to purchase and sell goods."[2] This is part of money's incentive. You can choose how and when to spend it, and saving it means that you aren't as vulnerable to having to adjust and respond to every minor or risky incentive that comes your way.

The discovery and reinforcement of a certain incentive can change our behavior. Like helping to build the mechanisms that allow elephants to remember how and where to find water over vast distances, we can create new neural pathways when obtaining rewards. Uncertain incentives, as well, can be beneficial to survival. Through studies of gambling and loyalty programs, researchers speculate that a tolerance for uncertain incentives is necessary because so many of our attempts to achieve something new fail on the first few tries.

The darker side of incentives is that sometimes pursuing our wants can rewire the brain so that these wants become requirements. This has been seen in studies examining drug addiction. After repeated chasing of an incentive because of the reward of feeling good, the brain pursues the incentive not because of how it feels to use drugs but because those wants have become hardwired to be their own reward. It's like getting the drug is what now gives the pleasure, beyond the actual use of the drug itself. Thus, incentives can have a powerful impact on our biology as well.

The Long-Term Influence of Short-Term Incentives

One of the main challenges with incentives is that they are a factor everywhere: with our needs, our wants, short-term interests, and long-term goals. In a basic survey of the people around us, humans do not generally appear to be able to prioritize incentives for deferred rewards over those that bring us immediate pleasure.

This is a problem in democracies, as Aristotle pointed out more than two thousand years ago. For all their political attractiveness, they are essentially governed by millions of people acting in their own self-interest. And those interests tend to be driven by incentives that offer immediate rewards.

Voters want to hear about policies that will have an immediate positive impact on their lives. Most have less interest in policies that won't have any obvious benefits for years or even generations. As Niall Ferguson writes in *Civilization,* "We love our grandchildren. But our great-great-grandchildren are harder to relate to." Politicians have no choice but to respond to the incentives to think short-term; otherwise, they won't gain voter support. They therefore present platforms highlighting the benefits that will miraculously occur should they win. Due to the relatively short term that people tend to hold political office, it's difficult for any particular politician to make significant positive change in that time. They're surrounded by rapid feedback loops that depend on them showing fast results—short election cycles, frequent opinion polls, media reports every minute of the day, and instant social media chatter. The result is a system in which politicians have little incentive to think beyond the current election cycle.

In a similar manner, publicly traded companies are incentivized to sacrifice long-term growth in the interest of showing profits on quarterly reports. The short tenure of CEOs and their large bonuses create perverse incentives. As a result, companies have difficulty investing in the sort of improvements that compound over time. For instance, many companies feel the need to jump on every new trend within their market to capitalize on the attention of their customers. This results in a hamster wheel of new tweaks rather than companies focusing on building timeless products and services.

Some large organizations have budgets that incentivize reckless spending. Federal agencies with use-it-or-lose-it budgets spend an average of 8.7 percent of those budgets during the last week of the fiscal year, nearly five times the typical weekly expenditure.[3] In addition, projects funded during the last week are between two and six times as likely to be rated as low quality as those from the rest of the year. Furthermore, variable pay for managers in these organizations is often tied to spending their budget.

Incentives have a powerful impact that spreads out like ripples on a pond. The short-term incentives in both politics and business impact every area of our lives. To change a system involving humans, we need to change the incentives.

Aligning Incentives

One of the challenges of leadership is aligning incentives. How do you get people to move in the same direction without being way-laid by immediate reward? Sun Tzu suggested more than two thousand years ago that a good leader "leads his men into battle like a man climbing to a height and kicking away the ladder."[4] When you can't go back, your motivation is to go forward together.

Manipulated by Incentive

We are vulnerable to the influence of incentives—whether from money, prestige, or power. Most insidious is when an incentive is designed to appeal to our personal narrative about the kind of person we are. No one wants to be thought of as bad, so we often perform intellectual contortions to justify our pursuit of an incentive as good.

Thalidomide is a drug with a tragic history. Discovered and developed by a West German drug manufacturer in the 1950s and widely marketed as a sedative and antinauseant, it was responsible for thousands of infant deaths and deformities. The story of how this happened exposes a lot of the nuances of incentives.

Thalidomide was first produced by the Chemie Grünenthal company. It was "a drug without a disease," and thus the first tests in animals and humans were actually to find something it could cure.[5] The scientists there could not find a dosage high enough to kill rats, and no side effects were observed on any animals tested. From this they concluded that the drug was completely nontoxic. They still didn't know what humans could use it to cure, but these original animal-testing results formed the foundation of their enduring belief that the drug couldn't hurt anyone.[6]

The Grünenthal company then began handing out free samples to doctors. There was no clinical trial as we understand it now. Instead, the initial users of the drug were the clinical trial. Thalidomide was put out into the world and "tested" on people without their knowledge or consent. The general population was the lab.[7]

As Trent D. Stephens and Rock Brynner explain in *Dark Remedy: The Impact of Thalidomide and Its Revival as a Vital Medicine,* the drug couldn't kill a rat, so Grünenthal thought it had to be safe. The company developed a large marketing campaign that sold thalidomide as a sedative. They partnered with manufacturers in other countries and brought the drug to market all over the world. In most countries it was available without a prescription. Doctors were routinely given marketing confirming the drug's safety—information that they passed on to their patients. Thalidomide was sold under various brand names, but with the assurance that it was like aspirin: mild, useful, and certainly not anything that could hurt you.

This, however, was not true. Slowly doctors in different countries began to notice physical impacts in which the only thing the patients had in common was their use of thalidomide. First it was permanent nerve damage in the hands and feet, and then it was significant birth defects in the fetuses of otherwise healthy mothers.

The research began to come together showing that thalidomide caused deformities in gestation that were so severe that babies could often not survive after birth. If they did, it was with debilitating and painful abnormalities, most often the lack of properly formed limbs. Grünenthal doubled down on their marketing, casting suspicion on the medical articles that discussed the dangers of thalidomide and attacking the credibility of the physicians who wrote them.[8]

At no point in the subsequent years did Grünenthal ever admit mistake or wrongdoing. All the drug manufacturers who sold thalidomide settled all compensation claims out of court. No company was ever held criminally responsible for selling a drug without verifying the claims they made about it, such as "safe for pregnant women."[9]

One way to understand how this happened is to look at the situation through the lens of incentives.

As you can imagine, there are financial incentives throughout the story of how thalidomide came to market. The heads of the team that discovered the drug were paid a percentage of the profits of its sales. And thalidomide was a big seller. There was a huge global market for sedatives, and in some countries it became the second-highest-selling drug.

There was also a significant financial incentive for drug companies to partner with Grünenthal. It meant that they could "avoid the cost of research, development, and testing."[10] And for Grünenthal itself, by not performing proper clinical trials on humans, it saved a ton of money.

Thalidomide's main competition as a sedative was a class of drugs called barbiturates. These had known undesirable side effects, and thus an incentive for doctors to recommend thalidomide was that it was purportedly safer than the alternative.

The drug companies regularly paid doctors for their endorsement, even going so far as to draft their lab articles.[11] This created more incentives. The first, financial incentive was payment, but then, once your name is linked with endorsement of a drug, you have an incentive to maintain your reputation by continuing to defend that drug.

In the later criminal trials and civil suits, a lot of drug company executives pointed out that their legal and moral responsibility was to their shareholders. The incentives to keep their shareholders happy in the form of large dividends were far more significant than fairly compensating victims.

One fascinating part of the thalidomide story is that it was never approved for sale in the United States. The Richardson-Merrell company had obtained the rights to distribute to the American market and so sought to obtain the approval of the Food and Drug Administration. The drug approval process in 1960 was not the same as it is today. The FDA had the responsibility of evaluating the safety and efficacy of all new drugs, powers that it had received in

1938 on account of another pharmaceutical tragedy.[12] But their efforts were often focused on drugs after they hit the market, with premarket testing and evaluation less regulated and more vulnerable to manipulation.

Unfortunately for Richardson-Merrell, and fortunately for the rest of the country, Dr. Frances Kelsey had just begun to work there. Having spent many years as a researcher, she was deeply concerned about the lack of evidence for the safety of the drug.[13] Neither Richardson-Merrell nor Grünenthal could provide any documentation to back up their claims of safety for both mother and fetus during pregnancy. Dr. Kelsey determined that there was no way they had done the research to show that thalidomide did not cross the placental barrier. She stalled approval as long as she could, sending back their application multiple times for being incomplete. She later explained that she had a very low incentive for approving the drug, as it was not a lifesaving one. The delay tactics worked, and she was able to keep thalidomide out of the American market until reports of its horrible effects were so widespread that countries began to take it off the shelves.[14]

> An incentive is a bullet, a key: an often tiny object with astonishing power to change a situation.
>
> —STEVEN D. LEVITT AND STEPHEN J. DUBNER[15]

How do incentives work to make people seemingly lose their minds—to make normal people double down on their immoral decisions? In light of how numbers of drug company executives and doctors never admitted that thalidomide caused such horrible effects, it is worth explaining more about the power of incentives.

The initial financial component is easy to understand. Money is desirable, and therefore it is a common incentive that modifies behavior everywhere. But money alone isn't often enough. Undoubtedly if you ask people whether they would harm thousands of children for money, most would say no. Therefore, in order to understand the real power of incentives, you have to look at the psychological condition they create.

Humans don't like cognitive dissonance—"the state of tension that occurs whenever a person holds two cognitions (ideas, attitudes, beliefs, opinions) that are psychologically inconsistent."[16] We engage in self-justifying rhetoric to reduce this dissonance. In the case of incentives for endorsements, the often subconscious thought process might go like this: "I am a good person. I supported this drug. A good person would not support a drug that is harmful. So, the drug can't be harmful because I am a good person." We don't see these connections laid out, and so what is produced is the opinion the drug is good without having a window into the mental gymnastics that got us there.

Carol Tavris and Elliot Aronson have written about the manifestation of cognitive dissonance due to incentives in the medical profession. "Physicians, like scientists, want to believe their integrity cannot be compromised. Yet every time physicians accept a few dollars or other incentives for performing certain tests and procedures, for channeling some of their patients into clinical trials, or for prescribing a new, expensive drug that is not better or safer than an older one, they are balancing their patients' welfare against their own concerns."[17]

Consider the story of Andrew Wakefield, the lead author on the paper published in *The Lancet* that claimed it had found a positive correlation between vaccines and autism. Later debunked, but not before causing a widespread drop in vaccinations that has resulted in needless deaths, the article was retracted. He did not sign the retraction. Why?

He had "a conflict of interest that he had failed to disclose to the journal: he was conducting research on behalf of lawyers representing parents of autistic children. Wakefield had been paid more than eight hundred thousand dollars to determine whether there were grounds for pursuing legal action."[18] Tavris and Aronson demonstrate that "unlike truly independent scientists, however, he had no incentive to look for disconfirming evidence of a correlation between vaccines and autism, and every incentive to overlook other explanations."[19]

This is why understanding the power of incentives is both critical and tricky. The acceptance of an initial incentive creates a psychological state whereby we become invested in maintaining whatever story brought about that incentive, so we can justify our acceptance of it.

> The greater danger to the public comes from the self-justifications of well-intentioned scientists and physicians who, because of their need to reduce dissonance, truly believe themselves to be above the influence of their corporate investors. Yet, like a plant turning toward the sun, they turn toward the interests of their sponsors without even being aware they are doing so.[20]

If we're not aware of the incentives that direct our behavior, we can end up doing things we might prefer not to. It's also important to be aware of how other people can incentivize us to do things that go against our wishes and values—much like those who sold thalidomide for the powerful incentive of money. By being aware of the incentives that may be directing our actions, we can recognize any unsavory influences and refocus by considering what we are really valuing. We may be driven by rewards like money, attention, and power, but we may actually value things like making a positive impact on the world, kindness, and honesty. We need not blindly follow incentives if they don't align with our values.

Motivated by Uncertainty

Humans can also be heavily motivated by uncertainty. There are particular situations in which we find it more compelling to go after a possible payoff instead of a sure thing. Why? Because it is often more stimulating, which is an incentive in itself. Think of getting together with a group of friends every Saturday to play board games. Numerous studies have shown that we would cease this behavior if we knew we were going to win every time. Winning is fun. Guaranteed winning is not.

The limit to this is when the value of the result outweighs the value of the process. Winning a game against your friends is not life-changing, and thus the incentive to have fun in the process of playing is more compelling than the incentive to be sure about winning. Conversely, if an amount of money were involved that would allow us to quit our jobs and travel around the world, we would go for the guaranteed win every time.

Conclusion

Incentives are the hidden engines that drive behavior. They're the unseen forces that shape our choices, the carrots and sticks that guide our actions.

Think of a business offering a bonus for hitting a sales target. The bonus is an incentive, the external reward that motivates the salesperson to excel. But incentives aren't always so obvious. They can be subtle, even subconscious—the social approval we seek, the habits we form, the desires we pursue.

Incentives are powerful because they tap into the fundamental wiring of the human brain. We're hardwired to seek reward and avoid punishment, to optimize for the outcomes that serve our interests. When the incentives align with our goals, we thrive. When they don't, we struggle.

In a classroom it's easy to say that we'll be motivated by doing the right thing; however, in reality, we're mostly driven by rewards. We have a hard time turning down the pleasure of immediate gains even if it takes us away from our ultimate goal.

Often short-term and long-term incentives differ. You might not feel like going to the gym today, but you want to be healthy as you age. Making choices to maximize your satisfaction today often leads to less reward down the road.

Poorly designed incentives backfire, encouraging short-term thinking, unethical behavior, or unintended consequences. The key is to craft incentives that reward the behaviors that lead to long-term success.

In the end, if you understand the incentive, you can predict the outcome. By shaping the incentives, we shape the outcomes. By aligning the incentives, we unlock the power of human potential.

Tendency to Minimize Energy Output

Least-effort principle.

Nature is thrifty in
all its actions.

—PIERRE LOUIS MAUPERTUIS[1]

All living beings require energy to perform their daily functions, including sleeping. Over time, species have developed different mechanisms to increase their energy efficiency. The tendency in organisms to conserve their energy is what ensures they will have extra to draw on in times of increased need. For humans, we have to be careful, though, to make sure minimizing our energy output increases our effectiveness and doesn't lead to laziness.

Saving It Up

There are many cold-blooded species. Without the biological requirement to maintain stable internal body temperatures, these animals do not need to expend energy for this purpose, allowing them to save energy for other activities. Some turtles, for example, can spend winters at the bottom of very cold bodies of water without moving because they have body parts that can maintain their integrity in extreme temperatures. Moreover, these turtles have powerful mechanisms to direct blood flow to essential organs during these times. They also have advanced energy-storage abilities that they make use of when they are in nutrient-deficient environments.

Sharkskin is another example of biological energy efficiency. The skin is composed of backward-structured scales that reduce water resistance. Along with the wavy motion in which sharks move, these scales allow them to swim at incredible speeds in an energy-efficient manner. There is a significant increase in survival potential for organisms that develop efficiency in handling the ongoing, repetitive requirements of their environments.

Change is costly for most organisms. It can be easier to keep doing whatever has guaranteed their survival thus far than to try something new that might fail and waste energy or endanger them. The instinct to minimize energy output can lead us to be resistant to change or risk-taking. Using this model as a lens can help us better understand our default thinking tendencies, and how our patterns of movement impact our physical environments.

Desire Paths

Cutting through forests, fields, snow, and debris are paths created by the feet of people who wanted to get between two points as efficiently as possible. Our tendency to minimize our energy output means that we don't always defer to the paths that have been set out for us. Sometimes these desire paths unwittingly trample on sensitive vegetation or cause other environmental fractures. But other times they are used by city or park planners to design traffic flows and the spaces around them. When designers and planners don't take into account our instinct to minimize energy expenditure, we end up with spaces that impede our movement, which we must use in a different way.

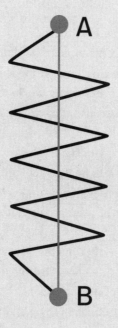

> The way people solve problems is first by having an enormous amount of commonsense knowledge, like maybe 50 million little anecdotes or entries, and then having some unknown system for finding among those 50 million old stories the 5 or 10 that seem most relevant to the situation. This is reasoning by analogy.
>
> —MARVIN MINSKY[2]

The Lazy Brain

Humans, like every other species, are energy minimizers—intensely so. Our brain has developed as an energy minimizer, as have the rest of our body parts.

Psychologists have a word for the efficiency mechanism in how we think: "heuristics." When we're thinking of making a decision, large or small, we use shortcuts developed from our long experience in the world; in chess terms, we do not consider ten million different moves but instead rapidly choose the two or three that are most likely to work.

Decisions carry a "cognitive load," meaning they require brainpower. Taking the time to analyze ten million moves requires significant effort, which uses significant energy. We cannot possibly stop in our day to do the work required to make the most optimal decision in all cases.

Heuristics are shortcuts and thus require us to expend less energy. The results may not always be the best (they usually aren't), but they are often good enough for whatever situation we are in. In a process known as "satisficing," we'll often search for the first thing in our brain that satisfies our minimum acceptable conditions. This saves time and energy, but it doesn't mean we get the best outcome.

Some heuristics develop based on previous experience. These are going to be the most reliable if the prior experiences are themselves fairly consistent. Heuristics are more likely to be accurate in situations with a stable environment, frequent exposure (large sample size), and immediate, unambiguous feedback.

In his studies of firefighters, for example, Gary Klein demonstrates the accuracy of the quick decisions that they make in the course of their jobs and how this accuracy increases over time.[3] Why? Fires are governed by rules of chemistry and physics, and thus exhibit consistent behaviors. The more you interact with fires, the more you will build knowledge that allows you to intuitively make good decisions in future fire situations.

The more unreliable the previous experience, such as by being too complex to identify true cause and effect or being based on too small a sample size, the more likely your heuristics aren't going to be particularly useful. Clinical therapy has this problem. The nature of the situation makes it hard to receive immediate feedback on the actual effectiveness of the therapy. There could be a host of other factors that contribute to eventual improvement, even simple regression to the mean. The confidential nature and often long duration of the therapy process makes it very hard for each individual practitioner to build experience over a large sample size.

Other heuristics seem to be built into how our brains operate. The most famous of these—anchoring, availability, and representativeness—were extensively studied by Daniel Kahneman and Amos Tversky. They demonstrated that these heuristics are essentially innate to the human brain. They are just how we do things, even when it's comparatively simple to demonstrate that they are often ineffective and filled with bias.

In *Thinking, Fast and Slow*, Kahneman describes the affect heuristic as a mental shortcut "in which people make judgments and decisions by consulting their emotions: Do I like it? Do I hate it? How strongly do I feel about it?" He explains that "the affect heuristic is an instance of substitution, in which the answer to an easy question (How do I feel about it?) serves as an answer to a much harder question (What do I think about it?)."[4] Answering the easier question is not necessarily a bad thing; we substitute our emotional response for a thinking response because we have to. We absolutely must react and trust our reactions in order to process the many interactions we have in a day. Our brain goes to the emotional reaction because it takes less energy to figure out how we feel about something than it takes to do the work to have an informed perspective. Often this is useful, as it lets us put minimal effort into decisions of little consequence, such as buying laundry detergent based on your love of its smell. Sometimes, however, we would increase our skills and knowledge if we put the effort into answering the harder question of what we think about something instead of relying on the emotional shortcut.

Heuristics exist because they are much more efficient—in terms of energy use, not necessarily in getting the most useful answer. As Kahneman explains, "A general 'law of least effort' applies to cognitive as well as physical exertion. The law asserts that if there are several ways of achieving the same goal, people will eventually gravitate to the least demanding course of action. In the economy of action, effort is a cost, and the acquisition of skill is driven by the balance of benefits and costs. Laziness is built deep into our nature."[5]

We often do what feels good. Using less energy often feels better than mentally taxing ourselves. We fall to the level of our evolutionary programming, not our best, often naive intentions. When we think we can overcome our basic instincts, we forget that our brains want to do the exact opposite.

The good news is, when we are willing to expend the energy, Kahneman offers a couple of corrections for the tendencies of heuristics: remember the base rates and pay attention to the quality of information.[6] If you know that 20 percent of people like chocolate ice cream and 80 percent like vanilla, you can easily guess that your new friend prefers vanilla. Even after you are exposed to a series of news stories about a current trend of athletes partaking in cocoa-avocado ice cream, you can still safely guess your friend's preference of vanilla. Always go back to the base rates and then ask if this new information you have could affect those rates substantially enough for you to change your guess. Without this vigilance, the availability of the news stories and the anchor of the word "cocoa" would likely prompt you to choose chocolate when asked to guess your new friend's favorite ice cream. But this new information has no relevance to your situation, unless the friend is a professional football player. Your best guess is the probability indicated by the base rates.

Thinking that expends the least amount of energy possible is often what feels most natural. Sometimes, though, we have to invest extra calories to get more relevant, useful results.

To Cubicle or Not to Cubicle

Designing environments for focus, to give people the space and time to do what they actually need to do, will allow for maximum energy efficiency. Like the hydrodynamic shark, whose scales allow for minimum water resistance, we need to develop mechanisms that promote efficiency in the ongoing, repetitive activities we undertake every day.

Open-plan homes can be beneficial in reducing energy expenditure. With an open-plan living space, you can cook dinner while keeping an eye on your kids. You can spot the keys you left in the hallway from the couch. You can move around with ease, transitioning between different spaces and activities without needing to open and close doors. Natural light can flood in from the right angles. Adapting the area to different needs, such as moving the living room furniture to make space for a dinner party, is simple.

But our homes are very different from our offices. They're a space where we're meant to be surrounded by people we trust, where we can let our guard down and relax. We can reshape them at will, and we're not confined by someone else's rules. Plus, even mostly open-plan homes tend to have private spaces, such as bedrooms, bathrooms, and studies, to retreat to.

When it comes to offices, open-plan layouts don't reduce overall energy expenditure. They may make it easier to move around, but they vastly increase the effort needed to focus and get work done—which is what matters most in an office. In an open office, workers have to ignore the constant onslaught of stimulus and disruptions—the ding of phones, the slurping of drinks, the sound of music leaking out of headphones, the clatter of feet, the sound of laughter, the annoyance of coworkers tapping on shoulders to ask questions, the slamming of doors, and so on. Not only are employees expending energy on their work, they're also expending energy on ignoring distractions, which means work is even more exhausting, without more getting done. Without control over when and where we interact, we get overloaded and drained.

Furthermore, people talking in an open office have no control over who is listening and who isn't. They can't form strong, one-on-one social ties. Social interactions become more superficial and performative when there's always an audience. When people need privacy and don't have spaces that allow it, they turn to means of communication that can't be overheard. This takes less effort than staying vigilant to see who is listening in.

A large part of the appeal of open offices to employers and designers is that they reduce costs. They also look impressive on the recruitment page of a website or when showing an investor around. However, any claims that they increase collaboration and reduce information silos tend not to be substantiated by research, which means that they actually are likely to increase costs in the long term. For example, face-to-face interactions decrease by as much as 70 percent, with more emails, messages, and other forms of digital communication making up the difference.[7]

What is interesting is that open-plan offices are far from modern and have indeed been the standard throughout much of history. Although their design has taken on many different iterations, their deficiencies are not new.

Frank Lloyd Wright, the iconic architect, designed the first modern open office in the 1930s for the Johnson Wax headquarters. The building featured incredibly high ceilings that let in natural light, with delicate supporting columns designed to evoke trees. Despite its industrial surroundings, the inside of the building felt airy and natural. Administrators had their own private offices on a mezzanine level so they could focus and enjoy privacy while still being part of the office floor. Wright designed the desks to be spread out enough to reduce distraction and enable free movement within the space.[8] The columns and filing cabinets acted as unofficial divisions too. With the success of the Johnson Wax headquarters, open-plan offices became increasingly popular, but they lacked the careful design and ample space of Wright's work and devolved into rows of cramped desks.

In the 1950s, a German design group created the "office landscape," with partitions dividing different parts of companies in a manner conducive to the way information needed to flow. Essentially, the office landscape was about minimizing the energy people needed to collaborate or to focus.[9] And if someone's needs changed, they could just move the partitions around.

In the 1960s, designer Robert Propst recognized the issues with open-office layouts. To improve upon the concept of office landscaping, he developed the Action Office system, which was intended to be a compromise between open and private workspaces. It involved flexible furniture and movable dividing walls that could be adapted to suit the day-to-day needs of employees. The Action Office was the perfect compromise to support both connection and privacy, but it was too expensive to become mainstream. Employers simply took the basic notion of dividing walls and ran with it, creating the notorious cubicle-farm office where everyone sat in tiny boxes, tapping away. Modern open offices were in part a means of stepping away from this imposed separation.

So, it's a cycle of open offices as a reaction against cubicles, then cubicles as a reaction to open offices. What's clear is that effective office design needs to recognize and honor the human tendency to minimize energy output in the same way Wright originally did. People need the space to focus as well as to move around, instead of environments that increase the energy required to get work done.

Conclusion

The tendency to limit energy output is the universal inclination to follow the path of least resistance. From the flow of a river to the behavior of a market, this tendency is the invisible hand that guides the actions of the world.

Sometimes our tendency to conserve energy helps us, and sometimes it hurts us. While minimizing our output ensures we will have extra to draw on in times of increased need, it can also get in the way of learning. Experience doesn't become learning without reflection, and reflection is an energy expenditure.

If we want to develop our thinking and get the most out of our environments, then we have to be aware of the natural tendency to minimize energy output and correct for it where doing so creates value.

Afterthoughts

The models in this book give you the tools that you need to better understand the world. We've explored fundamentals from physics, chemistry, and biology to show you how scientific concepts have wider applications in all sorts of everyday situations.

The more tools you have in your mental toolbox, the more likely you are to make better decisions. In turn, better decisions should free up your time and help you live a more meaningful life.

The world is fundamentally connected. However, the ideas in this volume are deliberately presented without connection, leaving you, the reader, to connect them to build your own latticework of mental models. While challenging, this is the work of assimilating information and making it usable. First you have to develop the models in your mind by learning about the fundamentals, applying them to situations in your life, and learning from the results. Then you have to keep using your latticework, refining and updating as you go. You must always be willing to adjust for new information but be knowledgeable enough to be selective about what you let in.

We recommend journaling to stimulate learning from your experiences. While most people assume that experience is the key to learning, the key is actually reflection. Journaling works because it prompts reflection. Keeping a journal, in which you chronicle your use of the models and your results, allows you to build a repertoire that you can rely on time and again. Using the models does get easier.

What is most important, however, is to find a method of reflection, feedback, and learning that works for you. Reread the chapters. Fill in the margins. Make a note about any relevance that pops into your mind. Usually when we finish a book that inspires us, we get excited and want to make changes right away. Then we get caught up in something else and forget about it. Before life gets in the way, take a step in the direction you were inspired to go. Pick one model and use it today. Test it out. Make the models in this book and in the rest of the series something you reach for in your everyday life. They're too useful to leave on a bookshelf.

The Great Mental Models is a four-volume series. The next book, volume 3, covers models from systems and mathematics. It presents the fundamentals from these two disciplines that govern our world and shows how we can harness them to improve our thinking and outcomes in a wide variety of situations. Systems and numeracy models have broad applicability and are the best source we have for trying to anticipate and plan for the future.

As the series goes out into the world, we will post resources on our website at fs.blog/tgmm to help you integrate the models into your thinking. Before long, when it comes to using mental models, you will be capitalizing on the powerful momentum you have created. These ideas will become such an integral part of the fabric of your thinking that it will be impossible to view any situation without the valuable lenses they provide.

Acknowledgments

I'm forever indebted to Charlie Munger, Peter D. Kaufman, Warren Buffett, and Peter Bevelin, who, to varying degrees, started me down the path of multidisciplinary thinking. I owe them a huge debt of gratitude.

Thank you to my coauthor, Rhiannon Beaubien, for making this series a reality. It's impossible to overstate her contributions to this volume and the entire series. Without her, you would not be holding this book in your hands.

This series would be lost without our talented illustrator, Marcia Mihotich. Thank you for seeing these words and ideas and bringing them to life in simple and exceptional ways.

While this is a revised volume 2, I wanted to give a special mention to Garvin Hirt and Morgwn Rimel for shaping the creativity of the original version. Working with you both has encouraged me to make things beautiful and timeless. And thank you to our OG editor Kristen Hall-Geisler for her willingness to dive in and ensure the material flows and comes together in the end.

The original version of this series would not have been possible without our partnership with Automattic and their incredible CEO, Matt Mullenweg. Thank you to Niki Papadopoulos and the entire team at Portfolio for rereleasing this series and supporting my efforts to make it as beautiful and as timeless as we can.

Thank you to Simon Hørup Eskildsen, Zachary Smith, Paul Ciampa, Devon Anderson, Alex Duncan, Vicky Cosenzo, Laurence Endersen, David Epstein, Ozan Gurcan, Will Bowers, Ran Klein, Sanjay Bakshi, Jeff Annello, Tara Small, Tina Cantrill, Nathan Taggart, Tim Bragassa, Yves Colomb, Rick Jones, Maria Petrova, and Dr. Gregory P. Moore for taking the time to review various books in this series. Your comments and contributions have helped make everything better.

Thank you to my sons, Will and Mack, for reminding me to continue to learn and grow along with you. This series was largely written for you and future generations.

Thank you to the entire FS team for your hard work and dedication over the years to bring this series to life.

And finally, thanks to you, the reader. I continue to be amazed by how many of you want to take this mental models journey with me. I hope this book is one you can reference time and again as you seek to better understand the world.

Notes

Introduction

1. Helen Czerski, *Storm in a Teacup: The Physics of Everyday Life* (New York: W. W. Norton and Company, 2016).
2. Ibid.
3. Ibid.

Physics

1. As quoted in Melvin A. Benarde, *Our Precarious Habitat: An Integrated Approach to Understanding Man's Effect on His Environment* (New York: Norton, 1973).

Relativity

1. Steven Strogatz, *The Calculus of Friendship* (Princeton, NJ: Princeton University Press, 2009).
2. Daniel L. Schacter and Scott D. Slotnick, "The Cognitive Neuroscience of Memory Distortion," *Neuron* 44, no. 1 (2004): 149–60.
3. David A. Neiwert, *Death on the Fourth of July: The Story of a Killing, a Trial, and Hate Crime in America* (New York: Palgrave Macmillan, 2004).
4. Timothy Egan, "A Racist Attack, a Town Plagued," *New York Times*, October 15, 2000.
5. Neiwert, *Death on the Fourth of July.*
6. Isaac Asimov, "The Relativity of Wrong," *Skeptical Inquirer*, 1989.
7. Rene Descartes, *Discourse on Method*, 4th ed., trans. Donald A. Cress (Indianapolis: Hackett, 1998).
8. Rifa'a Rafi' al-Tahtawi, *An Imam in Paris*, trans. Daniel L. Newman (London: Saqi Books, 2011).

Reciprocity

1. "Welcome to the Beginner's Guide to Propulsion," National Aeronautics and Space Administration, accessed August 12, 2019, https://www.grc.nasa.gov/www/k-12/airplane/bgp.html.
2. Jean Deslauriers and Denis Goulet, "The Medical Life of Henry Norman Bethune," *Canadian Respiratory Journal* 22, no. 6 (2015): e32–e42.
3. Ibid.
4. Ted Allan and Sydney Gordon, *The Scalpel, the Sword: The Story of Doctor Norman Bethune* (Toronto: Dundurn Press, 2009).
5. Jerf W. K. Yeung, Zhuoni Zang, and Tae Yeun Kim, "Volunteering and Health Benefits in General Adults: Cumulative Effects and Forms," *BMC Public Health* 18, no. 8 (2017).
6. J. D. Salinger, *The Catcher in the Rye* (New York: Back Bay Books, 2018).
7. Diana Britton, "The Loss Aversion Coefficient," *Wealth Management*, February 10, 2015, wealthmanagement.com/equities/loss-aversion-coefficient.
8. Daniel Kahneman, *Thinking, Fast and Slow* (Toronto: Anchor Canada, 2013).
9. Raymond Dawson, *Confucius: The Analects* (New York: Oxford University Press, 2003).
10. Trevor Bryce, "The 'Eternal Treaty' from the Hittite Perspective," British Museum Studies in Ancient Egypt and Sudan 6 (October 2006), webarchive.nationalarchives.gov.uk/ukgwa/20190801114433/https://www.britishmuseum.org/research/publications/online_journals/bmsaes/issue_6/bryce.aspx.
11. Ibid.
12. Ibid.
13. Ibid.
14. Richard H. Smith, *The Joy of Pain: Schadenfreude and the Dark Side of Human Nature* (New York: Oxford University Press, 2014).
15. Shensheng Wang, Scott O. Lilienfeld, and Philippe Rochat, "Schadenfreude Deconstructed and Reconstructed: A Tripartite Motivational Model," *New Ideas in Psychology* 52 (2019): 1–11.
16. Smith, *Joy of Pain*.
17. Wilco W. Van Dijk, Jaap W. Ouwerkerk, and Sjoerd Goslinga, "The Impact of Deservingness on Schadenfreude and Sympathy: Further Evidence," *Journal of Social Psychology* 149, no. 3 (2009): 390–2.

Thermodynamics

1. Peter Atkins, *The Laws of Thermodynamics: A Very Short Introduction* (Oxford: Oxford University Press, 2010).
2. Geerat J. Vermeij, *Nature: An Economic History* (Princeton, NJ: Princeton University Press, 2009).
3. Helen Czerski, *Storm in a Teacup: The Physics of Everyday Life* (New York: W. W. Norton and Company, 2016).

4. Tim Marshall, *Divided: Why We're Living in an Age of Walls* (New York: Simon and Schuster, 2018).
5. Adrian Keith Goldsworthy, *Hadrian's Wall* (New York: Basic Books, 2018).
6. Ibid.
7. Ibid.
8. Ibid.
9. Ken Wilber, *No Boundary: Eastern and Western Approaches to Personal Growth* (Boston: Shambhala, 2001).
10. Julia Lovell, *The Great Wall: China against the World 1000 BC–AD 2000* (New York: Grove Press, 2006).
11. Ibid.
12. Ibid.
13. Ibid.
14. Ibid.
15. Frederick Taylor, *The Berlin Wall: A World Divided, 1961–1989* (New York: HarperCollins, 2006).
16. Friedrich Nietzsche, *Twilight of the Idols* (London: Penguin, 2003).
17. Murray Gell-Mann, *The Quark and the Jaguar: Adventures in the Simple and the Complex* (New York: W. H. Freeman, 1993).
18. John Yorke, *Into the Woods: A Five-Act Journey into Story* (New York: Overlook Press, 2015).
19. Ibid.
20. Marina Warner, *Once Upon a Time: A Short History of Fairy Tale* (Oxford: Oxford University Press, 2014).
21. Ibid.
22. Ibid.
23. Yorke, *Into the Woods.*
24. Ibid.
25. Ibid

Inertia

1. Albert Einstein, *The New Quotable Einstein*, ed. Alice Calaprice (Princeton: Princeton University Press, 2005).
2. Rene Descartes, *The Principles of Philosophy*, trans. John Veitch (London: Forgotten Books, 2018).
3. Leonard Mlodinow, *Elastic: Flexible Thinking in a Constantly Changing World* (New York: Penguin Books, 2018).
4. *Encyclopædia Britannica*, s.v. "Newton's Laws of Motion," last modified January 1, 2024, britannica.com/science/Newtons-laws-of-motion.
5. "Alice Hamilton and the Development of Occupational Medicine," American Chemical Society, accessed May 30, 2018, acs.org/content/acs/en/education/whatischemistry/landmarks/alicehamilton.html.
6. Lars Öhrström, *The Last Alchemist in Paris: And Other Curious Tales from Chemistry* (Oxford, UK: Oxford University Press, 2013).

7. Kassia St. Clair, *The Secret Lives of Colour* (London: John Murray, 2016).

8. Ibid.

9. Ibid.

10. Ibid.

11. Ibid.

12. Hannah Arendt, *The Life of the Mind* (San Diego: Harcourt Brace Jovanovich, 1981).

13. Rafe Sagarin, *Learning from the Octopus* (New York: Basic Books, 2012).

14. Patricia Rife, "Lise Meitner," The Shalvi/Hyman Encyclopedia of Jewish Women, Jewish Women's Archive, accessed August 15, 2019, jwa.org/encyclopedia/article/meitner-lise.

15. Ibid.

16. Ruth Lewin Sime, *Lise Meitner: A Life in Physics* (Berkeley: University of California Press, 1996).

17. Ibid.

18. Ibid.

19. Ibid.

20. Rife, "Lise Meitner"; Susanne Kiewitz, "Portrait of Lise Meitner," Max-Planck-Gesellschaft, accessed August 15, 2019, mpg.de/11721986/Lise-Meitner.

21. Rife, "Lise Meitner"; Ashley G. Smart, Andrew Grant, and Greg Stasiewicz, "Physics Nobel Nominees, 1901–66," *Physics Today*, September 25, 2017, physicstoday.scitation.org/do/10.1063/PT.6.4.20170925a/full.

22. Rife, "Lise Meitner."

Friction and Viscosity

1. Susanna Kaysen, *Girl, Interrupted* (New York: Vintage Books, 1994).

2. Helen Czerski, *Storm in a Teacup: The Physics of Everyday Life* (New York: W. W. Norton and Company, 2016).

3. Ibid.

4. Stephen McCarthy, "Agnes Pockels: 175 Faces of Chemistry," Royal Society of Chemistry, November 2014, rsc.org/news-events/community/2016/may/women-in-science.

5. Ibid.

6. Serhii Plokhy, *Chernobyl: The History of a Nuclear Catastrophe* (New York: Basic Books, 2018).

7. Ibid.

8. Ibid.

9. Ibid.

10. Ibid.

11. Ibid.

12. Ibid.

13. James P. Womack, Daniel T. Jones, and Daniel Roos, *The Machine That Changed the World* (New York: Free Press, 2007).

14. Ibid.
15. Ibid.
16. Ibid.
17. Ibid.
18. Ibid.
19. Ibid.

Velocity

1. Seneca, *Letters from a Stoic*, trans. Robin Campbell (London: Penguin, 1969).
2. Andrew Roberts, *Napoleon: A Life* (New York: Penguin, 2014).
3. Adam Zamoyski, *Napoleon: A Life* (New York: Basic Books, 2018).
4. Roberts, *Napoleon*.
5. Ibid.
6. Zamoyski, *Napoleon*.
7. Ibid.
8. Roberts, *Napoleon*.
9. Zamoyski, *Napoleon*.
10. Roberts, *Napoleon*.
11. Zamoyski, *Napoleon*.
12. Carl von Clausewitz, *On War* (London: K. Paul, Trench, Trubner, 1918).
13. Ibid.
14. Emily Wortis Leider, *Becoming Mae West* (New York: Farrar, Straus and Giroux, 1997).
15. Paul Johnson, *Heroes* (New York: Harper Perennial, 2007).

Leverage

1. Aristotle, "Mechanical Problems" in *Minor Works*, trans. W. S. Hett (Cambridge: Harvard University Press, 1936), 353–35.
2. Ralph V. Turner, *Eleanor of Aquitaine: Queen of France, Queen of England* (New Haven, CT: Yale University Press, 2009).
3. Alison Weir, *Eleanor of Aquitaine: A Life* (New York: Ballantine, 1999).
4. Turner, *Eleanor of Aquitaine*.
5. Ibid.
6. Ibid.
7. Ibid.
8. Ibid.
9. Weir, *Eleanor of Aquitaine*.
10. Turner, *Eleanor of Aquitaine*.
11. Weir, *Eleanor of Aquitaine*.
12. Turner, *Eleanor of Aquitaine*.
13. David A. Corbin, *Life, Work, and Rebellion in the Coal Fields* (Morgantown: West Virginia University Press, 2015).

14. Ibid.
15. Corbin, *Life, Work, and Rebellion.*

Chemistry

1. Brenda Maddox, *Rosalind Franklin: The Dark Lady of DNA* (New York: Harper Perennial, 2023).

Activation Energy

1. Paul Graham (@paulg), "There's at least one time when it's ok to lie to yourself: to get the activation energy required to start a new project," X, January 10, 2023, https://x.com/paulg/status/1616453470114164736.
2. Ernest Harsch, *Thomas Sankara: An African Revolutionary* (Athens: Ohio University Press, 2014).
3. Ibid.
4. Ibid.
5. "Thomas Sankara: The Upright Man," California Newsreel, accessed June 7, 2019, newsreel.org/video/thomas-sankara-the-upright-man.
6. Harsch, *Thomas Sankara.*
7. Ibid.
8. "Thomas Sankara: The Upright Man."
9. Ibid.
10. Harsch, *Thomas Sankara.*
11. Ibid.
12. Ibid.
13. Joe Studwell, *How Asia Works* (New York: Grove Press, 2013).
14. Ibid.
15. Ibid.
16. Ibid.
17. Ibid.
18. Ibid.
19. Ibid.

Catalysts

1. Lars Öhrström, *The Last Alchemist in Paris: And Other Curious Tales from Chemistry* (Oxford: Oxford University Press, 2013).
2. Elizabeth L. Eisenstein, *The Printing Press as an Agent of Change* (Cambridge, UK: Cambridge University Press, 1979).
3. Peter Frankopan, *The Silk Roads: A New History of the World* (New York: Vintage Books, 2017).
4. Joan DeJean, *The Age of Comfort* (New York: Bloomsbury, 2009).
5. Ibid.

6. Ibid.
7. Ibid.

Alloying

1. Lars Öhrström, *The Last Alchemist in Paris: And Other Curious Tales from Chemistry* (Oxford, UK: Oxford University Press, 2013).
2. James Laxer, *Tecumseh and Brock: The War of 1812* (Toronto: Anansi Press, 2012).
3. Ibid.
4. Ibid.
5. Ibid.
6. "Philosophy of Technology," *Internet Encyclopedia of Philosophy*, accessed October 29, 2018, iep.utm.edu/technolo/#SH1a.
7. Walter Isaacson, *Leonardo da Vinci* (New York: Simon and Schuster, 2017).
8. Ibid.
9. Ibid.
10. Ibid.
11. Ibid.
12. Ibid.
13. Ibid.

Biology

1. Jacques Monod and Austryn Wainhouse, *Chance and Necessity: An Essay on the Natural Philosophy of Modern Biology* (London: Penguin, 1997).

Evolution Part One

1. Rafe Sagarin, *Learning from the Octopus* (New York: Basic Books, 2012).
2. Geerat J. Vermeij, *Nature: An Economic History* (Princeton, NJ: Princeton University Press, 2009).
3. Sagarin, *Learning from the Octopus*.
4. Vermeij, *Nature*.
5. Franck Courchamp, Luděk Berec, and Joanna Gascoigne, *Allee Effects in Ecology and Conservation* (New York: Oxford University Press, 2009).
6. Camilo Mora et al., "How Many Species Are There on Earth and in the Ocean?" *PloS Biology* 9, no. 8 (2011): e1001127.
7. David M. Raup, "Biological Extinction in Earth History," *Science* 231, no. 4745 (1986): 1528–33.
8. Chris Maser, "The Economics of Extinction," 2006, http://www.chrismaser.com/extinction.htm.
9. Dr. Roberta Bondar, accessed June 8, 2019, robertabondar.com.

10. Jean-Benoît Nadeau and Julie Barlow, *The Story of French* (Toronto: CNIB, 2009).

11. Ibid.

12. Ibid.

13. Ibid.

14. Ibid.

15. Ibid.

16. Ibid.

17. Donald Fairbairn, *Understanding Language: A Guide for Beginning Students of Greek and Latin* (Washington, DC: Catholic University of America Press, 2011).

Evolution Part Two

1. Geerat J. Vermeij, *Nature: An Economic History* (Princeton, NJ: Princeton University Press, 2009).

2. Ibid.

3. Rafe Sagarin, *Learning from the Octopus* (New York: Basic Books, 2012).

4. Peter Ungar, *Evolution's Bite: A Story of Teeth, Diet, and Human Origins* (Princeton, NJ: Princeton University Press, 2018).

5. Ibid.

6. Sagarin, *Learning from the Octopus.*

7. Margaret MacMillan, *Paris 1919* (New York: Random House, 2001).

8. Ibid.

9. B. H. Liddell Hart, *A History of the Second World War* (New York: Putnam, 1971).

10. Ibid.

11. Ibid.

12. Ibid.

13. Ibid.

14. Ibid.

15. Ibid.

16. Lewis Carroll, *Alice's Adventures in Wonderland and Through the Looking-Glass* (New York: Bantam Classic, 2006).

17. Vermeij, *Nature.*

18. Janice Moore and Randy Moore, *Evolution 101* (Westport, CT: Greenwood, 2007).

19. Jerry A. Coyne, *Why Evolution Is True* (New York: Penguin Books, 2010).

20. Vermeij, *Nature.*

21. Sagarin, *Learning from the Octopus.*

22. Vermeij, *Nature.*

23. Stephen Jay Gould and Elisabeth S. Vrba, "Exaptation—a Missing Term in the Science of Form," *Paleobiology* 8, no. 1 (1982): 4–15.

24. Vermeij, *Nature.*

25. FSTC, "The Mechanics of Banu Musa in the Light of Modern System and

Control Engineering," August 10, 2007, Muslim Heritage, muslimheritage .com/article/mechanics-of-banu-musa.

26. Steven Johnson, *Wonderland: How Play Made the Modern World* (New York: Random House, 2016).

27. Richard Rhodes, *Hedy's Folly* (New York: Doubleday, 2011).

28. Johnson, *Wonderland*.

29. Ibid.

30. Ibid.

31. Marie Curie, Lecture at Vassar College, Poughkeepsie, NY, May 14, 1921.

32. Monte Burke, "Wrap Star," *Forbes*, April 28, 2006.

33. Tara Winner, "The History of Play-Doh: Good, Clean Fun!" Strong National Museum of Play, November 3, 2016, museumofplay.org/blog/the-history -of-play-doh-good-clean-fun.

34. Dana Berkowitz, *Botox Nation* (New York: New York University Press, 2017).

35. Andrew M. Colman, *Game Theory and Its Applications in the Social and Biological Sciences* (Hove, UK: Psychology Press, 2017).

36. Donald W. Linzey, *Vertebrate Biology* (Baltimore: Johns Hopkins University Press, 2020).

37. Paul A. Keddy, *Competition* (Dordrecht, Netherlands: Kluwer Academic, 2001).

Ecosystem

1. John Gribbin, *Deep Simplicity: Bringing Order to Chaos and Complexity* (New York: Random House, 2004), xx.

2. "Fire Ecology," Pacific Biodiversity Institute, accessed August 13, 2019, pacificbio.org/initiatives/fire/fire_ecology.html.

3. Claire Asher, "Why We Should Let Raging Wildfires Burn," BBC, July 25, 2016.

4. "Status Check for African Elephants," NRDC, December 22, 2016.

5. "Asian Elephants," WWF, accessed August 13, 2019.

6. Nikorn Thongtip et al., "Successful Artificial Insemination in the Asian Elephant (Elephas Maximus) Using Chilled and Frozen-Thawed Semen," *Reproductive Biology and Endocrinology* 7, no. 1 (2009): 75.

7. Eric Scigliano, *Love, War and Circuses: The Age-Old Relationship between Elephants and Humans* (London: Bloomsbury, 2004).

8. Michael J. Berens, "Elephants Are Dying Out in America's Zoos," *Seattle Times*, December 1, 2012.

9. Geerat J. Vermeij, *Nature: An Economic History* (Princeton, NJ: Princeton University Press, 2009).

10. Guy Lasnier, "UCSC Study Shows How Urchin-Loving Otters Can Help Fight Global Warming," UC Santa Cruz, September 7, 2012.

11. Gary Hart, foreword to *Learning from the Octopus*, by Rafe Sagarin (New York: Basic Books, 2012).

12. Charles C. Mann, *1493* (New York: Vintage Books, 2011).

13. Ibid.

14. Ibid.

15. Ibid.
16. Ibid.
17. Ibid.
18. Sagarin, *Learning from the Octopus.*
19. Michael Lombardi, *Gridiron Genius* (New York: Crown Archetype, 2018).
20. David Harris, *The Genius* (New York: Random House, 2008).
21. Ibid.
22. Ibid.
23. Bill Walsh, Brian Billick, and James Peterson, *Finding the Winning Edge* (Champaign, IL: Sports Publishing, 1998).
24. Harris, *The Genius.*
25. Ibid.
26. Ibid.
27. Lombardi, *Gridiron Genius.*

Niches

1. Peter Ungar, *Evolution's Bite: A Story of Teeth, Diet, and Human Origins* (Princeton, NJ: Princeton University Press, 2018).
2. Geerat J. Vermeij, *Nature: An Economic History* (Princeton, NJ: Princeton University Press, 2009).
3. "Red Squirrels," Wildlife Trusts, accessed August 13, 2019, wildlifetrusts .org/on-land/red-squirrels.
4. Helen Keating, "Red Squirrel Facts," Woodland Trust, November 1, 2018, woodlandtrust.org.uk/blog/2018/11/red-squirrel-facts.
5. Ungar, *Evolution's Bite.*
6. Jonathan Coopersmith, *Faxed: The Rise and Fall of the Fax Machine* (Baltimore: Johns Hopkins University Press, 2016).
7. Ibid.
8. Ibid.
9. Ibid.
10. Ibid.
11. Ibid.
12. George R. McGhee, *Convergent Evolution: Limited Forms Most Beautiful* (Cambridge, MA: MIT Press, 2011).
13. C. Tristan Stayton, "What Does Convergent Evolution Mean? The Interpretation of Convergence and Its Implications in the Search for Limits to Evolution," *Interface Focus* 5, no. 6 (2015): 20150039.
14. Simon Conway Morris, "Evolutionary Convergence," *Current Biology* 16, no. 19 (2006): R826.
15. McGhee, *Convergent Evolution.*
16. Morris, "Evolutionary Convergence."
17. Michael Blanding, *The Coke Machine* (New York: Avery, 2010).
18. Ibid.

19. Ibid.
20. Ibid.
21. Ibid.
22. Ibid.

Self-Preservation

1. Samuel Butler, *The Note-Books of Samuel Butler* (New York: E. P. Dutton & Company, 1912).
2. Joseph Stromberg, "Video: A Drone Mates with a Queen Bee in Glorious Slow-Motion," *Smithsonian*, September 11, 2013, smithsonianmag.com /science-nature/video-a-drone-mates-with-a-queen-bee-in-glorious-slow -motion-6174953.
3. Olivia Judson, "The Selfless Gene," *Atlantic*, October 1, 2007.
4. Killian Fox, "Self-Destructive Species: From Exploding Ants to Postnatal Octopuses," *Guardian*, April 29, 2018.
5. Jonathan R. Potts and Mark A. Lewis, "How Do Animal Territories Form and Change? Lessons from 20 Years of Mechanistic Modelling," *Proceedings of the Royal Society B: Biological Sciences* 281, no. 1784 (2014): 20140231.
6. Gioconda Belli, *The Country Under My Skin* (New York: Anchor Books, 2002).
7. Ibid.
8. Ibid.
9. Ibid.
10. Ibid.
11. Ibid.
12. Ibid.
13. Ibid.
14. Ibid.
15. Ibid.
16. Ibid.
17. Ibid.
18. Patrick Hunt, *Ten Discoveries That Rewrote History* (New York: Plume, 2007).
19. Arnold C. Brackman, *The Luck of Nineveh* (New York: McGraw Hill Book Company, 1978).
20. Alan Weisman, *The World Without Us* (London: Virgin Digital, 2012).
21. Reşat Ulusay et al., eds., *Rock Mechanics and Rock Engineering: From the Past to the Future* (Boca Raton, FL: CRC Press, 2016).
22. Niki Evelpidou et al., *Natural Heritage from East to West: Case Studies from 6 EU Countries* (Berlin: Springer Berlin, 2014).
23. Eric Cooper, *Life and Society in Byzantine Cappadocia* (London: Palgrave Macmillan, 2014).
24. David Farley, *Underground Worlds: A Guide to Spectacular Subterranean Places* (New York: Running Press, 2018).

Replication

1. Jiddu Krishnamurt, *The First and Last Freedom* (New York: HarperCollins), Kindle ed., 40.
2. Geerat J. Vermeij, *Nature: An Economic History* (Princeton, NJ: Princeton University Press, 2009).
3. Ibid.
4. Benjamin Curtis, *The Habsburgs: The History of a Dynasty* (London: Continuum, 2013).
5. Razib Khan, "Inbreeding and the Downfall of the Spanish Hapsburgs," *Discover*, April 15, 2009.
6. Peter D. Gluckman et al., *Principles of Evolutionary Medicine* (Oxford, UK: Oxford University Press, 2016).
7. Alan Holland Bittles, *Consanguinity in Context* (Cambridge, UK: Cambridge University Press, 2012).
8. Ewen Callaway, "Inbred Royals Show Traces of Natural Selection," *Nature*, April 19, 2013.
9. Andrew Roberts, *Napoleon: A Life* (New York: Penguin, 2014).
10. Lawrence G. Shattuck, "Communicating Intent and Imparting Presence," *Military Review* (March–April 2000).
11. Ibid.
12. Vermeij, *Nature*.
13. Shattuck, "Communicating Intent."
14. Carl von Clausewitz, *On War* (London: K. Paul, Trench, Trubner, 1918).
15. Shattuck, "Communicating Intent."
16. Victor H. Mair and Erling Hoh, *The True History of Tea* (New York: Thames and Hudson, 2009).
17. Ibid.
18. Ibid.
19. Ibid.
20. Ibid.
21. Ibid.
22. Ibid.
23. Ibid.
24. Ibid.

Cooperation

1. Rafe Sagarin, *Learning from the Octopus* (New York: Basic Books, 2012).
2. Andrew J. Roger, Sergio A. Muñoz-Gómez, and Ryoma Kamikawa, "The Origin and Diversification of Mitochondria," *Current Biology* 27, no. 21 (2017): R1177–92.
3. Ibid.
4. Sagarin, *Learning from the Octopus*.

5. Alfred D. Chandler Jr., *The Visible Hand: The Managerial Revolution in American Business* (Cambridge, MA: Harvard University Press, 1977).
6. Ibid.
7. Geerat J. Vermeij, *Nature: An Economic History* (Princeton, NJ: Princeton University Press, 2009).
8. Sagarin, *Learning from the Octopus.*
9. Shane Parrish, "Alexander Shelley: The Architecture of Music," episode 9, 2016, in *Knowledge Project*, Farnam Street, 56:28, fs.blog/knowledge-project -podcast/alexander-shelley.
10. Ibid.
11. Tom Service, *Music as Alchemy* (London: Faber and Faber, 2012).
12. Ibid.
13. Ibid.
14. Maria Noriega Rachwal, *From Kitchen to Carnegie Hall* (Toronto: Second Story Press, 2015).
15. Ibid.
16. Ibid.
17. Ibid.
18. Yuval Noah Harari, *Sapiens: A Brief History of Humankind* (Toronto: Mc-Clelland and Stewart, 2014).
19. Ibid.
20. Ibid.
21. Robin Dunbar, "Neocortex Size as a Constraint on Group Size in Primates," *Journal of Human Evolution* 22, no. 6 (1992): 469–93.
22. Aleks Krotoski, "Robin Dunbar: We Can Only Ever Have 150 Friends at Most," *Guardian*, March 13, 2010.

Hierarchical Organization

1. From a July 2015 conversation with the author.
2. Ronald Heifetz, "Leadership," in *Political and Civic Leadership: A Reference Handbook*, ed. Richard A. Couto (Los Angeles: Sage Reference, 2010).
3. Yuval Noah Harari, *Sapiens: A Brief History of Humankind* (Toronto: Mc-Clelland and Stewart, 2014).
4. Rafe Sagarin, *Learning from the Octopus* (New York: Basic Books, 2012).
5. Charles Van Doren, *A History of Knowledge: Past, Present, and Future* (New York: Ballantine Books, 1993).
6. Colin Mooers, *The Making of Bourgeois Europe: Absolutism, Revolution, and the Rise of Capitalism in England, France, and Germany* (London: Verso, 1991).
7. Ian Davidson, *The French Revolution: From Enlightenment to Tyranny* (New York: W. W. Norton and Company, 2018).
8. Jean-Benoît Nadeau and Julie Barlow, *The Story of French* (Toronto: CNIB, 2009).

9. Ibid.
10. Sam Walker, *The Captain Class* (New York: Penguin Random House, 2017).
11. Ibid.
12. Nancy Etcoff, *Survival of the Prettiest: The Science of Beauty* (New York: Doubleday, 1999).
13. Harari, *Sapiens*.
14. Dana Thomas, *Deluxe: How Luxury Lost Its Luster* (New York: Penguin, 2008).
15. Etcoff, *Survival of the Prettiest*.
16. Ibid.
17. Amy C. Edmondson, Faaiza Rashid, and Herman "Dutch" Leonard, "The 2010 Chilean Mining Rescue A + B," prepared as a case study for Harvard Business School (2010).
18. Ibid.
19. Ibid.
20. Ibid.
21. Ibid.
22. Walker, *Captain Class*.
23. Ibid.
24. Edmondson, Rashid, and Leonard, "The 2010 Chilean Mining Rescue."
25. Ibid.
26. Heifetz, "Leadership."

Incentives

1. Charlie Munger, *Poor Charlie's Almanack: The Wit and Wisdom of Charles T. Munger*, comp. Peter D. Kaufman (New York: Donning Company Publishers, 2005).
2. Geerat J. Vermeij, *Nature: An Economic History* (Princeton, NJ: Princeton University Press, 2009).
3. Laurent Belsie, "Use-It-or-Lose-It Budget Rules," NBER Digest, National Bureau of Economic Research, March 1, 2014, nber.org/digest/mar14/use-it-or-lose-it-budget-rules.
4. Sun Tzu, *The Art of War*, trans. John Minford (New York: Penguin, 2002).
5. Trent D. Stephens and Rock Brynner, *Dark Remedy: The Impact of Thalidomide and Its Revival as a Vital Medicine* (Cambridge, MA: Perseus, 2001).
6. Ibid.
7. Ibid.
8. Ibid.
9. Ibid.
10. Ibid.
11. Ibid.
12. Thomas Hager, *The Demon Under the Microscope* (New York: Harmony Books, 2006).
13. Stephens and Brynner, *Dark Remedy*.

14. Ibid.
15. Steven D. Levitt and Stephen J. Dubner, *Freakonomics* (Rearsby, UK: Clipper Large Print, 2007).
16. Carol Tavris and Elliot Aronson, *Mistakes Were Made (but Not by Me)* (Boston: Mariner Books, 2015).
17. Ibid.
18. Ibid.
19. Ibid.
20. Ibid.

Tendency to Minimize Energy Output

1. Pierre Louis Maupertuis, *Essai de Cosmologie*, trans. John Doe (Paris: Académie Royale des Sciences, 1750), 123.
2. Susan Kruglinski, "Discover Interview: Marvin Minsky," *Discover*, January 13, 2007.
3. Gary Klein, "Insight," in *Thinking: The New Science of Decision-Making, Problem-Solving, and Prediction*, ed. John Brockman (New York: HarperCollins, 2013).
4. Daniel Kahneman, *Thinking, Fast and Slow* (Toronto: Anchor Canada, 2013).
5. Ibid.
6. Ibid.
7. Ethan S. Bernstein and Stephen Turban, "The Impact of the 'Open' Workspace on Human Collaboration," *Philosophical Transactions of the Royal Society B: Biological Sciences* 373, no. 1573 (2018): 20170239.
8. Eleanor Gibson, "Frank Lloyd Wright Designed the Johnson Wax Offices like a Forest Open to the Sky," *Dezeen*, June 14, 2017.
9. Anne D. Kroemer and Karl H. E. Kroemer, *Office Ergonomics: Ease and Efficiency at Work* (Boca Raton, FL: CRC Press, 2017).

Feed your brain in 5 minutes every week, for free.

The Brain Food newsletter delivers actionable ideas and timeless insights every Sunday.

fs.blog/newsletter

PORTFOLIO

Also by Shane Parrish

"An indispensable guide to making smarter decisions each day."
James Clear, bestselling author of *Atomic Habits*

SHANE PARRISH

NEW YORK TIMES
BESTSELLER

CLEAR THINKING

**Turning Ordinary Moments
into Extraordinary Results**

PORTFOLIO

The Knowledge Project Podcast is one of the most popular podcasts in the world.

Join host Shane Parrish as he uncovers the strategies, mindsets, and hard-earned secrets the very best use to achieve remarkable results.

Listen at

fs.blog/podcast

or search for "the knowledge project" wherever you listen to podcasts.

PORTFOLIO